# GOD, THE JOY OF MY LIFE:

## A BIOGRAPHY
of
## SAINT TERESA
OF JESUS OF THE ANDES

By
Michael D. Griffin, O.C.D.
With the Saint's
**SPIRITUAL DIARY**

IGNATIUS PRESS　　　SAN FRANCISCO

First edition published in 1989 by Teresian Charism Press, Hubertus, Wisconsin

ISBN 978-1-58617-453-8

Printed in the United States of America

COVER ART DONE BY NANCY GURGANUS.
THE PICTURE OF THE SAINT ON THE
COVER WAS TAKEN A FEW MONTHS
BEFORE ENTERING THE CONVENT.

The official canonization picture. It was created by the well-known Chilean artist, Gonzalo Correa.

# CONTENTS

# FOREWORD

Blessed be God who has spoken through His Church. The canonization of Saint Teresa of The Andes, the youngest saint of the Carmelite Order and the newest model for the youth of our times, has made a revised and enlarged edition of **God, the Joy of My Life** imperative. It is a fitting tribute to the new honors bestowed on her by the Church.

The task of writing a foreword or preface to this second edition is actually twofold: first, to state the meaning and arrangement of the book; and then to express my thanks to all who made this book possible.

**God, The Joy Of My Life** was written to introduce English speaking readers to Saint Teresa of Jesus of the Andes, a young Chilean Carmelite nun and mystic who is being referred to abroad as "the newest star in the firmament of Carmel." The book is arranged so that the first biography of this Carmelite ever to appear in English is followed by my own translation of her *Intimate Spiritual Diary,* which she kept from age 15 until her untimely death three months short of her twentieth birthday. The Diary is then followed by *A Biographical Guide* to the principal events of her life. Both of these texts have been taken from *Teresa de Los Andes Diario Y Cartas,* the definitive edition of the saint's works compiled by Father Marino Purroy Remon, O.C.D., biographer and vice-postulator of her Cause, and published by Las Madres Carmelitas of the Carmel of Los Andes, Chile, 1983. An English translation of the Papal Homilies preached by Pope John Paul II in Spanish at her beatification and canonization have been included.

English translations of both talks appeared in the English version of *L'Osservatore Romano*. Reflections of the Superior General of the Carmelite Order on this important saint brings the book to a close. And some select photographs of the Saint have been added.

Expressing my gratitude to those who made this book possible is the second task of this foreword. **God, The Joy of My Life** owes boundless debts of gratitude to many people. First of all to Father Felipe Sainz de Baranda, Superior General of the Discalced Carmelite Order. It was he who, on a pastoral visit to the Carmelite Monastery in Washington, D.C. made me aware of the existence as well as the spiritual importance of Teresa of the Andes. These providential talks with Father General during the summer prior to her beatification immensely enriched my spiritual life and made me want to offer this book to English-speaking readers.

My mind and heart next turn to the Discalced Carmelite Nuns of the Monastery of Los Andes, Chile, the foundation to which Saint Teresa belonged. To these wonderful Sisters the book owes everything. These lovely Sisters gave me full permission to translate all the texts of their new Saint's writings. My admiration for the Community of Los Andes has soared again and again as I see them carrying on and living the spiritual legacy and the spirit of joy of the first Carmelite of the "New World" to be honored as a Saint of the universal Church.

Nor must I forget Sister Guadalupe Torres, a professed Religious of the Sacred Heart for more than 50 years, who many years ago taught me Spanish. For her kindness, for her friendship and her patience in inspiring me in so many ways I now want to pay public and deserved tribute.

And how can I overlook Consuelo Powell, a native of Santiago, Chile and for many years a member of the Chilean Embassy here in Washington, D.C.? Patiently she checked over my translation of Teresa of the Andes' *Intimate Spiritual Diary*. I am likewise deeply indebted to Doctor Leticia Bercerra de Ríos at the Clinical Center of the National Institutes of Health - originally from Guadalajara, Mexico - who was good enough to look over my translation and give me a second opinion regarding its accuracy. This she did cheerfully and willingly, astutely pointing out a number of inaccuracies in my initial version.

But there are more who contributed to this success of this second version. Mary Rainey helped me in countless ways as I struggled to get this text readied for the printer. To her, I am deeply indebted. And, finally, to Thomas Blummer, my editor, I want to express heartfelt appreciation for his patience, skill and valuable suggestions as well as for his enthusiastic devotion for our new Saint.

And last, but by no means least it is to Saint Teresa of the Andes herself that I owe more than words can ever express. The story of this charming Carmelite who lived in the beginning of this century makes me realize and appreciate how valid is the contemplative Carmelite charism of joy and intimacy with God for the Church, my Order and for the men and women who stand at the threshold of the third millennium of human history. To one and all, and to the whole Church and the whole world Teresa of the Andes spontaneously sings her new canticle: "God is infinite joy. In Him alone can we find happiness." To share this message with others has been the guiding light that has directed all my work.

Michael D. Griffin, O.C.D.
Shrine of Mary Help of Christians
Holy Hill, Wisconsin.

# THE LIFE OF
# TERESA OF THE ANDES

## INTRODUCTION

St Teresa's life was brief but remarkable. At the time of her death, she was 19 years and 9 months old, still a teenager. Although her years were few, she did, however, become a Discalced Carmelite nun. She lived that life for 11 months at the Monastery of the Holy Spirit in Los Andes, Chile, with heroic love and fortitude.

Sister Teresa of the Andes is referred to as the newest star in the spiritual firmament of Carmel. During a pastoral visit to Chile in 1987 at an outdoor ceremony at O'Higgins Park in Santiago, Pope John Paul II beatified the saintly Chilean Carmelite known for her spiritual message of divine joy.

After Teresa's beatification, devotion to her steadily and significantly deepened and increased. A miracle, sign of God's approval, was confirmed to have been granted though her intercession. Rome, after due deliberation, was convinced that God was calling His Church to take the final step of declaring Blessed Teresa of the Andes a Saint. The solemn canonization took place in the Vatican on March 21, 1993. For all time, Juanita Fernández Solar will forever be known in the Church and the world as Saint Teresa of Jesus of the Andes.

1

This first Carmelite Saint from the New World now takes her place alongside three other Discalced Carmelite saints who bear the name of Teresa.

## Her Identity

Let's begin with the question, who is Teresa of the Andes? This is the most obvious question for people of the English-speaking world to ask. Until now, few have ever heard of this Carmelite nun from Los Andes. Some know she is from Chile, but not all are aware that she lived in a Carmelite Monastery close to the famous statue of Christ of the Andes perched on the summit of the Andes Mountains between Chile and Argentina. Is there any symbolic connection between Christ of the Andes and this new Carmelite saint of the Andes?

## Christ of the Andes

In Chile in the foothills of the Andes and not too far from the famous statue, is a poor Carmelite Monastery dedicated to the Holy Spirit where Teresa of the Andes lived her life of prayer and sacrifice, attaining the highest degrees of transforming union with Christ. Totally aware that of herself she could do nothing, she looked to Christ for help. Moved by His grace and strength, she offered her life as a sacrifice of adoration and praise to God. Through her life lived in union with Jesus, she looked to Him and sought His rich blessings for the world.

This image of Teresa of the Andes imploring Christ for the needs of the Church, and asking that more and more men and women will come to know God's boundless love in the depths of their hearts, well expresses the true meaning and power of the prayerful life of the Chilean Saint.

## The Name Teresa

The Church has canonized four Carmelites who carry the name Saint Teresa. On March 12, 1622, Gregory XV proclaimed Teresa of Avila, the holy foundress of the reformed Carmel, to be a Saint. During the Holy Year of 1925, Pius XI proclaimed Thérèse of the Child Jesus and of the Holy Face a Saint. Millions know her as the Little Flower. Nine years later, in 1934, Pius XI declared Teresa Margharita of the Sacred Heart a Saint. This Saint Teresa is often referred to as the Lily of Florence.

When the beatification process began for Sister Teresa of Jesus, there was immediate confusion over her name. It was difficult to keep Teresa of the Andes mentally separated and distinct from the other three illustrious Carmelite women who bear the same name. At the outset of the canonical proceedings, a simple, practical solution was reached. She would officially be called Teresa of the Andes. Throughout the trials, this rule was deliberately followed and simplified matters for the judges.

The name was officially confirmed during the beatification ceremonies when Pope John Paul II referred to her, at least a dozen times, as Sister Teresa of the Andes. In the Pope's beautiful canonization homily, however, the Pontiff consistently referred to her as Saint Teresa of Jesus of the Andes, precisely because this name identifies her so perfectly. When Juanita took the Carmelite habit at the Monastery of Los Andes, she herself chose to be called Sister Teresa of Jesus, for this name accurately reflects the theme of her short life. In fact, by the time of her death she had become Teresa of Jesus in every sense of the term.

# Part One:
# Her Life on Earth

**Born in South America**

Teresa of the Andes was born at 1352 Rosas Street in Santiago, Chile, on July 13, 1900, the daughter of a wealthy and aristocratic family. Her parents were Miguel Fernández Jarequemada and Lucía Solar Armstrong. Two days later, on the vigil of the feast of Our Lady of Mount Carmel, the little girl was baptized in the Church of Saint Ann and given the name Juana Enriqueta Josefina de los Sagrados Corazones. But in her family and among her friends she was always affectionately called Juanita.

Juanita was the fourth child in the family. Lucía, the oldest, was Juanita's senior by 7 years. Her brother Miguel was 4 years older; her brother Luís 2 years older. A sister, Juana, died just a few hours after birth. Rebecca, her other sister, was born a year and 8 months after Juanita. Ignacio was the youngest.

**Baptismal Name**

Before Juanita came into this world, there was a family dispute about the name she was to receive. Following a strong biblical tradition, her parents wanted her to be named after one of her grandmothers. But which one? Her father wanted her named after his own mother, Enriqueta Jaraquemada Vargas. What could be more natural since the child was to be baptized on the feast of Saint Henry?

But Lucía, his wife, insisted that the child be given the first name of her own mother, Juana Armstrong Gana, who had died just three years previously. This was very pleasing to her maternal grandfather, Eulogio Solar, a medical doctor and a member of the aristocracy.

It was finally decided that the newborn girl would be called Juana Henrietta Josephine of the Sacred Hearts. Her mother was delighted that she was named Juana, the name Henrietta was added to please her father, and she was given the name Josephine because of her mother's special devotion to Saint Joseph, the guardian of virgins, and the title "of the Sacred Hearts" because both of her parents were devoted to the Sacred Heart of Jesus and to Mary whose heart was so closely united to her Son.

## Not Born in Poverty

"Jesus did not desire me to be born poor like himself; I was born in the midst of riches, spoiled by all," she wrote in her Diary. The family was a wealthy farming family and could afford every possible comfort. In this closely knit family, Juanita was loved by all. From the very beginning she enjoyed and maintained a basic, healthy trust in the goodness of life and people.

Her family surrounded her with human as well as religious love and affection. They possessed a deep spirit of faith. Her home environment was Christian in every way, offering the help she needed to acquire authentic religious feelings and sentiments that were to remain with her throughout life.

From the time Juanita was 5, she never tired of hearing others, especially priests or nuns, talk about God and sacred things. She delighted in asking questions about religious matters, for this reminded her of the God she loved. She longed to know how to go to heaven. On one occasion when she asked about this, the parish priest pointed his hand in the direction of the Andes Mountains. But the young priest, fearing that he might be misunderstood, added that the secret of the way to heaven was not to be found in a place above that gorgeous and majestic chain of mountains in South America, but that the way by which one can go to heaven was to be found in the Tabernacle, for Jesus alone is the true way to heaven. Juanita always treasured these words since they told her how she would find her way to see God.

### "My Life Is Divided Into Two Periods"

Describing her own life in a journal she called her *Intimate Diary*, she writes:

*My life is divided into two periods: (the first is) more or less from the time I attained the age of reason until my first Communion. Jesus filled me with favors both in the first period as well as in the second, from my first Communion till now. Or better still, till my soul enters the harbor of Carmel.*

Her early life was lived in the family home in Santiago, the capital city of Chile, or at the magnificent 23,000 acre hacienda of her maternal grandfather, Don Eulogio, at Chacabuco. She was especially close to her affectionate younger sister Rebecca, and both were doted on by their grandfather, who encouraged them to go horseback riding every evening. He loved being with the two girls, and they loved being spoiled by him.

When her beloved grandfather died, Juanita experienced a deep sense of loss. She experienced grief for the first time. The dear old man died, according to

Juanita's account, just as Mass was being offered in the chapel on his estate. During the elevation of the host his soul took flight from this world. His death made a deep and lasting impression on little Juanita, filling her with sadness and making her see how all good things here on earth must eventually pass away.

## Before Her First Communion

No one is born a saint. It takes time and effort to become one. "God made us without ourselves," to repeat the much-quoted saying of Saint Augustine, "but He cannot sanctify us without ourselves." Sanctity is a long and arduous process, similar to that of scaling a very high, rugged mountain. Each person is made in the image and likeness of God, which is the basis of all human dignity, but it is only with time and effort that men and women give evidence of becoming more like God by keeping the commandments and walking in the footsteps of Jesus.

## "The Good and the Beautiful"

There are fundamental obstacles to achieving a life of true holiness. Each of us has a divided heart. At one moment our hearts are taken up with the highest and most noble aspirations for good, and moments later are consumed with enormous selfishness or savage egotism. There are times when we feel noble only to discover a short time later that we can be very ruthless. This often causes great distress of soul and leaves us puzzled and afraid. But until these faults of our nature are cured, we are unable to be guided consistently by the higher principles of love, which affirm that we do not belong to nature but to the transcendent maker of nature, the God of love and the source of all joy and happiness.

7

Juanita Fernández was no exception to this rule of human nature. She had her faults. She had to struggle, and she had to keep struggling throughout her life. When she was still quite young, certain faults quickly became evident. In her *Diary* she speaks of the need to overcome vanity. She tells us that many family members indiscreetly said she was the prettiest one - though they did not speak this way in the presence of her mother, for Señora Fernández disapproved.

This lively and at times strong-minded young girl also had a predisposition to anger. She acknowledges to herself in her *Diary* that at times she found persons and things bothersome and annoying, which tempted her to anger. She writes that certain things or people make "my blood boil." She even describes in great detail a "ferocious fit of anger and rage" that swept over her when she was vacationing at Chacabuco and was not allowed to have her own way.

It took this lively young Chilean girl a long time to overcome her inclination to anger and to gain dominion over these disorderly forces in her life. And it was not easy. After describing the depths of her struggle, she expressed her discovery that "the good and the beautiful always cost tears."

**Daily Mass**

From the time Juanita was 6 years old, her mother and her aunt Juana took her to daily Mass. Concerning this stage in her life, she writes in her *Diary*: "After the earthquake in 1906, Jesus took my heart to be His own." From that day, her desire to receive Communion grew stronger. She began to plead with her mother and aunt to let her approach the altar rail, but her continued pleas were unavailing. Each time Juanita was given the same reply: "You are too young."

This was a setback for Juanita, but she did not allow herself to become excessively discouraged or despondent. Instead, she tells us that she was aware that her soul was in need of deeper purification and preparation. So she began intensifying her efforts to overcome her faults and failings, convinced that this was the best way to prepare herself to approach the blessed table of the Lord. Despite her best efforts and intentions, the longed-for permission was not immediately granted. Only a few years later were her mother and aunt fully satisfied. At last, they did give their permission, but on the condition that she allow herself to be prepared by the Religious of the Sacred Heart, who conducted a school in Santiago. The Sisters who prepared her were Mothers Julia Ríos and Ramona Gumucio, assisted by the Jesuit Fathers Colom and Falgueras.

## Devotion to the Blessed Virgin

A distinctive feature and grace of Juanita's entire life was her tender devotion to the Virgin Mary. It began when she was about 6 years old. What is admirable about her Marian devotion - and what produced solid fruit in her life - was that this devotion to Mary was not based on empty sentimentality but rather was biblically well-grounded. Hence it brought Juanita to live her life more perfectly for Jesus. The touchstone of all authentic Marian devotion is found in those who strive to be blessed like Mary by "hearing the Word of God and keeping it." Devotion of this kind is true devotion to Mary and impels one to live out the Marian injunction to the servants at the wedding feast of Cana to "do whatever He tells you to do."

One way Juanita practiced her devotion to Mary was the daily recitation of the rosary, "the holy Rosary" as she called it. Her brother Luís, who was 2 years her senior, taught her how to say the rosary. They made a pact to recite the beads every day, a promise Juanita faithfully fulfilled, "except one time," as she tells us, "when I forgot."

## Statue of the Virgin

One special statue of the Virgin meant a great deal to her. When this devout little child was at Chacabuco for the last time, she became very sick. Juanita was having a particularly hard time taking the unpleasant medicines prescribed by her physician. To help her overcome this repugnance, Aunt Juana made a deal with Juanita, "if you take your medicine faithfully I will give you a porcelain statue of the Virgin Mary that you love." It was a deal that couldn't be refused. The little girl drank her medicine and was given the statue, which became exceedingly dear to her and which always remained by her bedside.

Before leaving home for Carmel, Juanita gave this beautiful statue of the Virgin, "who never failed to console me and listen to me," to her brother Luís. In a letter dated April 1919, Juanita wrote:

*Luís, before leaving, I bequeath to you as a seal of our perpetual fraternity, the statue of the Most Holy Virgin, which has been my inseparable companion. She has been my intimate confidante from the tenderest years of my life. She used to listen to me when I told her of my joys and sorrows. So many times she comforted my heart when it was weighed down with sorrow.*

## Temperament

Juanita had a very sweet disposition and was loved by all. But she was nevertheless a lively, strong and courageous girl. Hence on occasion she did become irascible. Before her First Communion she sometimes displayed fits of anger when she didn't get her own way. Juanita relates that she couldn't stand a cousin of her mother, Rosenda Luco Solar, who lived with the Fernández family. Her mother Lucía likewise recalled how Juanita would get into fights with her younger sister Rebecca, and how it cost her dearly to put aside her anger and obey. This was particularly true when she was young, especially when she was told to do something that went contrary to her will. Then she would deliberately take her time in doing what she was told to do. Little by little she learned to bring her anger under control, although even at the end of her life she still had to struggle with her emotional reactions to anger.

Precisely because she had a sweet disposition and was good natured, her brothers and sisters often teased her and tried to provoke her to anger. But Juanita, now resolved to practice virtue to prepare for her First Communion, struggled courageously to master herself and refused to fall into their trap. The others soon discovered that no matter what they did she wouldn't lose her temper.

When Juanita was 6 she began to attend the school of the Teresianist Sisters each afternoon. She learned how to read at that school, even though she only went there for a month.

In 1907 she became a day student at the school of the Religious of the Sacred Heart located on the Alameda, the most famous street in Santiago. The Fernández family was at the time living at 164 Saint Dominic Street.

The Sisters at that school prepared Juanita for her First Confession. From that time, the young girl tried even harder to overcome her faults. She implored God's help, acknowledging that alone she was unable to heal the divisions of her own heart. She doubled her efforts to be rid of her faults and also redoubled her pleadings with her mother and Aunt Juana to be allowed to go to Communion. They still would not yield to her request.

## Perseverance in Prayer

Juanita faithfully kept on seeking and knocking until her heart-felt prayer was at last heard. Her mother finally gave consent but on the condition that a year of preparation precede her reception of the Holy Eucharist. It seemed as though that year would never end, so intense were Juanita's longing for the great Sacrament. But she kept preparing her soul and reports that "during this time the Virgin helped me cleanse my heart of every imperfection." The days seemed to pass very slowly but finally the year ended and when she was 10 years old, Juanita made her First Communion.

## General Confession

The night before this very special event, she made a general confession of all her sins. When she returned home, Juanita relates how she went to each member of the household and begged pardon for all her faults against them. She first went to her father, who with tears in his eyes took her into his arms and told her he had never had any reason to be displeased with her and how happy he felt to see how good she was. Next she went to her mother, who also received her with tears of joy. She then went to each of her brothers and sisters and then to all the servants in the house, begging their forgiveness. Understandably, all were deeply moved in the presence of one who had the strength and graciousness to beg pardon for all her faults as a gift and a blessing from God.

### "A Cloudless Day, the Happiest of My Life"

The long-awaited day of her First Communion was one of the most glorious of her life. The event took place on September 11, 1910, which happened to be a national holiday as well as the first centenary of the independence of her country. "It was a cloudless day," she writes in her *Diary*, "the happiest of my life."

Her mother helped her dress for the occasion. Juanita was thinking of nothing else but Jesus. Everything else was a matter of indifference to her and, as a matter of fact, she didn't even look at herself in the mirror when they told her how precious she looked in her white dress.

Monsignor Angel Jara preached a moving sermon and then gave her Communion, together with 29 other girls. Like Thérèse of Lisieux, Juanita was able to say that her first Communion was truly a fusion between Jesus and her soul. Words are quite naturally powerless to express adequately what transpired in the depths of her soul "when she heard His [Jesus'] sweet voice for the first time." No wonder, it was the most beautiful day of her life! From that day till the end of her life the Eucharist remained her preferred devotion, for in the Eucharist Jesus showed her that He took her to be His own.

She wrote to Father Falgueras that:

*From the time I made my first Communion, Our Lord spoke to me after Communion. He told me things that I never dreamed of, and even when I asked Him, He told me things that were to happen and they actually happened.*

13

Those familiar with the lives of the saintly Carmelites Thérèse of Lisieux and Elizabeth of the Trinity will detect similarities in their lives and in the life of Teresa of the Andes. This is particularly so regarding the first reception of Holy Communion, which brought about deep and lasting effects in the lives of all three. After Juanita's death, her older brother Luís wrote in a published biography of his sister that "after her First Communion all noticed changes in Juanita's conduct. Until then she had some defects: her character was a bit irascible and she found it difficult to obey."

Juanita herself tells us the cause of these noticeable changes that came over her soul. "From that first embrace," she writes, "Jesus did not let me go but took me to Himself." She went to Communion every day. Whenever she went to Communion, she wrote in her journal: "Jesus spoke with me for a long time." In her charming simplicity and innocence, she thought Jesus was speaking with everyone during the time of Communion in the same remarkable and special mystical way He was speaking with her. As a result, one day she ingenuously mentioned this grace to her mother, who, in turn, became alarmed and advised the little girl to go and discuss this matter with Father Colom. The 10 year old admits, however, that she was too frightened and ashamed to do so.

### Frequent Illnesses

Juanita was no stranger to sickness. She was often ill, especially on the feast of the Immaculate Conception. Though extremely devoted to the Virgin and while Mary helped and comforted her in many ways, Juanita began to entertain the idea that it would be on the feast of the Immaculate Conception, December eighth, that the

Virgin would obtain for her the grace to leave this mortal life and be admitted to the joys heaven. Her dream didn't come to pass.

At the age of 13 Juanita was stricken with a serious attack of appendicitis which required surgery at Saint Vincent's Hospital. Her mother feared Juanita was going to die. On the day of the operation Juanita received Communion very early that morning. Then in her Diary she reports, "I asked Our Lord to give me courage and serenity."

On the appointed day, the attendants soon came to take the patient down to surgery. Just before Juanita was taken to the operating room, she informs us, "I took my statue of the Virgin, I embraced my crucifix, I kissed them and said to them: 'Soon I will contemplate you face to face. Farewell.'" The attendants then took her to the operating room, where the anesthesiologist administered chloroform, a highly toxic anesthesia frequently administered in the early years of this century. Although the operation was successful, Juanita developed serious postoperative complications because of this anesthetic.

## Challenged by Death

This close experience with death neither disturbed nor depressed her; instead, it made her think more seriously about the meaning and the sacredness of human life. She allowed herself to be challenged by this brush with death and consequently came out of this experience a deeper and more mature person. The young Chilean girl rose to the challenge and joyfully resolved to live her life and her faith more seriously and more intensely, and more courageously too.

## To Suffer and to Love

Juanita has a remarkable saying in her *Diary*: "My life is composed of two things: suffering and love." Suffering played a major role in her life, and she never flinched from it nor did she try to escape it. Instead, she saw suffering as an indispensable means for living her life fully, as long as it was always permeated with love and based on the imitation of Christ.

In her *Diario Intimo* Juanita writes of her personal desire to embrace suffering. This desire was neither morbid nor unhealthy. Her desire to pass through the crucible of suffering was based on the teachings of her faith, which showed her how to grow in love for and imitation of the Crucified Jesus. She wanted to be like the One she loved, and was fully aware He had travelled the lonely road of suffering.

She says that Our Lord told her, "if you want to be like Me, then take up your cross with love and joy." Moved by these words, she explains the deep reasons that drew her to seek suffering:

*Suffering pleases me for two reasons: because Jesus preferred suffering from his birth till his death on the cross. It must then be something very great since the All-Powerful One sought to suffer always. And suffering also pleases me because it is in the crucible of sorrow that souls are formed and because Jesus gives this gift to the souls He loves the most."*

## Can't You Suffer One Moment of Solitude?

The little girl who was born in Santiago, a beautiful city located midway between the Pacific Ocean and the Andes Mountains, shares with us a revealing experience that occurred when she was 14 years old. She was ill at

16

home, and one of the family servants was caring for her as well as for several other members who were sick. Because she was not getting all the attention she craved, Juanita began feeling sorry for herself and broke down in tears. Just then her tear-filled eyes caught sight of a picture of the Sacred Heart in her room, and she confesses to her Diary: "I heard a very sweet voice saying to me: 'How is this possible? I am alone on the altar for love of you, and can't you even suffer one moment of solitude?'"

From that time on she spent longer hours conversing with Christ in prayer, and He taught her how to suffer and never complain. He also spoke to her about intimate union with Himself and assured her that she would become a Carmelite. She also began to keep a discreet silence about her inner life but evidently, as Mother Angelica wrote later in the Circular-Letter traditionally sent to all Carmels after the death of a Carmelite sister, "this did not prevent other persons who dealt with her, even if it was just once, from detecting in her something extraordinary and from noting the great influence she had for attracting other souls to goodness."

## Juanita's Education

From grade school through high school, Juanita attended institutions conducted by the Religious of the Sacred Heart. Both schools had been founded by members of the Society of the Sacred Heart, a Congregation founded in France by Saint Madeleine Sophie Barat about 1800.

From the first, the schools of the Religious of the Sacred Heart in Santiago were held in the highest esteem, and their reputation was justly deserved. The foundress of this Society had only been recently beatified (May 24, 1903) by Pope Leo XIII and was to be canonized by Pope Pius XI on May 25, 1925.

The schools of the Religious of the Sacred Heart have always enjoyed and continue to enjoy a superior reputation, no doubt chiefly because of their academic excellence and even more because of the spiritual values they instill. The teachers of these schools had faith in young people and were able to love them in a holy way and educate them into the great ideals of the Christian life. It was precisely for these reasons that Señor and Señora Fernández chose these schools for their gifted daughter. Juanita was aware of the value of such an education and was grateful. She makes an interesting entry in her *Diary*, noting that "the education of women is even more important than that of men, for the woman will educate the man."

### College of the Sacred Heart

In Juanita's time two "colleges" were conducted by the Religious of the Sacred Heart in Santiago. It was common then to call schools conducted by religious sisters Colleges, particularly when the chief emphasis of the training was on religion and if all the girls wore uniforms. The first Sacred Heart college, the elementary school Juanita attended as an extern or day student, was opened in 1885 and closed in 1969. The school itself was located on the Alameda, a beautiful street that has existed since colonial times. In Juanita's day this street was lined with lovely elm trees and named the *Alameda de las Delicias*. Today its official name is the Alameda of Bernardo O'Higgins, though it is usually just called the Alameda.

18

When Juanita was studying there - from 1907 to 1914 - the Fernández family was living nearby at 475 Ejercito Street. The appearance of the school was most impressive and around 250 students attended classes there. Juanita did very well in all her classes and was especially delighted because she could live at home. All in all, Juanita received an excellent humanistic and religious education and it was in the magnificent chapel of this school that she received her First Communion.

Juanita studied at the second Sacred Heart "college" during her high school years, 1915 to 1918. This school was located on Maestranza Street, today known as Portugal Street. At the time the Fernández family was living at 92 Vergara Street, which is quite a distance from the school. It was partly for this reason that Juanita was made to become an intern student, a boarder. Both schools, unfortunately, are no longer in existence, though the school on Maestranza Street has been preserved as a national monument because of its architectural value.

The Sacred Heart school on the Alameda was referred to as the French School, because the Sisters who founded it had come directly from France and also because the French language was stressed. People generally referred to the boarding school on Maestranza as the English School because the Sisters who originally made that foundation had previously lived in the United States and stressed the teaching of English. For a long time the people in Santiago called these religious the English Nuns.

## An Excellent Student

As she was growing up, it soon became apparent that Juanita was a gifted student. She had all the endowments and talents necessary to excel. Diligent in her studies, she also fully appreciated the educational opportunities her parents were providing for her. She strove to make them happy and proud by using her talents to the fullest. In some of her classes she was awarded the highest marks.

Juanita, like all good students, had to work hard at her studies. Success in studies is always the fruit of great effort. One of her classmates informs us that Juanita had a particular dislike for chemistry but was determined to do her utmost to attain a good grade to make her parents happy. Despite her repugnance for the subject, she did her best and obtained the highest mark.

When she was 18 she graduated with high honors. Some of her high school compositions are still preserved today. In these papers, written in her own hand, one can immediately see why she had been accorded first prize in penmanship. In the handwriting of this attractive young girl and in her compositions, we can't help but be struck by the beauty of her character as well as by the keenness of her mind and her giftedness of soul.

## Child of Mary

Juanita thanked God for her academic achievements in high school, but what she treasured even more was that on June 15, 1917, she and seven other girls were admitted to become *Children of Mary*. This high honor was awarded to the girls in a very solemn ceremony. Jesuit Father Ramon Font celebrated the Mass at Maestranza Street. It was followed by Benediction of the Blessed Sacrament. When the medals were awarded it was made clear that they were bestowed as the school's highest distinction to students who were "exemplary in their piety, in the fulfillment of their duties and for their excellent conduct." In all the schools conducted by the Religious of the Sacred Heart, this custom and practice is still honored. Juanita was so proud of this honor that sometimes in her *Diary* (but much more frequently in her letters) she signed her name Juana and then added the initials H. M., the Spanish initials for a Child of Mary.

Her high school had an honor system in which outstanding students were given medals or ribbons of different colors. Juana received the medal awarded to the most dedicated students, the ones most remarkable and consistent in the fulfillment of their scholarly obligations. That's why she was accorded the blue ribbon which was granted to students for outstanding conduct.

Such medals were bestowed twice a year for those who received the highest marks in their class and were worn at special ceremonies as a sign of academic achievement, a cooperative attitude, and overall excellence.

## Put in Charge of Younger Students

Because of her evident leadership qualities, Juanita was put in charge of some of the younger girls in the school. For Juanita neither her academic excellence nor such duties were a cause for vanity. Rather they were always a challenge to imitate the virtues of Mary more perfectly, for in truth she cherished her medal as a Child of Mary more than any of her other medals or ribbons of distinction.

This is seen clearly on a day in 1917 when Juanita was entrusted with the task of taking care of some of the younger girls. The girls were misbehaving at table. When Juanita tried to correct them, they paid no attention to her. This made Juanita very upset or, as she so often expresses it in her *Diary*, it made "her blood boil." She expressed her anger to the children in no uncertain terms.

Juanita very quickly repented of her fault and begged pardon of the little ones. In her *Diary* she wonders if Jesus would have acted toward the children in that way, and she especially deplores her behavior as being unworthy of a true Child of Mary.


## Friendships

During her life, Juanita was blessed with many wonderful friends. She surely had all the attributes required of a perfect and devoted friend. She was warmhearted and sympathetic; she loved to communicate with others and respected the sacredness of the personality of others; and she willingly shared her goodness with them and had that inner goodness that is the true foundation of sound and lasting friendships.

In the official "Relatio" prepared for the Beatification of Sister Teresa of the Andes, we read that many people testified that in friendship "she was a stupendous, amiable and discreet friend." This shows that in her human relations as well as in her high school apostolic activities she possessed all the human qualities and attractive virtues that make a young girl appealing in her character as well as effective in her work.

Today Juanita strikes us as especially modern and appealing in her great love of sports. She seems to be so South American in this. We are told that she was an excellent swimmer and loved to go horseback riding when vacationing at Chacabuco or Bucalemu. Being an accomplished equestrienne, we are told she could ride for hours on end.

She says that horseback riding was a great passion for her; there was nothing she liked to do more. Her great regret when recuperating from her appendicitis operation was that the doctors had forbidden horseback riding for some weeks. In her *Diary* and letters she also reports that some of the other girls were so impressed with her ability and stamina in riding for many hours at a time that they described her as "a real Amazon." Others testified that she played tennis "furiously." Since she was well coordinated, she also became an excellent swimmer and won many matches.

## The Gift of Music

She was also gifted musically. She played the piano and harmonium very well and had a pleasing voice. Her older brother informs us in his account of her life that the family possessed a beautiful organ in their private chapel at Chacabuco. Eventually this summer home had to be sold; but, since the harmonium had been in the Solar family for generations, it was given to Juanita. She kept it in her bedroom in Santiago. Luís, her brother, tells us that every morning, while the others were still asleep, she played this harmonium ever so softly and beautifully. Because his bedroom was next to hers, he had the pleasure of hearing these soft strains of music at dawning of each day. On one occasion he questioned her about this, and with great simplicity she told him: "It is such a joy when I awaken to salute God by singing." Since she was blessed musically, it is little wonder that she later confessed she felt a kinship with Blessed Elizabeth of the Trinity, a Carmelite sister who excelled in music and had studied at the Dijon Conservatory of Music in France.

Juanita was tall and graceful, attractive and filled with charm.  A collection of her photographs reveals that she had fair skin and light hair.  One biographer describes her as "being tall among the tall."  She was also graced with beautiful blue eyes, which can no doubt be attributed to her British ancestry; her maternal grandmother was an Armstrong.

## Desire to Become a Carmelite

When Juanita was only 15 years old she was fully convinced that she was being called to consecrate herself to God in the religious life.  But like many a teenager in high school, she struggled to discern her true calling in life and the shape and form her vocation should take.  Juanita's vocational choices narrowed down to this: should I enter the Society of the Sacred Heart, which had been founded in Paris by Saint Madeleine Sophie Barat?  Or, should I become a Carmelite according to the charism lived by Saint Teresa of Avila?  Juanita literally wrestled with and prayed earnestly over this question.  Only during her final year of high school did she satisfactorily resolve the question in her own mind.  Her greatest fear was that she might be too delicate to endure the austerities of Carmel.  In the meantime, she could do nothing but place the matter in the merciful hands of God and pray to Saint Thérèse, asking the French Carmelite to intercede that she be granted the health needed for the austere life in Carmel.

## The Decisive Interview

It was at this time, when she turned 15, that Juanita had what she describes in her *Diary* as the decisive interview with her spiritual director, Mother Julia Ríos.

In this interview she raised the issue for the first time with Mother Ríos regarding her intention to become a Carmelite. She told Mother that she had never personally met a Carmelite, but that she had read Saint Thérèse of Lisieux's The Story of a Soul several times and had drawn great profit from it. Juanita added that

> Thérèse's soul has points in common with my own. Like her, I have received many favors from Our Lord, that made her come to perfection in a short time; but I have repaid Jesus very poorly."

## Vow of Perfect Virginity

The long, intimate conversations she had with Jesus each day in Communion and prayer were producing deep and lasting effects in her young soul. His love was inviting and drawing her to express her gratitude and dedication to God in a more precise way. At 15 Juanita was able to state with full conviction: "I have understood that only in God can I find happiness, the satisfaction of my desires, the possession of all good things, because He is Truth and infinite Goodness." Consequently, she decided to consecrate her whole life to God by making a vow of virginity, but she had the good sense and prudent insight first to seek the counsel of others in a matter so serious. Even then she only made a temporary vow of chastity, which she was later given permission to do on a more permanent basis.

Juanita made her vow of virginity on the feast of the Immaculate Conception of Mary when she was 15 years old. This was not done impulsively or in haste. Instead, Juanita proceeded with great deliberation. She wrote out her vow of perpetual virginity very solemnly, promising to dedicate her entire life to God with undivided heart. This is the form that her actual vow took:

*Today, the eighth of December 1915, at the age of fifteen, I make a vow before the Most Holy Trinity and in the presence of the Virgin Mary and all the saints in heaven, to admit no other Spouse but my Lord Jesus Christ, whom I love with all my heart and whom I want to serve till the last moment of my life.*

## Letter to Her Sister Rebecca

Some months later Juanita wrote her famous letter to her younger sister, Rebecca, in which she explains that she had decided to enter Carmel. Juanita chose Rebecca's fourteenth birthday to write this letter. She begins the letter by congratulating her sister on another year of life, and tells Rebecca that now "at 14 one understands one's vocation. You hear a voice and a light shows you the path of your life." And then continues rhapsodizing about her vocation: "That beacon shone for me when I was 14 years old. I changed my course and I determined on the path that I had to follow and now I come to share with you my secrets and the ideal projects I have forged."

For some time Juanita had been convinced and enthralled that the Lord was calling her to follow in the footsteps of Saint Teresa of Avila. What is amazing, however, is that she had a firm awareness of the nature and demands of the charism of life she would vow in the Teresian Carmel. In addition, Juanita was fully aware of how much generosity and courage were needed in this vocation. Desiring to give herself to God fully, she was determined to exert every effort necessary and was aware of the inexorable law of divine love expressed so trenchantly by the Saint of Avila, who tells us that "God cannot give Himself to a soul fully until the soul gives herself fully to Him."

In her exquisite letter to Rebecca, the affectionate companion of her youth, Juanita lyrically but accurately spells out the nature of the Carmelite vocation. She writes:

*I have been caught in the loving nets of the Divine Fisherman. I see that my vocation is very great: to save souls, to provide workers for the vineyard of Christ. I, as his bride, must be thirsty for souls. I must offer my Bridegroom the blood that He shed for each soul.*

## To Become a Victim of Love

Later, after having read the writings of Saint Thérèse and Elizabeth of the Trinity, Juanita writes very explicitly that she wants to become a "victim soul." She "wants to suffer to save souls and to aid in the sanctification of priests."

Offering her sacrifices to God and detaching herself from all personal comforts and from everything in this world, Juanita generously entered religious life, instinctively intuiting what Saint Teresa of Jesus says in *The Way of Perfection,* that "this life can be heaven on earth for those who seek God alone."

But there was one great obstacle to her dream. She was troubled by one deep regret: the sorrow she felt at the thought of leaving her own family, the ones who were the dearest ties that bound her to this earth. She hated to leave her own mother, to whom she owed so much and to whom she was very deeply attached. She especially regretted leaving Rebecca, the faithful echo of her soul. As a matter of fact, the dreaded separation from her whole family became a real sacrifice to the Lord. And each family member, in turn, deeply regretted Juanita's departure.

## Boarding School

For many years Juanita was content in attending Sacred Heart school on the Alameda as a day student. She was pleased with her school and with her teachers; and, more importantly, she had the additional joy of being able to live at home with her family. It was then that her parents decided to send her to the school on Maestranza Street as a full-time boarder for her last years of high school. This turn of events came about because Doña Lucía, her mother, was becoming uneasy about Juanita. Each day when going to school her daughter would pass by Saint Ignatius High School and the young men liked to admire the young girls, especially Juanita who was especially beautiful. Juanita did nothing more than be kind and gracious to everyone, but still her mother's anxieties were increasing. A final decision was made by the mother to enroll Juanita and Rebecca as boarders during the last days of July, 1915.

At first, Juanita was less than pleased with this arrangement. She found it especially difficult to make the changes required to become a boarder. She herself tells us "it cost me dearly" to adjust to the discipline of the school. We can see how hard it was for Juanita when she, who normally was so well balanced, was plunged into sadness over the prospect of going back to school at the end of the summer vacation, which in the South American Hemisphere comprises the months of December, January and February. She was gripped by sadness, which was increasing and almost taking possession of her soul. So great was her distress and so much did it disturb her happiness to even think of going back to school, that she wrote: "The place is like a dungeon or a jail. The school should be reduced to ashes!"

But two years later by graduation time her mood had completely changed. By that time she had become very close to and deeply loved by many of the Sisters who had been kind and good to her. She also enjoyed the friendship and esteem of many of her fellow students. Now this grateful and affectionate young girl found that the thought of leaving "her beloved school" was especially painful. She could look back on all the blessings she had enjoyed there and consequently regretted that the time had come to terminate this preparatory phase of her life. She could now more clearly see how the time spent as a boarder at the school had preserved the virtue and innocence of her youth and had prepared her to live away from her family, which was an excellent preparation for her entrance into Carmel.

But, above all, she was fully convinced that it was now time to get on with her life, and to pursue her true vocation to live for God alone in Carmel.

Juanita was afforded a very fine education at the high school located on Maestranza Street. Because of the extreme depth of the writings of Saint Teresa of Chile, it is evident that she had received a good classical education. Hence, it might then be good to pause and examine the curriculum of her school.

We are fortunate to have Anita's Rucker's testimony on this matter. Anita Rucker was a cousin of Juanita. They both attended high school together. In an interview which was reported in *El Mercurio*, Santiago's leading newspaper, Anita assures us that it was a true convent school, had strict discipline and the girls were initiated into religious exercises as well as into academic matters. There were eighty boarding students on Maestranza Street. But the primary purpose of the school, in Anita Rucker's own words, was the sanctification of the student. And adding her own personal conviction, Anita continued, "That's why I always say that where Juanita became a saint was here in the college, and that's why she entered Carmel as a saint."

What was the curriculum like? Anita, who was one year older than Juanita and privileged to go to Rome at the age of 93 to attend her cousin's canonization, makes the following observations. Each day there was a class in handwriting, and all the girls had to learn to use the famous script of the Religious of the Sacred Heart. Juanita won first prize in handwriting. There was one year dedicated to ancient history, another to medieval history, a year of modern history and one to the history of Chile. Philosophical courses were given at the school. There was a year of logic, one of ontology or metaphysics; one year of psychology and a year of history of philosophy. Religion and literature were stressed. On the other hand, the physical sciences were not stressed in those days the way they are today. Juanita had to take chemistry. But Juanita, though she did not like chemistry and had trouble with the formulas, took top honors in her class.

What were Juanita's favorite subjects, Anita Rucker was asked by the reporter. She replied, "religion above all, but she loved literature and philosophy." She was proficient in Latin and could speak French fluently.


## Parties and Dancing

Any normal South American girl in her teens naturally looks forward to and enjoys parties and dancing. Did young Juanita Fernández feel the same way? Her brother Luís, who eventually became a distinguished lawyer in Santiago, informs us that Juanita generally shunned such activities. But Señora Fernández insisted that Juanita be in attendance at all the parties and dances given at their home. And Juanita complied with this command.

Still, Juanita was hesitant, reluctant. Something made her feel deeply uneasy. The source of her conflict was the vow of perfect virginity that Juanita, drawn by grace, had chosen to make. She was a naturally cheerful and joyful young lady and people were naturally drawn to her, but Luís affirms that he never saw her alone with any boy. He also assures us that he himself used to bring many young men home. While Juanita was always very gracious toward them, she never showed special interest in any of them.

Still we can't overlook one particularly interesting entry she made in her *Diary* about one young lad who was attracted to her and showed great interest. The young lad even brought her a bouquet of flowers. She very appreciatively expressed her thanks with a gracious smile for his kindness. She was naturally pleased and touched by this delicate gesture. He, too, was so pleased that he began "to come around to her house and began to walk up and down the block with her, as they then used to say."

This leads her to speak of her affection in this very innocent courtship. In translating her Diary it is difficult to correctly translate the word she used to describe these attachments. The precise word she uses is the word *pololeo,* a uniquely Chilean word that is not found in ordinary Spanish Dictionaries. It can mean many things and is an especially difficult word to translate into English.

Pololeo is generally used to describe a friendship between a boy and girl that has grown and may in time lead to courtship, but the two friends cannot be said to be engaged or even going steady as yet. During Juanita's lifetime, the ritual in Chile that she describes consisted of the boy sending flowers to the girl and then walking up and down in front of her house with her. The girl, of course, was pleased with the attention and affection.

Juanita uses pololeo to describe her natural warmth and affection, but also because this occasioned inner spiritual conflict. She almost fears that by showing any mark of affection to a boy, she might be compromising her fidelity to the Lord and her vow of life-long virginity. In what she called her *decisive interview* with her spiritual director, we find Mother Julia Ríos taking a very dim view of this matter, carefully reminding young Juanita that she had promised herself to the Lord not just for a day but forever. Mother Ríos does this not because she is trying to make a severe pronunciamento on Juanita's problem, but because, as a spiritual director, she is trying to lead the young girl to Christian perfection and strengthen her resolve to remain faithful to the promises she made to her Lord and Spouse.

Regarding parties and dancing she was required to attend and where problems might arise, Juanita acted with prudence, carefully harmonizing these situations with her vow of virginity. She was careful not to draw undue attention to herself or appear to be singular. Therefore, she contributed to the festivities and enjoyment of these events by playing the piano or guitar, or else by singing in her delightful contralto voice. She was not antisocial in any way nor was she opposed to such normal gatherings for healthy entertainment. It was just that in her heart of hearts she cherished this strong sense of loyalty and fidelity to her Lord, to whom she had solemnly pledged "to have no other Spouse but our Lord Jesus Christ." Juanita fully and faithfully lived the vow she had made, because she saw it as her personal mystery of truth in love.

## Carmelite Saints, Her Role Models

In Juanita's now famous *decisive interview* with Mother Ríos concerning her vocation, she was struggling to discern if God was truly calling her to enter Carmel. Juanita confided to her sister Rebecca how strongly she felt drawn to Carmel. But Mother Ríos, eager that this generous young woman not let herself be carried away by her enthusiasm and imagination, reminded her that the life of Carmel is austere and difficult. Since Juanita's health was delicate, Mother Ríos asked the young student, "Do you think you have the necessary health? Do you feel strong enough for this vocation?"

Mother Ríos earnestly encouraged Juanita to read the writings of three Carmelites: *The Story of a Soul* by Saint Thérèse of the Child Jesus, *The Autobiography* of Saint Teresa of Avila, and finally, *The Praise of Glory* by Blessed Elizabeth of the Trinity, the young French Carmelite who died at Dijon when Juanita was 6 years old. After reading these books, Juanita was more convinced than ever of her Carmelite vocation. Her keen mind and ardent heart drew deep spiritual nourishment from these Carmelite women for whom she felt such affinity and attraction.

From the time she was 15, Juanita read the writings of these Carmelite women, drawing much light and inspiration from their contemplative lifestyle. She used their lives and examples as her role models to prepare herself for life in a Carmelite Monastery. The young Santiago student didn't overlook the fact that these women had also experienced the call to enter Carmel when they were quite young, and had to overcome strong parental objections to achieve their goal.

## Apostolic Activities

By temperament, Juanita was a very happy person. She was even-tempered and was not subject to excessive highs or lows. Those who knew her also tell us she wasn't given to ostentation or affectation. While attractive and gracious, she never sought to draw undue attention to herself. Instead, she was always kind and sympathetic and at boarding school tended to reach out to those who were in need of encouragement. She possessed the happy gift of saying the right thing at the right time, especially to those in trouble, and always doing so with particular tact and good grace.

From the time of her First Communion, she strove for Christian perfection as proposed to us in the Gospel. She never limited herself to seeking merely her own self-fulfillment or perfection. Juanita realized that we are all called to reach out with a true Christian spirit of love of neighbor to all the children of God in need.

## Caring for Juanito, a Little Abandoned Orphan

A good example of her preferential love for the poor was the case of Juanito, an abandoned orphan, who came to the Fernández home begging for food and clothing. Juanita took the little boy in, fed him and even saw to it that he was given lodging with neighbors. Little Juanito was always allowed to come for lunch. Juanita personally served him, often saving her dessert or special things for him. She even pawned her watch on one occasion when he was in need of a pair of shoes. She writes in 1917: "I was given 30 pesos for my feast day

*(Saint John the Baptizer, June 24th).* I'm going to buy shoes for Juanito and the rest I'll give to my mother so that she can give it to the poor." She concludes her account of this episode by telling us she is convinced that "it is so rich to give to the poor!"

Far from being self-centered, she loved to reach out to others. Even on her First Communion day, which she describes as "the happiest day of my life," she didn't forget the poor. She and the other girls, after they made their post-Communion thanksgiving, gave some of the money they received as gifts that day to the poor.

## Spiritual Works of Mercy

As Juanita grew older she loved to practice not only the corporal works of mercy but the spiritual ones as well. She especially and earnestly loved to share her faith with others. She taught catechism to little children during a Mission when she was vacationing with her close friend, Elisita Valdés, who was then aspiring to enter the Carmel of Valparaíso. In a letter written from Santiago in November 1918 to Mother Angelica, she describes the success of the Mission conducted at her friend's summer estate at Cunaco, which is situated several hundred miles south of Santiago. Juanita was vacationing there with the Valdés family, who were very close to Juanita's family.

The future Carmelites took a very active part in that Mission. Both acted as sacristans; and, every night when they prepared the sanctuary lamp, "we resolved to leave our hearts with Him for the whole night." The Mission was a huge success. "God moved many hearts," Juanita later wrote. More than 1,300 hosts were distributed, and 76 children were prepared for their First Communion.

## Keeping an Intimate Spiritual Diary

Truly extraordinary and inspiring are the writings Juanita left us. They give us rare insight into the growth, development and personality of the young Chilean saint. Through her writings Juanita shares with us not only the events of her short but rich life but also the inspirations that guided her to maturity and holiness.

We can now see that one of the most important and providential things that happened during Juanita's school days was keeping her renowned *Diario Intimo*. This came about almost by accident. Madre Julia Ríos, her spiritual director, asked her to write down the graces and favors God was bestowing on her soul. Obedient to this command, Juanita Fernández began writing down the intimate secrets of her interior life which have become an acknowledged part of the history of spirituality and mysticism.

A careful perusal of this *Intimate Diary* reveals the life of a young girl that is deep and rich, graced with special insight and beauty. She has the style and grace of the great ones, and her writing shows signs of exceptional maturity. But throughout she always retains that charm and simplicity which are the special privilege of the young. In going through her journal, one is struck by the fact that her innocent heart and loving soul reached perfect psychological and spiritual equilibrium in the springtime of her life.

How fortunate we are that Juanita did not keep her spiritual treasures to herself. Happiness is born a twin, they say, and Juanita did not jealously keep her blessings and the roots of her good life hidden under a basket. On the contrary, by writing down her thoughts she has become a beacon of light and radiant goodness for others, thus sharing and bringing a greater fullness of life to others.

In this precious and delightful *Diary* one finds easy access to the beautiful soul of our little Chilean Carmelite. At the very beginning of her journal, she dispels any thought that we are going to read just an interesting story of the life of a teenage girl or of the interesting events that happened during her lifetime. Instead, she candidly promises us at the outset that we are about to read "the intimate life of a poor soul, who, without any merit on her part, Jesus Christ loved in a special way and filled abundantly with His favors and graces." This sums up the remarkable power and beauty of the book.

Going through the pages of her journal we are able to follow Juanita's spiritual journey to God in holiness. She is aware that God has always been the center of her life and has filled it with His sunshine and love since she was a little child. We discern that holiness was the overriding concern and ambition of her brief life and that she dedicated every ounce of her strength to this goal. By the end of the volume, we have no doubt that she has been totally transformed into Christ and, to paraphrase Saint Paul's famous words, that Juanita lives no longer, but Christ lives in her.

Juanita exerted herself and strove for Christian holiness. Each day she better understood that holiness is not just doing difficult and unpleasant things or even suffering a great deal (although there was a good deal of suffering in her young life). True holiness, she is fully aware, primarily consists not of our efforts but in being loved and cherished by God and allowing God to fill our lives with the fullness of His love. It means being conformed to Christ. It means taking on Christ's mind and heart, and allowing the Holy Spirit to fill our lives with His divine fruits, the unmistakable sign of God's loving presence. This is what this young girl did or, rather, this is how "the young virgin of the Andes," to quote the words of Pope John Paul II, "proclaims to us the beauty and happiness that comes from a pure heart." In a word, she invited and allowed the Holy Spirit to make her a shining witness and model of the holiness of Christ.

Mother Angelica, Juanita's Prioress and Novice Mistress, makes this wise observation about the merits of the *Intimate Diary.*

*We see in her copy book her diligence in the practice of the virtues, how she made her examination of conscience, how she spiritualized all things: studies, dealing with other students, keeping the rules of the school, and her recreation.*

Finally, we find in her *Diary* an account of the many ways God was drawing her to ever-closer degrees of union with Himself. Some entries, especially the retreat to the Holy Spirit and the retreat of 1919, contain truly mystical graces in the strict sense of the term. They enable us to see how lofty and sublime was her union with Christ. It can be said with full confidence that she arrived at some of those elevated stages of the spiritual life that are described by her patron saint, Saint Teresa of Avila and by Saint John of the Cross.

Still, in the name of prudence, it can and must be stressed that one can never be sure or fully satisfied in judging such mystical graces, and even less is it permitted to use them as "proof" that the person who experienced them is a saint. This sound principle is in accord with time-honored traditions of the Church and follows the sagacious norms proposed by Pope Benedict XIV. It is to be remembered that these sound norms are still honored today in causes for beatification and canonization. But, becoming more specific and more practical, the same Pope Benedict observed that when an *official decree* has been issued by the Church which proves beyond a shadow of doubt that a Servant of God has practiced the Christian virtues to an heroic degree, then *these mystical accounts* must be given their full weight and appropriate credence.

## Letters to Mother Angelica

When she was 17 Juanita initiated a steady correspondence with Mother Angelica of the Most Blessed Sacrament, Prioress of the Carmelite Monastery of Los Andes, Chile. The young girl wrote these letters with the hope of being accepted as a novice in that community.

Fortunately, the 20 letters written to Mother Angelica have been preserved; and are extremely helpful in following Juanita's growth in her Carmelite vocation. The young girl from Santiago opens her soul to Mother Angelica completely. So much so that with complete honesty she candidly acknowledges even her faults and shortcomings. And in these letters, in a true spirit of docility, Juanita seeks advice from the Prioress as to how she can fully understand and spiritually prepare herself for her Carmelite vocation.

Juanita also describes the struggles she encounters in preparing herself to enter Carmel where, to use her own words, "behind the grilles of Carmel I will encounter horizons without limits, divine horizons that the world cannot comprehend." Being honest, she tells Reverend Mother about how God in His infinite love is helping her overcome her faults. She also assures Mother that in her desire to become a Carmelite,

> *I am not seeking Tabor, but Calvary, for I understand that the life of a Carmelite is a continual abnegation, not only of the flesh but of the will.*

She sums up her understanding of the meaning of the Carmelite vocation by stating that,

> *I have asked nothing else than to love Him, and nothing more; that I, his soldier, follow him till death, but always on the condition that He assist me with His grace. The life of a Carmelite is to suffer, love and pray, and in this I find my ideal. Reverend Mother, Jesus has taught me these three things since I was a child.*

In another letter, Juanita informs Mother Angelica Teresa that she has recently joined the Priestly Reparation Society, whose goal is to pray for priests who need prayers so badly. She finds the aims of the society to be a truly Carmelite devotion, since a Carmelite nun must sacrifice herself for priests. "This was the reason that moved me to join this society," she wrote.

## Her Little Niece

In writing to Mother Angelica, who previously had been a member of the Valparaíso Carmel and who had helped found the Los Andes Carmel, Juanita does not hesitate to share with her future superior the joy that now fills her heart in being close to Luz, her newborn niece. She says that she finds her niece enchanting, especially as she contemplates that this little child is the temple of the Holy Spirit. She confesses, "I love her very dearly and am enchanted when I hold her in my arms."

## Leaving School

After a rough beginning, Juanita became very happy at the boarding school on Maestranza Street. Her school was often referred to as A Normal Training School or Teacher's College because the last two years corresponded by modern standards to two years in college. When a student finished these classes, she was usually recognized by the state as having requirements to teach. Many students left before completing their last year of high school and it seems that it was thus that St. Teresa completed her education.

When the time approached for Juanita to finish her schooling, she was filled with apprehension. She hated the thought of leaving school. She realized she would no longer get the constant spiritual assistance and guidance she had enjoyed there. And, more important still, she would no longer enjoy the privilege of living under the same roof with Jesus in the Blessed Sacrament, which meant so much to her. She would have to give up her hours of adoration and thanksgiving in the chapel. Instead of these benefits, she would now have to take her place in the world. So, despite the innumerable graces and advantages of her "dear school," as she calls it, in August 1919 she returned to her home located at 475 Ejército Street.

Life is never without paradoxes. Together with her regrets at leaving school, she tells us that in another way she was glad to be going home. The thought of her home made Juanita happy because she was greatly loved by her family. She was also eager for the opportunity to help her mother run the house now that her older sister Lucía had married. And she was pleased to be able to serve everyone in the house in return for all they had done for her.

41

## Problems in the Fernández Household

The Fernández family was a good and deeply Christian family. Still, no family is without its problems, and Juanita's family was certainly no exception. Her father, for example, was forced to be away from home for long stretches of time. As with so many families, this was due to economics. He had to provide for his family and their needs.

Don Miguel, Juanita's father, unknowingly had not managed the family fortunes too wisely or skillfully. This forced a reduction in his family's affluent lifestyle, a style of living to which they had become accustomed. Naturally, this brought dissatisfaction into his family. Some members of the household bitterly resented this loss, though Juanita herself was able to accept the situation with more than good grace.

Juanita's father was a morally good and upright man, never guilty of any serious offenses or scandals. But he had not had a good education like Don Eulogio Solar, his father-in-law. Don Eulogio was a physician and had accumulated the vast family fortune.

His lack of economic adeptness caused Don Miguel to make poor investments. His wife Lucía, who was such a blessing to and so important in Juanita's early formation, was the more gifted of her parents, but Lucía, according to her biographers, could also be rather fastidious and demanding. This only added to Don Miguel's problems. To avoid disputes and problems with his family, Juanita's father spent long periods of time away from home on lands he had rented and was cultivating. His absence was deeply felt by Juanita. Though pained by this trial, she wrote him beautiful, touching letters that are still extant. She told him how his family celebrated and enjoyed the holidays but confides that all would have been much happier and more joyful had he been home.

Juanita also revealed to him that she felt sad when she saw other girls her own age have their fathers home for the holidays, while her own father was absent. She expressed her deep affection for him and encouraged him in every way. Her deep concerns for him are conveyed in these letters, and she begged him not to work too hard and not to be afraid to take time off so he could spend time with the family. Juanita was not only concerned with her own loss, she also worried about her father's soul because of his long absences from home.It seems that when he was out in the country, the head of the Fernández family had not gone to the Sacraments for a year or so. Juanita took this alarming news very much to heart and encouraged her father, tactfully but gently, to return to the full practice of his faith.

## About Her Brother Miguel

There was another vexing family problem. In addition to her concern for her father, Juanita had even more reason to be concerned for the spiritual welfare of her oldest brother. Miguel was a very gifted young man and loved to write poetry, but lived a Bohemian style of life. He also drank excessively. Because of this he became a constant source of worry to the whole family and was accordingly treated as the black sheep of the family.

Although Juanita's mother Lucía was an exceptionally good and pious woman, she found the lifestyle of her son to be almost unbearable. She often reproved him bitterly for his faults. Later, when Juanita had already been in the convent for a few months, Lucía wrote to tell her that she was praying "that God would quickly take Miguel to Himself before he became a total disgrace to the whole family."

The situation was an embarrassment to the family and caused Juanita great grief. Sister Teresa alludes to this in her *Diary* and explained how she found the situation especially disturbing, particularly "because this is my own flesh and blood." Nevertheless, being the middle child in her family she was a skillful negotiator and handled the situation with more gentleness and understanding than did her mother. Juanita always encouraged her mother to correct Miguel with more kindness.

Juanita's gentle and sure method of dealing with the correction of the faults of others was always appreciated. This did not always come easily to Juanita, nor does it come easily to anyone. She had to conquer her unruly feelings and keep her head. But strength came to her from habitually striving to do everything in the name of love.

From the magnificent Condor, which is the national bird of Chile, Juanita tells us she learned the important lesson of rising above the trying and weighty burdens of life through love of God. "I sometimes feel like a little bird without wings," she wrote, and wondered who would give her the wings of love she needed. She described her secret discovery in these words:

*Even though birds, like the Condor, have wings and feathers that are heavy, they climb to great heights despite the rains, etc., and in the same way the soul extends its wings and rises up. And these wings are the love of God.*

### First Visit to the Monastery of Los Andes

Juanita continued to carry on her intense and very fruitful correspondence with Mother Angelica, the Prioress of the Carmelite Monastery in the little Chilean town of Los Andes. This lovely town, today about a one hour drive from Santiago, is situated at the foot of the Andes Mountains, a very impressive range of mountains that begins in Panama and runs down to the tip of South America. The beautiful town of Los Andes is not too far from the world-famous statue of Christ of the Andes which commemorates a peace treaty that prevented Chile and Argentina from going to war in the early days of this century.

In letters to this Prioress, Juanita expressed her strong desires to embrace the Carmelite way of life and to walk in the footsteps of the great Saint Teresa of Avila. Impressed with the correspondence of this sincere high school girl, Mother Prioress invited Juanita to visit the Los Andes Carmel for an interview.

The long-awaited invitation filled Juanita's soul with delight. On January 11, 1919, the young Carmelite aspirant and her mother took the train from Santiago to Los Andes, planning to spend the whole day with Mother Angelica and the community. They left from Mapocho Station in Santiago on a train that went toward Valparaíso; but, at Llay-Llay Station they boarded another train that took them to Los Andes.

The full name of the town where the Carmelite Monastery is located is Santa Rosa de Los Andes. It was founded toward the end of the 18th century by Don Ambrosio Higgins, Governor of Chile and later Viceroy of Peru. He was the father of Bernardo O'Higgins, the Liberator of Chile. Today no one calls the town Santa Rosa de Los Andes but simply Los Andes. As the young aspirant to Carmel stepped down from the train, she learned that the Carmelite Monastery was only four blocks away. In a matter of minutes her eager eyes caught sight of her future home.

Juanita's first impressions of the Monastery were gratifying, almost overwhelming. Later, when she was able to put her feelings into words, she wrote: "When we got there I found a poor, old house that was to be my little Convent. Its poverty spoke to my heart, and I felt attracted to it." When she went inside the Carmel, she was welcomed by Teresita Montes, a friend from Santiago, and was told that Reverend Mother would be able to speak with her after lunch.

Juanita and her mother were served lunch in a dining room outside the cloister, after which time they awaited their visit with Mother Prioress.

### Origin of the Monastery of Los Andes

From the chronicles of the Carmel of Los Andes we learn that this Monastery was founded in 1898 by Mother Margarite of Saint John of the Cross (Vial Guzmán). Mother Margarite had been professed in the Monastery of Saint Joseph in Santiago, and from there she founded the Carmelite Monastery of the Sacred Heart in Viña del Mar.

In those days Viña del Mar was a seashore resort, but it was not too well populated and lacked resources. As a result, the community was forced to transfer to Valparaíso in 1895. Thus the founders of Los Andes came from the Monastery of the Sacred Heart that was then in Valparaíso. After a fire totally destroyed their Monastery, the Valparaíso community returned to Viña in 1912.

The Carmelite Nuns of the Valparaíso Carmel attempted to make a foundation in Curimon, but the people of that small town were unable to support them. Therefore, the Sisters soon moved to town of Los Andes and started a Carmel there which was named in honor of the Holy Spirit. Mother Margarite of Saint John of the Cross brought Mother Angelica of the Most Blessed Sacrament from Curimon to be the Prioress of the Los Andes community. She is the holy woman who had been corresponding with Juanita and now had the satisfaction of greeting her on the aspirant's first visit to the Carmel.

Later, in 1924, after the death of Sister Teresa of the Andes, a larger Carmel was built. It housed the Carmelite Nuns until October 18, 1987, when they moved 10 miles away to Rinconada de Los Andes. The present Carmelite Monastery of Los Andes is actually situated on land that was part of Juanita's maternal grandfather's hacienda where Juanita spent many delightful vacations as a child.

It was in this original Carmel of Los Andes in the Diocese of Alconcagua that Juanita Fernández Solar lived her religious life. The Monastery where Juanita actually lived, which had been seriously damaged in an earthquake, has unfortunately been sold. At the time of the sale few realized that Sister Teresa would one day be canonized. That Monastery was eventually destroyed and the land is now being used by a company that exports fruit.

Meeting Mother Angelica and the Community

Her first meeting with Mother Angelica, a very holy and gifted religious woman, impressed Juanita deeply. In meeting Mother Angelica Teresa, the young girl immediately felt happy and eagerly listened as the

Superior began to explain the life of Carmel, with all its rich traditions and practices. In her *Diary*, Juanita shares with us this important conversation: "Mother Angelica began to speak of the love of God with an eloquence that seemed to come from the depths of her soul; she made me see the great goodness of God in calling me and how all that I was came from God."

Such conversation was uplifting to Juanita's soul; she would have been willing to continue it indefinitely. But in her *Diary* she tells us she spoke with Mother Prioress until 4:30. After speaking with Mother Angelica, first together with her own mother and then alone, Juanita was invited by Teresita Montes to take share in the *visit of visits*. This is a term used by the Los Andes Carmel, which simply means the young candidate was invited to meet with the whole community. Such a meeting, of course, offered the community an opportunity to evaluate her vocation.

The meeting proved to be very satisfying to both the community and Juanita. The expectations of both sides were met and even surpassed. When the Sisters entered the speak room each greeted Juanita, filling her with unspeakable delight. She reports that "each one with her veil raised came and greeted me with such affection that I was confounded. In the beginning my emotion was such that I could scarcely talk, but then we began to speak with the greatest confidence."

A very positive sign that the Sisters of the community were pleased with their new candidate from Santiago was that they began to ask her how soon she could come to become part of their Monastery. An agreement was reached that she would come during the first week of May. Then one of the Sister rushed out of the room to find a calendar to determine whether the feast of Saint Joseph or the Holy Spirit came first. She brought back the news that the feast of Saint Joseph came first. It turned out that May 7th, the long awaited day, was the feast of the Solemnity of Saint Joseph, the protector of Carmel.

On this happy note her visit to the Monastery ended and an amazing peace flooded her soul. This inner peace she attributed to the working of the Holy Spirit, and considered it a divine sign that confirmed the process she had been living through, the process of trying to ascertain if it was the will of God that she should enter Carmel. It was wonderful to have divine assurance that this was the place to which God was calling her. Now she could and did return home with confidence and trust.

The train that was to take them back to Santiago was late, so Juanita and her mother arrived about 11:30 that night. Only Rebecca, who knew the true nature of their trip, waited up to welcome them home. It was so good for Juanita to see Rebecca again and to share her joy and happiness with "the faithful echo of her soul" and to be able to put into words the marvelous things that had occurred during the visit to Los Andes.

### Inundated With Divine Peace

While still in high school and still in her teens, Juanita had at last resolved the major problem that kept her soul unsettled for several years. An intolerable burden had finally been lifted from her mind and heart. Now she could forge ahead with full certainty that Carmel was the true vocation given to her by God. She now knew where she was going and was certain she belonged behind the grilles of Carmel. Assured that she had been accepted for entrance, she now began to make her final preparations to enter her beloved and poor Carmel of Los Andes.

It is important to note that there was a well-known Carmelite Monastery in Santiago, called the *Carmen Alto*. It was then located on Saint Lucy Hill which today is called Valdivia Street. Some might wonder why Juanita chose not to enter there as it was not far from her home. Juanita tells us that she chose the Los Andes Carmel first of all because it was a poor Carmel. And poor it was indeed! It did not even have electricity or hot running water or other conveniences. Secondly, Juanita was particularly impressed by the joyful spirit of the Sisters of the Los Andes Carmel. They had the spirit of joy that the great Saint Teresa wanted to prevail in all her Carmels. Joy is one of the hallmarks of the Gospel, and it must also be a distinguishing characteristic of a truly contemplative vocation.

But there was another motive, a deeper and more important motive that guided Juanita's choice. To make her sacrifice more complete and perfect, she wanted to live in a Carmel that would fully separate her from the family she loved so dearly. Being separated from her family, Juanita assures us, was the greatest sacrifice she had to make in following her true vocation. But she was prepared to sacrifice everything to follow Christ perfectly.

## More Problems in Her Path

The days began to pass by quickly but not quickly enough. Juanita wanted to give herself totally to God in Carmel, and she wanted to do this as soon as possible. But her spiritual longings of anticipated joy were being overshadowed by additional obstacles. First and most importantly, she did not have her father's permission, and she didn't want to leave home without his blessing.

There was also a question as to whether he would provide the dowry which was then required to enter a poor cloistered community of nuns.

In school Juanita excelled in history and literature. According to historical sources, Chile was first seen by the great explorer Ferdinand Magellan in 1520. The city of Santiago was founded on February 12,1541, by the Spanish conqueror, Captain Pedro Valdivia. The magnificence of this city was brought about by people who had vision and courage and wanted to make the world a better place in which to live. Before Juanita entered Carmel, she saw fresh evidence in Chile that the world was continuing to grow and change for the better. We can easily sense this from her emotion and enthusiasm in a 1917 letter to her father, telling him how excited she was that on the very next day she was going to see an airplane take off. This was very exciting, since obviously people were not accustomed to see airplanes flying in the Chilean skies every day during the final years of World War I. But the very fact that she writes of her appreciation of airplanes makes us somehow feel closer to Juanita, who lived during those early days of aviation.

Exactly 14 years previously, Orville and Wilbur Wright made their first successful air flight at Kitty Hawk, North Carolina. That first airplane flight in 1903 forever changed the face of our world and paved the way for men and women to go further up into the sky and then on into outer space.

These events inspired Juanita's motivation. She herself longs to do even more than such giants as the Wright brothers or Charles Lindbergh. But it was in quite another sphere that she would excel. She was determined to make her own mighty and rightful contributions to the transformation of this world. But how? With what means? She seeks to bring about her revolution not through the powers of statesmanship or through scientific discoveries, great and noble as these achievements may be. She aspires to do more; or, better yet, from within the depths of her soul she was being drawn by the grace of God to desire to do more.

Today, the astronauts of outer space command our attention and fire our imagination because of their signal bravery and courage. The efforts of these men and women herald a brighter tomorrow for all. In the popular imagination, it is as though astronauts are the ultimate in bravery. Jean Guitton, however, the Sorbonne poet and philosopher, asks whether it takes more daring and courage to journey into outer space or whether one must be just as daring or even more so to become "cosmonauts of the spirit" and journey into the infinite depths of our spirit, braving all spiritual trials to find the God who is absolutely infinite? This is the precise challenge the little saint of Santiago undertook, this is what Juanita longed to do: she longed for the greatest intimacy with the living God who is infinitely good and infinitely holy.

Could anything be greater and more daring than to seek perfect union with the all Holy God? And to brave the stresses of the most authentic closeness and intimacy with God? And to seek this because it is the most direct way to help others draw ever closer to their God? God was calling this young girl to this spiritual vocation, and she sensed that it would bring her the greatest fulfillment. She was already convinced that her vocation would lead her to the fullness of love and that in Carmel she would experience what Saint John of the Cross discussed in *The Living Flame of Love* when he describes the soul that has been perfected in divine love by the Holy Spirit. In that book the Mystical Doctor wrote of the deeds of those who have been transformed into this divine life. He says, their "acts of love are most precious; one of them is more meritorious and valuable than all the deeds a person may have performed in his whole life without this transformation, however great they may have been."

This is the life Juanita desired in Carmel. In a celebrated letter to Mother Angelica, she wrote that she would be prepared to walk through fire to become His bride. Put another way, she would like to be like the Magdalene sitting at the feet of Jesus in adoration, listening to every word that comes from His divine lips and responding with all the love of her heart. More, she aspired to imitate Mary, her mirror, the Mother of the Lord, who cherished every word that came from the mouth of her Son. And she wanted to sacrifice herself like Mary who stood at the foot of the Cross and identified herself with His life-work and achievements. Juanita did not accomplish her daring dreams as others do, amid the activities of the world or in the marketplace, but she achieved eternal and everlasting greatness because she dared to do what few men or women have dared do. She dared resolutely to do what is most stressful to human beings: she braved the possibility and danger of entering into the deepest closeness and intimacy with the all-holy, living God. Could there be anything more daring? Could there be anything that required more ardent love? Or, better still, could she have aspired to anything the world is more in need of or that brings down more divine love to humankind? This is the essence of the vocation she envisioned when she was on the threshold of entering the Camel of Los Andes.

## Her Father Gives His Consent

On April third she wrote a very moving letter to her father, beseeching him to give his consent and his blessing on her entrance to the Carmel of Los Andes. She confided to Don Miguel that she kept this secret in her heart for a long time and only now could she confidently share it with him. Assuring her beloved father how much she has appreciated all the sacrifices he had already made for his children, and mindful that this would be even more costly for him, she was confident that he would make this sacrifice out of love for her. And she avowed that she is not taking this step of separation from him "for another man," but for God alone, only for the One who has an absolute right over our hearts. No human being has placed this idea in my head, she assures him, it is due only to the God who disposes things in His own way. And, finally, she lovingly assured him that her vocation would never separate him from her love because "those who love one another can never be separated!"

When he received her message, her father was away at his farm at San Javier in Loncomilla, more than 300 miles south of Santiago. The letter caused him pain and many mixed emotions. For whatever reason, her father didn't answer her letter immediately, thus causing the girl great sorrow. But in due time Don Miguel did write, not directly to Juanita but instead to his wife, telling her that he was trying to make up his mind.

When at last her father gave his consent Juanita was relieved and delighted. But permission was given only when her father came to Santiago for the birth of his niece. At first Don Miguel made every effort to avoid being alone with Juanita because he felt awkward about discussing this emotion-filled matter with his daughter.

In a letter written from Santiago to Father Artemio Colom, and dated April 1919, Juanita described how at last her father came to her room and gave his permission. She told her confessor that it was the "permission of a truly Christian father." Señor Fernández said to Juanita: "If it's the Will of God, I will not oppose it, since that will bring you happiness." Then with tears streaming down his face he asked when she was planning to leave. Juanita told him "in the month of May." He just said to her, "Do as you see fit." The young Carmelite candidate added these words in her letter to her director:

*How great were those moments, Reverend Father! And what thanksgiving blossomed in my soul in that moment for God and for my dear father. I will never be able to repay him as I ought.*

In a joyful letter to Mother Angelica, Juanita simply reports,

*Last Sunday my father gave his consent. Saint Joseph is the one who obtained this miracle.*

## Family Reluctance

One final hurdle still had to be overcome: the reluctance of the rest of the family. As the other members of the household learned of her intention to leave home forever, they became deeply saddened. Some openly expressed their anger. Juanita had to bear their dejected looks and put up with their sad laments. One of her brothers so resented her decision that he bitterly expressed his displeasure to Don Miguel in her presence. Typically, Juanita tells us how proud and happy she was when her father took her part and insisted that her older brother express no more of his anger.

All this, of course, is perfectly understandable. Juanita herself was so convinced of her vocation and that she was answering the inner, loving invitation of Christ calling her to be His bride in Carmel that her heart was overflowing with happiness. She was looking at matters from within. Her family, on the other hand, could only look at things from without, considering all that they were losing. Aided by God's grace and inner light, she easily understood the beauty of God's invitation. They regretted the thought of losing Juanita, whom they considered to be "the pearl, the joy, the sunshine of the household." But, their generous love gradually brought them around to acceptance of and support for her noble decision. Perhaps it would be more precise to say that all came to recognize that Juanita had a God-given vocation and felt proud that she was following it so generously.

## A Dark Night of the Soul

Curiously, the good news of her father's approval arrived at the very time Juanita was going through what spiritual writers call "a dark night of the soul." In simpler terms this is a very difficult and painful stage of prayer and spiritual growth. During this stage of mystical prayer, the soul is being led more deeply and directly into God's love. It is, however, experienced by the soul as a painful, spiritual trial. But it is a trial that is indispensable for the grace of transforming union with God. Clearly, Juanita was now being led to a more mature way of receiving God's love and of appropriately responding "to the vigor and warmth of the love of her Spouse," to use a phrase from Saint John of the Cross. This stage of purification and interiorization is necessary for the soul to reach the sublime goals for which Juanita was craving so ardently. The dark night "will lead her to die to self in order to begin the sweet and delightful life of love with God," as the Mystical Doctor of Carmel explained.

In retrospect, it was a joyful but painful experience. It was more than a trial; it was the victory of God's grace over her spirit. This trial deeply purified her soul and paved the way for the deepest possible union with God. Yes, even when Juanita was passing through the darkest of nights, there was a strange and sure awareness in her heart that she "was being guided by a light from within," and was aware, too, that this divine light was leading her to greater and greater intimacy and closeness with God. Temporarily, she was unable to pray the way she wanted because, as she tells us, "There is a dark cloud that is hiding the Beloved of my heart and I long to plunge myself into His divine Being, but I am unable to do so." She experienced no consolation. Nor did that matter. What really counted was that her heavenly Bridegroom was with her still and that in a curious way she felt His nearness more than ever before. But she was still perplexed.

In the very last entry written into her *Diary* before entering the cloister, she informs us that in her distress she went to see Father Falgueras, her confessor. He brought her comfort and helped her see that it was only a trial she was passing through, albeit a very painful trial, but that she need only remain faithful to her prayer and await God's deliverance. Calm did eventually return to her soul and it became clear that she had grown and matured through this ordeal. At the same time her love for God had undergone considerable purification and wonderful elevation.

## Her Habitual State of Prayer

When Juanita wrote to her confessor, she opened her soul to him with full candor and trust. What is especially noteworthy here is the way she describes to him her habitual state of prayer. She wrote:

*My prayer consists almost always of an intimate conversation with Our Lord; I imagine that I am like Magdalene as His feet, listening to Him, and He tells me what I must do to please Him.*

She continues:

*Sometimes I am very recollected in prayer and have been completely absorbed, contemplating the infinite perfections of God, above all those that are manifested in the mystery of the Incarnation.*

And she then goes on to say how God made her understand His grandeur and her nothingness. She truly delighted in His greatness, but was always aware that she was, in her own inimitable words, "a nothingness, more still, a criminal nothingness *(una nada criminal)*." In Juanita's lexicon the emphasis is on the supreme excellence and goodness of God and how undeserving anyone is of that love, but through everything she was never unmindful that she "was favored and loved."

## Photographed in the Carmelite Habit

Before Juanita entered Carmel, she had her picture taken in the Carmelite habit. Today this may strike us as unusual. But in those days it was a custom for a young girl to have her picture taken in the habit of the Order before she entered a Monastery. One copy of this photograph was to be kept in the archives of the Monastery, and the other copy given to her family as a remembrance of the girl, because no photographic equipment was allowed in the Monastery in those days.

The picture in question was taken at a professional photography studio in Santiago. Juanita borrowed the habit from Sister Carmel of Saint Francis Xavier (Bruner Prieto) at the Saint Joseph Monastery of the Discalced Carmelite Nuns in Santiago. On this same occasion, Juanita posed for the well-known photo in secular clothes, a picture that captures so well the quiet elegance and expressive beauty of her soul. In a letter to Mother Angelica dated just 7 days before entering Carmel, Juanita spoke of all the photos she posed for that day, and added: "In everyone's opinion, the best picture was of me as a Carmelite." She then goes on to say how grateful she was that "the Carmel of Saint Joseph made this possible." (*Juanita did receive the Carmelite habit with the white veil of a novice, but did not live long enough to receive the black veil of a fully professed sister.*)

## Should I Burn My Diary?

Juanita had been keeping her *Intimate Diary* for several years, writing down graces and favors God had been granting her. Only her spiritual directors and some close family members were aware the *Diary* existed. Since the time was fast approaching her entrance into Carmel, Juanita wondered what to do with the four memorable copy books. It would have been natural to take the books to Carmel. Instead, she seriously thought of destroying them forever.

In a letter to Father José Blanch, who had succeeded Father Artemio Colom as her spiritual director, she sought his advice as to whether it would be advisable to leave the books with her mother. Doña Lucía was strongly urging Juanita to leave the books in her possession as a constant reminder of her beloved daughter. Señora Fernández was convinced that the *Diary* would bring her soul much good. Rebecca, too, had asked for the books, promising that she would not read them but only preserve them. Juanita was convinced that she could trust Rebecca, who later entered the Carmel of Los Andes. She believed Rebecca would be true to her promised word and not read the books.

"My own personal preference," wrote Juanita, "is to throw the book into the fire so it will disappear forever; but, again, I worry that if they do read it they will see the goodness of the Divine Master who has loved me so much even though I have been so ungrateful and am so sinful, but even for that reason I would be glad if they did read it." But she would be embarrassed if anyone read the secrets of her intimate prayer experiences, which she recorded only at the command of her confessors. She concluded a letter to Father Blanch, written on April 28, 1919, (only 8 days before entering Carmel) with these words: "There are things, Reverend Father, as you yourself have told me, that only God and the soul must be aware of, as well as the confessor. In short, tell me what I should do, since that will be the will of God." Fortunately, Father Blanch allowed her to keep the *Diary* and thus, providentially, a precious spiritual treasure was forever preserved.

On the very eve of Juanita's departure, her brother Luís, who had taught her devotion to the Virgin when she was young and had made a pact with her to recite the rosary every day, still found it impossible to accept her decision. He wrote her a long letter, using the same forceful forensic skills that were later to make him a successful lawyer. He told the sister he dearly loved that she was making a terrible mistake, that she was

60

throwing away her talents and her beauty and that she should remain at home. He told her she need not marry, if that be her wish, but he argued that she could do so much more good in the world than in the cloister.

When she read his letter, Juanita immediately understood. She knew he wrote it out of love, and she knew his words were the words of a brother who had always been very close to her. Luís would later record his own as well as the feelings of the whole family with these words: "She loved us unselfishly. She was the angel of our home, the treasure of our household."

Juanita put his letter down and then took up her pen. In what must be regarded as one of her finest letters that has come down to us she was easily able to refute all his arguments and assured him that she would always be close to him and to the family in love. She reminded this brother who was exceptionally close to her that the greatest way she could glorify God on earth would be to use all the talents and gifts God gave her to know Him and to love Him. And, referring to his statement that she was throwing away her natural beauty, she intrepidly asserted:

*I have no beauty. But if I did possess any, I wouldn't hesitate to offer that to Him too, because the good and the beautiful is what He deserves.*

## Farewell Santiago

Don Miguel's favorite child had previously always been Lucía, his firstborn, but in later years he came to understand Juanita better and learned to appreciate her gracious qualities more and more. Juanita dearly loved her father and hoped above everything that he would be home when she left, so that she could give him her last affectionate embrace. Don Miguel liked to avoid emotional situations. Even though his love for her was very tender and never wavered, he didn't have the strength or the courage to bid this final farewell to his daughter. Her love for him remained deep, as a result she had to struggle to accept this new and very painful cross.

Juanita was grateful that her father was considerate, understanding and had given his blessing on her vocation. So, she took special pains to write him a letter on April 17, 1919, thanking him and telling him how happy he had made her. But she added that her feelings were mixed because for the first time "I have been the cause of your tears." She expressed her conviction that God would give him the necessary strength and that he would feel deep satisfaction in his soul now that he had given her to God. Because of him, she said, and because of his blessing on her vocation, she would be eternally grateful and happy.

A few hours later, Juanita hastened to write to Mother Angelica to report her father's permission had been obtained, and she would soon be arriving at the Monastery.

The night before Juanita left for the convent, the family gathered for her final meal with them. Doña Lucía, who had previously had 10 servants to run the house, now could afford just three due to financial reverses in the family. Eager that things would go well she made sure that the last dinner at home was well prepared and well served. It was; but the mood was strained. There was uneasiness in the room; all were not their usual selves. Doña Lucía tried to be matter-of-fact, Rebecca was engrossed in herself, and Miguel, who was usually very talkative, had little to say.

The night seemed endless. There was a terrible electrical storm causing many trees to be down. Someone called to suggest that perhaps the train would not leave the next day. Rebecca was inconsolable, causing Juanita to get very little sleep that night. Luís, whom she always called Lucho at home, was very down in spirit. Recalling that Juanita had always said she would find heaven in the Carmelite life, this very thought only added to his woes. He said to her, "You will have everything but I will have nothing - not even God!" Knowing that he was referring to his struggles with his faith, his favorite sister put her arm around his shoulder and tried to comfort him as best she could. Sleep finally did come to Juanita that night, but not until a few hours before it was time to get up.

## Leaving Home Forever

On May 7, 1919, the feast of the Patronage of Saint Joseph, Juanita rose early and went to Mass with her mother. She then said goodbye to her home and family forever. At the time they were living at 92 Vergara Street. At the preordained time Juanita, her mother, Rebecca, Luís her brother, Aunt Juana, and a close friend boarded the express train at the Central Station of Santiago for the little town of Los Andes. They arrived in Los Andes at 11:30 A.M.

The future Carmelite was very elated to be so close to her goal, but was mindful that, according to Mother Angelica's instructions, they were not due at the Monastery this early. So, they all went to have lunch at a nearby restaurant, taking as much time as they could. All then made their last affectionate farewells. Juanita then went to the Carmel to give herself to her All.

The young and fervent aspirant was admitted to the community as a postulant. From the start, Juanita was very happy in this Chilean Monastery of the daughters of Saint Teresa of Avila. This can be clearly seen in going through the letters she wrote from the Monastery, letters that express overflowing spiritual joy. Just 8 days after bidding a final farewell to her family, she wrote:

*It is 8 days since I have been in Carmel, 8 days of heaven; I feel the divine love to be so great that there are moments when I feel I'm unable to resist.*

Because she had been well prepared spiritually since her earliest years and had conscientiously practiced the evangelical virtues as a way of imitating Christ, she found it easy to adjust to the life of Carmel. She immediately felt at home and loved the prayerful and silent atmosphere of the cloister, as well as the poverty and simplicity of Carmelite life. She enjoyed and eagerly treasured the time spent alone in her cell with her Beloved. The cloistered life was everything she had longed for, and even more.

## The Novice

After an initiation period called the postulancy, Juanita was formally received into the Order. When she received the habit she was given the name Sister Teresa of Jesus. During her novitiate she was very happy. She summed up her new life by calling it a life of "prayer, work and laughter." More and more in Carmel she experienced the joy of being united with God in untiring love. Like Saint Teresa of Avila, she instinctively knew that gloom was not appropriate in Carmel, for the holy foundress wanted all her Sisters to be joyful and to find their delight in the Lord. Sister Teresa reports in her *Diary* that on the feast of Saint Martha, according to an ancient custom of the Order, the novices gave the lay Sisters the day off from their customary tasks.

The novices generally enjoy this, she tells us. Sister Teresa was asked to help some of the other novices with the kitchen work that day. What actually transpired is told in this cheerful account:

*Imagine if you can how much we enjoyed preparing the meal. Our laughter became uncontrollable as we saw tears streaming down from our eyes when we peeled the onions. In Carmel everything is done with joy because everywhere we have Jesus, who is our infinite joy.*

Sister Teresa, even when young and going to school, was always joyful and cheerful. She herself tells us that there were times, especially during vacations, when her relatives and girl friends were at table that all got into fits of giggling and laughing. On one of these occasions things got so out of hand that the priest who was visiting was unable to say the grace after meals, probably much to his confusion and annoyance. Juanita, though she was leading a very contemplative life, even in high school, was long remembered for her giggling fits.

## "Captured in the
### Loving Nets of the Divine Fisherman"

When Juanita was 15 she wrote to her youngest sister, Rebecca, about the meaning of the vocation she wanted to live in Carmel. These are her exact words:

*I long for the day when I can go to Carmel to concern myself only with Him, to abase myself in Him and so to live His life alone: to love and suffer to save souls. Yes, I thirst for souls because I know that it is what my Jesus craves more than anything else. Oh, how I love Him!*

Juanita knew full well and clearly spelled out for her sister Rebecca a truth that is often forgotten, that "a vocation is the greatest blessing that God can grant a creature." She assured her sister that the central feature of her vocation is that "the God who has captured my heart is filling it with happiness and joy and I cannot refuse Him."

Then she continued:

*Who can refuse the hand of the All Powerful One who abases Himself to the most unworthy of His creatures? How happy I am, my dear sister! I have been captured in the loving nets of the divine Fisherman. I would like to make you understand this happiness.*

## The Fullness of Love in Carmel

Gradually she learned to explain her own vocation in clearer words and more fully. Let us allow her to do this in her own words:

*I can also be a martyr in Carmel, dying to self at every instant. That is the vocation of the Carmelite: to be a pure host who constantly offers herself to God for the sinful world.*

*How beautiful is our vocation! We are redeemers in union with our Lord. We are hosts where Jesus dwells, in whom He lives, prays and sacrifices Himself for this sinful world. We are co-redeemers of the world. But the redemption of souls is not accomplished without the cross. My idea of being a Carmelite is to be a victim, constantly immolated for souls.*

This is exactly how she lived her beautiful life during her 11 months in Carmel. And this is how she attained the fullness of holiness.

## Letters of Joy

From the time she came to Carmel, she wrote numerous letters. And in almost all of her letters she is tireless in repeating that in Carmel she has found everything she had been seeking. Father Marino Purroy, her most noted biographer, has captured the meaning and significance of her life in Carmel. He wrote: "In reality, from her entrance into the convent, she never ceases to proclaim in her correspondence the 'peace and happiness that inundated her soul'. Not only that but she called her convent 'a little anticipated heaven'." She believed she was "the happiest creature in the world." And she assured us: "I have found the most complete happiness." She found her complete happiness because she experienced that God is infinite joy."

The same Chilean Father Purroy wrote of her:

*Hidden in the cloister, she nevertheless carries on an intense apostolate, not only by means of the mysterious fruitfulness of sacrifice and prayer, but also through her letters. By means of these letters she enkindles in her family and friends her own love of Christ, of the Eucharist and of the Most Holy Virgin, and at the same time manifests her happiness and joy and shows that her love and affection for her own family keep growing every day.*

In an article which appeared in *L'Osservatore Romano*, Father Roberto Moretti gives his evaluation of the saint's letters:

*Writing to her mother, she says: 'You cannot imagine, Madrecita, the change that I already feel in myself. He has transformed me. He is opening the veils that have kept Him hidden. Each time He seems more beautiful to me, more tender, and more crazy.... I don't want to continue, because when I begin to speak of the Lord, I can't restrain my pen.'*

That is how the young Carmelite of Los Andes writes, continues Father Moretti:

*She has pages vibrating with humanity; shining, fiery pages that set us ablaze with an enthusiasm that leads to the heights, pages that fill us with joy. Here is how she writes to a friend: 'I am happy, in fact, the happiest creature in the world. I'm beginning a heavenly life of adoration, of praise and of continuing love: God is infinite joy'.*

Concerning the young Chilean saint's correspondence, Father Moretti concludes his evaluation with the words:

*This is the spiritual experience of this young Carmelite. We can also say that this is her spirituality. It is a message that is particularly relevant to our times. We can quickly read her message, a message that seems particularly helpful to those of us who are advancing in years.*

## On the Cross with Jesus

"There is an interchange of love that takes place only on the Cross," Elizabeth of the Trinity had written only 14 years before our Chilean Carmelite Sister entered Carmel. Those words are the law of following Christ who said of His own sufferings and death: "Is it not fitting that the Son of man should suffer and thus enter into His glory?" Sister Teresa fully believed and cherished these words as well as another saying of Elizabeths, "It is on the Cross that He gives me life."

Now, Sister Teresa of the Andes is about to experience the full truth of those words as well as the mystery and reality of being totally configured to Christ.

During Lent, 1920, the young novice, one of the "white veils" as Carmelite novices are referred to, was taking to heart the moving lessons of that solemn penitential season. She was careful to remain recollected, careful to keep her thoughts centered on her crucified Lord and on the great needs of His Church. She poured her life into her vocation and into the graces of the holy penitential season.

## Holy Week, 1920

Things are now about to change. In fact, during the last week of Lent they would change radically. In Holy Week, the sufferings, humiliations, mockery and death of Christ on the Cross are solemnly recalled by Christians. How true the words of John's Gospel: "If I be lifted up, I will draw all people to Myself!" How eagerly the novice united herself to the fate of her Spouse during this most solemn week of the liturgical year. Her heart was aflame with love for the One who, in her moving words, was "crimsoned with love for me." The true spirit and graces of Holy Week kept streaming into her heart, kept bonding her souls most closely to the Crucified One.

Previously she had written "I want to be His little Cyrenian." This is how ardently she wanted to take up the cross and accompany Christ in His Passion. It is in the Gospel of Matthew where we read the account of the Cyrenian who was forced to help Jesus carry His cross to Calvary. In this scene of the Gospel, the Evangelist is not merely offering us factual information, he is inviting all Christians to consider the sufferings of Christ and, like the Cyrenian, to enter fully into helping Christ carry

His cross. Sister Teresa, the young novice in the Los Andes Carmel, fully grasped this invitation to stay close to the suffering Christ, and she thrills at the thought of being His loving "little Cyrenian."

Sister Teresa remained absorbed in the sufferings of her Spouse throughout Holy Week of 1920. But she also began to sense that something was wrong. She did not feel well. And, indeed, something *was* wrong, terribly wrong. The ardent young novice had contracted typhus, a fleaborne disease for which there was then no cure. In fact, no cure was discovered for typhus until many years after her death. Even today, unless this deadly disease is detected early and medication administered immediately, the patient can be expected to live no more than a few weeks. It has been said that more people have died of typhus than have been killed in all the wars since the death of Christ.

Modern physicians do tell us that the deadly disease of typhus runs through four phases. During phase one, the patient is infected with the disease; this is normally followed by the second phase, an incubation period of about 2 weeks. It is generally during the third stage that the patient begins to become aware of the serious nature of the disease. In the fourth and final stage the deadly disease races to its inevitable, fatal conclusion. The sufferings that accompany this disease are simply unbearable.

## Holy Thursday

Holy Thursday was a day always dear to Sister Teresa. On this Holy particular Holy Thursday the young Sister was beginning to experience the first signs of her illness. She did not complain nor did she ask to be dispensed from the community exercises. That day, she spent long hours on her knees in prayer before the Blessed Sacrament. But that night she felt quite exhausted - too weary, in fact, to fall asleep. She did finally get to sleep, but was unable to sleep more than four hours.

The next day she assisted at all community exercises and even attended the preaching of the Seven Last Words. But late on Good Friday, the Novice Mistress first noticed how ill Sister Teresa was and immediately ordered her to bed. Sister Teresa was running an abnormally high fever. The doctor was summoned immediately but was unable to reduce her fever. His prognosis was very unfavorable. Sister Teresa had to admit to him that she had not been feeling well for several weeks.

Mother Angelica had Sara Urbistondo telephone Señora Lucía to advise her of her daughter's condition. She, in turn, dispatched her personal physician, Doctor Diaz Lira, to care for Sister Teresa.

### Death Bed

The grieving community loved their novice and kept constant vigil by her bedside. Everything possible was done to help her, but the doctors admitted that it was already too late. Her case had passed beyond the limits of medical science, beyond the capabilities of human help. On Monday, April 5, 1920, she requested the last Sacraments and received them with the greatest joy and comfort.

Because of high fever, she was in and out of fits of delirium. The community feared the end was near. During a period when Sister Teresa was not delirious, Mother Angelica suggested to the young novice that she make her religious vows in the Carmelite Order. It took

71

place shortly after midnight. According to the ancient practice of the Church and in accord with the norms of canon law recently promulgated in 1918 by Pope Benedict XV, Sister Teresa was allowed, although still a novice, to make her Profession in the Carmelite Order.

Those who were present assure us that she made her Profession with great joy. Then she prayerfully repeated the formula three more times with great emotion, and then thanked all the Sisters for having allowed her to make her Religious Profession. She was now fully living what she had previously written of: "the victim of love must ascend Calvary with her Lord." Later that day she was given Holy Viaticum.

In 1917, she had offered herself to any kind of death the Lord would permit. She even offered to suffer "the abandonment of Calvary." God accepted her offering. Her mystical purification continued, especially that Saturday night. She felt some of the abandonment Christ suffered on the Cross. There were moments of doubt and of mortal anguish. During her delirium, she told those present that she felt abandoned by God and condemned for not having responded faithfully to the graces the Lord gave her. Despite these feelings, she remained abandoned into God's merciful arms and in the deepest depths of her heart she knew she was safe and secure.

On Monday, April 12, at 7:15 P.M., she sweetly fell asleep in the arms of God. Her earthly life was ended. She had passed through the portals of death and was taken into eternal, everlasting life with her Lord. She had never feared death. Previously she wrote, "To die is to be eternally immersed in Love." Now she was with the risen Jesus. Her Spouse has taken her into that reality and fullness of Love, and she forever beholds the Face of the living God, the God who is Infinite Joy.

When death overtook her she was only 19 years and 9 months old; she had not yet reached her 20th birthday. She had lived in the Monastery of Los Andes 11 months and had been a member of the Discalced Carmelite Order for 6 months, since she had taken the habit of the Order in October 1919. She made Profession only 5 days before leaving this mortal life. During her 5 days as a professed religious she lived that profession in union with her Spouse in transforming suffering and love.

## The Viewing

The Fernández family assembled at the Monastery of Los Andes and were brought to the grates so they could view the body. Sister Teresa of the Andes was laid out in her habit, with the white veil of a novice. The Sisters put a crown of roses on her head and white roses over her body. Doña Lucía approached first and paid her final respects. She was, of course, heartbroken for the loss of her daughter. Don Miguel had the courage to come to the funeral. He approached the grille and took a last look at his dear Juanita. He held his wife's hand for support and she asked him to be brave for the sake of the children. Rebecca came next; the loss for her was devastating. More and more she had been considering the possibility of entering the Los Andes Carmel to take her sister's place, which is exactly what she would do in a matter of months.

Luís also came to see his sister for the last time. He was not only grief-stricken but filled with confusion. He had not yet resolved his religious doubts, but eventually he would write that he was her "greatest moral miracle." The young law student was amazed that so many people

73

came to the funeral. His unerring instincts told him an important story was taking place. He was right, for it was the story of a young girl who, in the fullness of her youth, sought to live a hidden life with Christ, and now she was receiving the veneration of many. He was delighted, but could find no natural explanation for what was happening. In reality, was any natural explanation possible?

All commented on how angelic she looked. Sister Gabriel of the Child Jesus was to write: "She seemed to sleep so gently. Her face, with the majesty of death, seemed to keep an expression of supernatural peace that inspired veneration in those who beheld it." The family recalled that Sister Teresa died as she desired, as a Carmelite and as a bride of Christ. And they would always remember that she had been filled with exceeding joy and happiness in her Carmelite vocation.

## The Funeral

On April 14th her funeral Mass was celebrated in the chapel of the Carmelite Monastery of Los Andes by Father Epiphanius of the Purification, the Vicar Provincial of the Discalced Carmelites in Chile. All the Sisters of the Monastery and the entire Fernández family, as well as many other religious and priests, were in attendance.

Since Sister Teresa had been a cloistered nun and unknown to the people of the Los Andes area, everyone was surprised at the large crowds of people who came to her funeral Mass, even though nothing had been done to publicize the services. It was even more surprising that so many priests came, but this was fitting for one who had lived her life and offered her sufferings for the sanctification of priests.

Her brother Luís also marvelled that when the funeral services were ended, people didn't go home. Many stayed at the Chapel; many passed their rosaries or medals into the Sisters, asking to have them touched to her body. Everyone was convinced that this was something unexpected and out of the ordinary.

During the days following her death an unusual amount of mail poured into the Monastery of Los Andes as well as into the Fernández home in Santiago. What was judged most remarkable about this phenomenon was that not a single one was a letter of condolence; instead, all were congratulatory letters, thanking God for giving us a new saint.

## With Us Still

When the funeral was over the Sisters, the family and the rest of the people began walking back to their homes. As they did so, they kept marvelling and praising God for the life of this very young Carmelite nun. Her life had been so short, so simple, so seemingly uneventful, yet there was something beautifully mysterious and out of the ordinary about that short life. That her life had been special and even extraordinary, no one attempted to deny; that her life was destined to help many people, was just about to be revealed. Everyone had the conviction that a saint had just been buried.

There was another point on which a consensus was building among the people. People were convinced that the saintly Chilean Carmelite somehow lived on and was still with them; they were sure the little Carmelite was with God and would never leave them. In the final analysis, that is what really mattered the most.

## Her Legacy to All

When the events of her life unfolded and her writings became known, a better understanding of the significance and importance of her life slowly emerged, slowly became clearer. Her simple writings shed great light and are now a blessing for all. Teresa of the Andes had been granted that very rare grace of understanding "with remarkable clarity and truth" the meaning of her own life; and she was given deep insight into the unfathomable mystery of the goodness of human life and existence. It is just this vision, so greatly needed in human life, that makes her important.

When all is said and done, every man and woman, young or old, is faced with the same questions and doubts about the meaning of human life. Everyone asks the same questions: Who am I? What is the meaning of my life? Why did I come into this world? What makes life full and worthwhile? All ask such questions because each one is seeking joy and happiness that is true and that will last forever. Teresa of the Andes was blessed to have been granted an adequate answer to her questions.

Many have been led to discover an answer to their own questions by considering the life and teachings of Teresa of the Andes. They are able to see that she truly understood who she was and why human life is so precious. In the opening paragraph of her *Intimate Diary* she explained the deepest secret of her life:

*You think you are going to find an interesting story. I do not want you to be deceived. The story you are going to read is not the story of my life, but the intimate life of a poor soul who, without any merit on her part, Jesus Christ loved in a special way and filled abundantly with His favors and graces.*

To be loved and appreciated by another is a great blessing, but to be loved by God surpasses everything else. Shouldn't God's boundless love for me become the basis of my life? Hasn't God loved and favored each of us far beyond our understanding and imaginings? Do we strive to understand His favors? Remembering the love God has shown me in Christ is what makes me feel I am important, that my life is special, complete and worthwhile. Her two words, "loved and favored," explain everything. It is Sister Teresa of the Andes' joyful and abiding legacy. It will do so much for all, provided, of course, each one comes to the realization in their hearts that they are God's loved and favored ones! This divine assurance brings joy to the heart, a joy no one can take away.

## Final Farewell of Her "Dear College"

In Santiago the news of the young Carmelite's death spread rapidly throughout the faculty and student body of Sacred Heart school on Maestranza Street. A very solemn commemorative ceremony was held for Juanita, their beloved alumna. Bells tolled solemnly for Sister Teresa after Mother Maria Teresa Alaysa spoke eloquently of the deceased graduate.

In her eulogy, Mother Alaysa, R.C.S.J. captured the true feelings of everyone present when she spoke of their common sorrow. She told her listeners,

*We must give the Lord everything and increase our love for Him. And we must do it doubly because here on earth there is now emptiness. Gone is a little soul who glorified Him so. True, this is exactly what she is doing now in heaven, but Jesus looking down from heaven on this earth sees a little less love.*

When they went to the Chapel, the Mass in her honor began. She was remembered fondly and many said, "The little saint is now in heaven."

# Part Two:
# Her Life in Heaven

## Reputation of Holiness After Death

During the early years following her death, there was much talk about the meaning and significance of Sister Teresa's life. All agreed that her life was extraordinary and suffused with the beauty of holiness. And all agreed that this teenage girl had touched the lives of many people and that her loving influence still continued long after her death.

Not only was talk increasing about the young Carmelite's reputation for holiness, but a peak of popular fervor was reached that could not be stopped. Claims were even being made of miracles and spiritual favors granted through her intercession. She was, people were saying, like a radiant star that had suddenly risen in the firmament and demanded attention. The time now appeared ripe to present the whole matter to the bishop of the Diocese of Alconcagua for the Church's definitive study and judgment. After mature deliberation with his staff, the bishop of Santiago decided to consider the cause of Sister Teresa of the Andes in a juridical trial.

Matters came to this state because a Jesuit priest had visited Mother Angelica two years after Sister Teresa's death. He told the Superior that she had a moral obligation to introduce this cause for consideration. He also said that he had become convinced that she was truly worthy of canonization because he was living with Father Colom, who had been Juanita's confessor when she was young. Father Colom liked to speak of her and often told me, he repeated to Mother Angelica, that the young Sister was extremely holy. He also said that he never kept letters written to him, except in the case of this young girl. In fact, he said, he now wouldn't part with the four beautiful letters she had written to him. In actual fact, Father Colom eventually did hand these letters over to the Carmelite Monastery.

Mother Angelica listened to this suggestion with more than common interest. She truly believed in the extraordinary holiness of the young Carmelite novice and we now know that she had carefully preserved intact all Sister Teresa's personal effects. Nevertheless she hesitated to advance the cause, fearing she might be lacking in prudence or that the time was not right. Obviously, Rev. Mother was pleased and encouraged by the Jesuit's advice. Now with a good conscience she could and did act on the priest's counsel.

The primary purpose of the Canonical trial in question was to examine whether the life of Teresa of the Andes was fully and truly Christian; and whether it was totally lived in accord with the demands of the Gospel. It was also necessary to demonstrate that people considered her to be a saint, or that she enjoyed a reputation of holiness (the technical term is "fama sanctitatis") from the time of her death. The court was commissioned to carefully examine the foundation and extent of this judgment on the part of the faithful. They needed to be able to show that in her life the fruits of the Gospel were so outstanding in nature that she could rightly be placed on the altar for the veneration of the faithful. In other words, it had to be proved beyond any shadow of a doubt that the life of Sister Teresa of Jesus of the Carmel of Los Andes had been an outstanding and authentic witness to the holiness of Christ and the Church.

Any alleged miracles must also be examined scrupulously and their validity ascertained. If it could be demonstrated that the miracles in question were authentic and attributable to the intercession of this servant of God, they would of necessity lend great weight to a favorable outcome. Miracles, in the lapidary phrase of Pius XI, are said to be "the voice of God" and in such cases are viewed as a divine confirmation of the holiness of God's servants.

## The Road to Beatification

The first official trial that would eventually lead to her beatification was begun in 1947, 27 years after Teresita's death. Fortunately, 14 eye witnesses were still living who were able to give first-hand testimony. Needless to say, during this trial and all the ones that succeeded it, every aspect of her life, both positive and negative, was submitted to the scrutiny of norms prescribed by Canon Law to determine whether or not Sister Teresa had practiced authentic Christian virtues to an heroic degree. The sound norms of discernment always followed in these cases are guided by the words of the Gospel, which assure us that "by their fruits you will know them."

### Negative Points of the Saint's Life

During the trial, negative or unfavorable points were raised, challenging the claim that Juanita Fernández Solar was a saint and had practiced Christian virtues heroically. The charges, however, while true, were for the most part the very same ones she had levelled against herself when she wrote her *Intimate Diary*.

Before going to bed at night, the young girl sometimes found a little time to write in her *Diary*, not only accounts of the favors the Lord had granted her but also of the faults her conscience accused her of. For example, she admitted to having had fits of temper, and she wrote that there were times when her "blood would boil in anger." She also admits to being vain and excessively sentimental.

She confesses that she felt irritated when she was overlooked by others or when the attention she was seeking was paid to others. And she chronicled the time when she curried the special favor of Mother Popelair, one of the teachers at her Sacred Heart school, and the sadness that ensued when she felt overlooked or misunderstood by this Sister. Her resentment was particularly great the day one of the Sisters at the school passed out a box of candy to the students and Juanita was given a very small piece of candy by the Sister. She became so indignant that she threw it on the ground and refused to eat it.

In the Canonical trial, all these and other faults were acknowledged to be factual; but it was proved satisfactorily that for the most part her faults were attributable to the inexperience of youth and not to any malice or hardness of character. It was also felt that while these were points she had to struggle against throughout her life, she had made constant efforts to overcome herself and her weaknesses in order to grow in holiness and be transformed into Christ.

The record shows that all her faults were faced openly and honestly by the judges of the Canonical Trials. No attempt was made to tone them down or resort to the use of harmless euphemisms when discussing them. The court thoroughly studied the incident at the swimming pool at Chacabuco when Juanita was 8 or 9 years old, especially looking into her anger and disobedience to her mother. Juanita herself gave us a full report of this incident in her *Intimate Diary*. She tells us that because of this display of anger, her own mother was so irritated that she threatened to go back to Santiago that night "so she would not be around such an angry child." Needless to say, Juanita was soon contrite and after shedding many repentant tears, she writes: "I believe that for this sin I had perfect contrition."

Her brother Luís, in a delightful book of personal reminiscences of his sister and the events of her life, assures us that his sister had a number of faults when she was young, but that after her First Communion all noticed a remarkable transformation produced in his sister's life.

## Official Evaluation of These Negative Qualities

The Official Acts of the trials demonstrate convincingly that "When all the negative aspects of her character were put together, they were in reality, without doubt small, and were more expressions of the limitations of adolescence than hardness of character." The Acts continue, "But it would be unjust if we did not reveal that often the witnesses, after having emphasized her strong character, went on to add: 'she learned to overcome herself;' 'her character became sweeter through her victories over self;' and they all stressed that 'she learned to conquer herself'."

## Spiritual Infantilism?

One important question was raised and, in fact, could not be overlooked or dismissed in her trial. Since her life was so short, it was inevitable that the judges would probe to see if Juanita matured or whether she remained spiritually infantile. Did she? Basically the question of her spiritual infantilism was reduced to this: Was her life just a romantic, though very beautiful, dream of a teenage girl? Was it just childish emotion or was her life grounded and filled with the substance of true holiness? Was it a mature Christian life? Teenagers are at that special season of life when some of life's most beautiful dreams are spun in a young girl's mind and heart, but did this young girl who never lived beyond her teens attain the maturity of full Christian holiness? The fullness of Christian holiness requires a child-like disposition since all graces and favors are gifts of God, but it also requires the courageous love of a mature person. It has been established that Juanita had "a strong temperament, as well as profound convictions."

All the witnesses at her canonical trials were unanimous in rejecting the idea that infantilism ruled the life of Sister Teresa. By definition, infantilism denotes the retention of childish emotional qualities. It suggests lack of proper maturity as well as a failure to come to grips with the full reality of life. The charge of infantilism was investigated because Sister Teresa's life was so short. Remember, the same charge was often unsuccessfully raised during the causes of many young men and women who are now officially canonized.

All finally agreed that it was ridiculous to imagine that she remained infantile. Witnesses were easily able to refute these charges by stressing her remarkable growth in virtue, demonstrating that she had remarkable strength of character or outstanding Christian personality strengths, which is what the infused virtues are. Her personality profile indicates a young woman who was courageous in acknowledging and overcoming her weaknesses, who rose above self and lived generously for higher ideals and for others. And she did this not by relying on her own power but under the inspiration and with the help of the Holy Spirit.

In short, it is clear that her character was very balanced and not given to exaggerations; her highs were generally never too high, her lows not too low. She was a delightful person to be with, it was agreed, and as a result, she had many friends. She was a source of strength and inspiration to those who associated with her. Her virtues were strong and many, and were enriched with what Saint Paul refers to as "the good fragrance of Christ." It is evident to all that during her young life she achieved perfect psychic and spiritual equilibrium. She fully understood the grandeur as well as the serious demands of the religious vocation she chose to follow. As a matter of fact, everything in her life was the fruit of her asceticism and prayer.

## Was Teresa of the Andes a Mystic?

Since Sister Teresa lived in a Discalced Carmelite Monastery for only 11 months, inevitably the question was raised as to whether she was a true contemplative and whether she was a true mystic. This question could be avoided in the case of one who wrote to her confessor that she intended to take the name of Teresa of Jesus in honor of the great Saint Teresa of Avila, and then added:

"This is the name of a great saint, and therefore I will have to become a great saint!" If it can be shown that the answer to our question is affirmative, then an additional question must be asked: in what sense was she a contemplative and a mystic?

This question is legitimate and fair and arises instinctively when we recall that her role models in high school were contemplative Carmelites. She was moved and enamored by reading the lives of Saints Teresa of Avila and Thérèse of Lisieux as well as of Blessed Elizabeth of the Trinity. After carefully reading the spiritual writings of these holy women, the fervent teenage girl asserted that she was going to walk in their footsteps and embrace the same way of life. Above all else, she was decisively influenced by Saint Teresa of Avila through reading the Saint's *Autobiography* and *The Way of Perfection.*

Of special interest in the question of whether Teresa of the Andes was a contemplative and a mystic and was moved by the special influence of the Carmelite, Elizabeth of the Trinity. Saint Teresa of Jesus of the Andes is the first canonized devotee of Elizabeth, who less than weeks before her death had expressed the purpose of her mission in these clear words: "I think that in heaven my mission will be to draw souls by helping them to go out of themselves in order to cling to God by a wholly simple and loving movement, and to keep them in this great silence within, which will allow God to communicate Himself to them and to transform them into Himself."

Bear in mind that Juanita was reading Elizabeth's *Praise of Glory* when she was a sixteen year old, and that she was reading it just ten years after the death of the renowned French Carmelite. Deeply moved by reading this book Juanita was led to hope that she could live the spiritual legacy of Elizabeth, who told us: "I am leaving you my faith in the presence of God, the God who is all love, dwelling in our souls. I confide to you that it is this intimacy with Him that has been the bright sunshine lighting up my life, making it already an anticipated heaven." These quotations and many others fill the *Diary* and *Letters* of the first Chilean Saint, revealing the strong influence of one young saintly Carmelite on another.

## A Contemplative

First of all, Sister Teresa of the Andes, it is acknowledged, was a contemplative soul, not only when she lived in the Carmelite cloister but even while she was a high school student. By the term *contemplative* we mean one who had a very deep prayer life, a very special life of prayerful and personal intimacy with God. About that there can be no doubt. True contemplatives experience God much more by loving than by knowing. They are able to go out of themselves and gaze at God with the love of a friend for a friend or of a lover for the beloved. The grace of contemplation leads souls to a deep and direct understanding of the living God. For the contemplative, God alone, not ideas or concepts about God, is the all-important thing. The effects of this loving knowledge of God powerfully change and transform a soul.

But a further question must be raised: if it be granted that Sister Teresa of Jesus was a mystic, we must also ask was she also a mystic in the sense that St Paul was a mystic? In the sense that Saint Teresa of Avila is considered to be a mystic? Perhaps we must first define what a mystic is. To be quite brief in this very complicated matter, I will just compare the way mysticism is dealt with by Saint Paul and by Saint Teresa of Avila.

## Pauline Mysticism

In Saint Paul's Letters, the question of mysticism is very real and very important. Paul on occasion mentions his own mystical graces, not to praise himself but to give praise to the Lord who is the author of all such graces. He tells us that the Risen Lord appeared to him on his way to Damascus, and 14 years later he reports to the Corinthians how he was caught up into paradise and there heard words so secret that human lips are powerless to repeat them. These were personal favors bestowed on Paul, not experiences promised to every Christian in this life. These mystical experiences transformed Paul and spiritually strengthened him to carry out effectively the apostolic work the Lord had commanded him to perform.

From Paul's writings, we can also glean his conviction that every Christian is a mystic. This is known as the "Pauline mysticism," the Apostle's teaching on the mystical union of every Christian with Christ. Paul himself was a mystic, presumably one of the greatest, and that is why his teachings on mysticism are so important. In Baptism, Paul sees that we have all been plunged into the death and resurrection of Christ; thus, for Paul, every Christian is a mystic, since every Christian has the deep, hidden life of union with God that Paul refers to as "life in Christ" or "life in Christ Jesus."

Does this mean that Paul teaches that the Christian is always aware of a personal union with Christ and God? While it is perfectly true that a Christian is one with God through Baptism, and equally true that one is united with Christ as members are united with the body of which Christ is the head, in Pauline doctrine the Christian is aware of this only through faith, and knows this only through the public revelation of the Church. Without a special grace or a special revelation, one cannot have the direct, immediate and remarkable awareness of one's union with God that Saint Paul had when he was taken up into paradise. According to the Christian mysticism Saint Paul normally describes, the Christian can only know of his or her union with God through faith and with the certitude of faith.

## Everyday Mysticism

Perhaps not the most elegant term, but Karl Rahner's "everyday mysticism" guides the lives of most men and women. Actually, everyday mysticism is a less forbidding but a very down to earth term for Pauline mysticism. Many Christians have no "extraordinary awareness" of God's presence and workings in their lives, and yet they can attain the fullness of Gospel holiness. The saintly Pope John XXIII, for example, the Pope of goodness and the Pope of the New Pentecost, lived this kind of a life of exceptional Christian holiness; and many were convinced that, like the Baptizer, "he was truly a man sent by God, whose name was John." Despite all this, in his *Journal of A Soul*, no extraordinary technical, mystical phenomena are every mentioned. Steadily and surely he walked the path of Christian holiness.

In the Pope's ordinary, every day life he was constantly able to find God; was ever living with, in and for God. And to many it was evident that God was with Him. Being ever surrendered to God's will, his life became a perfect reflection of Paul's vision of the true Christian life. Writing to the Colossians, Paul stated: "Whatever you do in word or deed, do everything in the name of the Lord Jesus, giving thanks to god the FAther through Him. (Col:1:17) And so, Pope John kept trusting that God would be his strength and the joy of his heart.

Towards the end of his life the Pope was able to write: "The course of my life over these last two years shows a spontaneous and whole-hearted intensification of union with Christ, with the Church, and with the heaven which awaits me." This is the powerful mysticism of ordinary, everyday life; this is the mysticism which lead millions of God's people to the heights.

## Mysticism of Teresa of Avila

Saint Teresa of Avila, the first woman ever declared a Doctor of the universal Church also speaks of mysticism, and at great length, but she always discusses it from the standpoint of her own personal experience. She stresses that she herself was often granted a very special awareness of the nearness or closeness of God in her own soul. At times, she tells us, she was aware that God was present to her or that Christ was speaking to or appearing to her. Once in the *Autobiography* she says that for more than two years she was always aware that Christ in His humanity was present at her side. She keeps stressing that this did not happen at all times. When it did occur, the certitude did not come from her own faculties but was given to her by God. That is why she could not doubt its truth

When we ask whether Saint Teresa of the Andes was a mystic, we take for granted that she and all of us can be mystics in the Pauline sense. Here we are pressing for an answer to a very precise question: does Saint Teresa of the Andes meet the requirements for a true mystic as described in the writings of Saint Teresa of Avila and Saint John of the Cross?

It would be difficult in these few pages to collate all the experiences of the newly canonized Saint of Chile with those described by Saint Teresa of Avila. But there are solid grounds to assert that Teresa of the Andes did experience some of the very elevated stages of infused contemplative prayer described by the Saint of Avila. She furthermore certainly did arrive of the grace of perfect transforming union with God that Saint John of the Cross describes in *The Living Flame of Love*. Her age did not preclude this young woman from attaining the mystical marriage Teresa of Avila and John of the Cross describe. We have the assurance of Saint Teresa of Avila that while it generally takes many years before one arrives at this stage of perfection, still God is not bound to this rule and can and often does make exceptions.

What we do know from Juanita's *Diary* is that from her First Communion on she was at times distinctly aware of Jesus conversing with her. We cannot evaluate her after-Communion experiences scientifically, but in February 1919 she clearly had a profound mystical experience of the Most Blessed Trinity. In addition to this, we have her own testimony in her own handwriting in the *Diario Intimo* of special experiences. These cannot be described as anything other than mystical. She received them during her retreat in preparation for the feast of Pentecost; the retreat began on the Feast of the Ascension, May 29, 1919.

She tells us that on one occasion during this retreat she became so inflamed with divine love that when the community evening hour of mental prayer ended, she was at first unable to rise and follow her Sisters to the refectory. She says she begged our Lord that others would not become aware of this grace. Still, she was too absorbed in God to leave the choir. In her *Diary*, she also tells us of being graced with a transport into God that left her powerless to move or even to resist. Clearly she was then given an understanding that was an activity far above the truths she ordinarily knew and held by faith.

So we can confidently answer the question as to whether or not she was a mystic by responding to the question in the affirmative, being guided more by the outstanding spiritual effects produced in her soul than by merely academic or scholastic reasons. Effects produced in her soul were an increase in humility and fortitude, a greater desire to sacrifice herself for the good

90

of the Church, the salvation of souls and the sanctification of priests. She was in no way precluded by her extreme youth. God does not exclude the young from His choicest unitive graces and favors.

## Her Writings

The writings Juanita left us are extraordinary and inspiring. They afford a rare insight into her growth, development and personality. Through her writings, Teresa of the Andes has moved the souls of many men and women, as she shares with others her short but rich life as well as the heavenly inspirations that guided her.

A careful perusal of her *Intimate Diary*, for instance, reveals a young girl's life that is deep, rich, and graced with unusual insight and beauty. Throughout her writings there is simplicity of style and grace, and she often evidences signs of remarkable maturity. In addition, she retains the charm and simplicity that are delightful features of hearts that are young and generous.

Gabriel Marcel, the Christian existential thinker, wisely observes that the way to evaluate the life of a man or woman is not to consider only whether it is good or bad, but also to *ascertain whether it is full or empty*. Accordingly, one can see in Juanita a fullness and completeness of human and God-given life that is so wholesome and above the ordinary that it compels our admiration. Her life was filled with love, and overflowed with springtime love for her Beloved and for all others.

Juanita, fortunately, was not one to keep her riches to herself. But she did know that many things are not to be broadcast indiscriminately. It was not her intention to make her *Diary* public and; in fact, she never dreamed it would be seen by other eyes. She herself writes in her 52nd entry in her *Diary* that there are things so intimate to the soul that no other should be allowed to penetrate them. And she then adds this astonishing statement: "there are enclosed in the pages of this book favors that

God grants to *chosen souls* that others should not know about." We today have access to her inner secrets because the young teenager wrote these matters in her *Diary,* and did so only out of obedience to her spiritual directors. In God's Providence the loving secrets He communicated to her in the privacy of her soul were not to remain concealed but have now been trumpeted to the whole world. By following the inspirations that were granted to her at the time, she has become a beacon and a light of radiant goodness, bringing greater fullness to the lives of others. And through her writings, especially her *Diary* and *Letters,* she continues to let her light shine before us so we may glorify our Father in heaven.

## The Intimate Diary

What is the greatest of Saint Teresa of Chile's writings? Actually, it is hard to choose among them, but undoubtedly her *Intimate Diary,* which is her spiritual autobiography, is immediately the most helpful. As the *Autobiography* is a foundational book for understanding the personality and spirituality of the Saint of Avila, so Saint Teresita's Diary enjoys a similar role. It helps us structure her life and get a better understanding of the workings of her personality. As we read it we are aware that, like Moses, we on are sacred ground and must remove our ordinary shoes to ascend to her special religious level, a level of spiritual fullness that is all too infrequently achieved in this life.

Through this precious and delightful book we are given easy access to the soul of this Chilean Carmelite. At the outset she dispels any idea that we are about to read just an interesting story of the life of a teenage girl or her views about interesting events of her times. Instead, she tells us that we are going to read "the intimate life of a poor soul who, without any merit on her part, Jesus Christ loved in a special way and filled abundantly with His favors and graces." In this sense and only in this sense is her *Diary* Teresita's authentic autobiography. In this book, she sings the praises of mercies of God.

In other words, in this journal Teresa of the Andes describes her graced spiritual journey to God in holiness. She is fully aware that, from her childhood, God is the one who filled her life with sunshine and love. In this book we can see how God was the central and dominant concern of her short but beautiful life. And this is to be expected, for she was so attached to Christ who told us that He came that we may have life and the fullness of divine life. No other love had Teresa of the Andes than her love of Christ, and through Him for all others united with Christ. Indeed, there was no other life she ever craved or desired.

Not only do we find Juanita confessing the great mercies the Lord graced her life with, but we also see her diligently and unrelentingly working to become, as she says, "a good copy of Jesus." She carefully writes down in those precious copy books the recommendations of her confessors as well as the many notes taken during her retreats with exercises suggested by and in the spirit of the *Spiritual Exercises* of Saint Ignatius. In this sense, the Diary often turns into a very practical spiritual workbook, reminiscent of the inspiring *Journal of a Soul*, which is the spiritual autobiography of the beloved Pope John XXIII, the Pope of the New Pentecost in the Church.

"My soul is in the pages of this book," are the words with which Pope John XXIII, the Pope of goodness described to Monsignor Loris Capovilla the significance of his journal as he hesitantly handed it over to him for printing after his death. Sister Teresa of the Andes can say the same. She as much as says to us, in this book I am allowing you to read my soul. It is a transparent and permanent record for all to see that the overriding concern of my life was to love God at all costs and to work for the spreading of the reign of God throughout the world.

93

## Spiritual Evaluation of the Intimate Diary

Already the *Diary* and *Letters* of Saint Teresa de Los Andes are recognized as spiritual classics and have done marvels for souls. Many important spiritual leaders and thinkers have commented on their depth and timeliness. Let us consider just a few who have done so:

A) Pope John Paul II:

In his beautiful beatification homily, Pope John Paul II said,

*In her brief autobiographical writings she has left us the witness of a simple and attainable holiness centered on the core of the Gospel: love, suffer, pray and serve. The secret of her life completely directed toward holiness is summarized in familiarity with Christ, as a friend who is constantly present, and with the Virgin, a close and loving mother.*

B) Father Valentine Macca, O.C.D.:

A more extensive and penetrating analysis of her writings has been done by Carmelite Father Valentine Macca, author of the final "Relatio," the last working paper used to summarize all the data that came to light during Canonical trials held in Santiago, Valparaíso and Rome.

Because of the importance and authority of Father Macca's comments, a longer quote will be given to present his full thought on the central meaning of her writings:

*It is possible to see in her writings an almost complete spiritual autobiographical synthesis of her spiritual life or the way in which she uninterruptedly strove to be transformed by the love of Christ. In her Diary we see not only how she was inspired but also how she strove to be*

94

*guided by God in everything she did. Her letters, especially her letters to her father and mother and her brother Luís, unmistakably betray her march toward the holiness of the Gospel.*

*Especially rich and revealing are the letters she wrote to her spiritual directors. There we can see that she fully comprehended the demands of the spiritual life and we can also see in her letters that she had a tenacious will to fulfill all that the life of grace and union with God required of her.*

*Considering the limited number of years in the life of this servant of God, the writings take on additional importance, especially when we consider that it is in these writings of hers that we can see how this charming and delightful young girl took her life of union with God so seriously and inspires us to do the same. That we are not romanticizing the life of young Juanita Fernández Solar nor attempting to write a fairy tale of her beautiful and gracious life is, happily, demonstrated ably and convincingly by the witnesses who gave testimony concerning her life and virtues and the remarkable way she fulfilled the commandments of the Gospel.*

C) Father Marino Purroy, O.C.D.:

Father Purroy, a Discalced Carmelite, was the Vice-Postulator of her cause and her outstanding biographer. In his *Introduction to her Diary and Letters* he assures us that her writings have awakened an extraordinary hunger and thirst for God. He suggests that this is the outstanding mission of this young Carmelite to a world taken up with secularism and materialism, and forgetful of spiritual values.

He finds that perhaps what is most outstanding in her writings is to read the testimony of a young girl who felt called and loved by God and responded

95

wholeheartedly to this call. Thus she tells us of the emptiness experienced by many, an emptiness that is only counteracted when one totally gives oneself to God and, above all, when one remains faithful in this gift of self.

Father Purroy is well aware of the cultural differences between Saint Teresa's time and our own age. He notes that often, in her writings, she is relating the ideas of retreat directors and her own spiritual directors. But despite this, the message that comes through loud and clear and quite appealingly is her unreserved gift of self and total surrender to the will of God in all things. This was the goal of her life; this was the goal that led her to the fullness of divine joy and happiness.

### Declared a Servant of God

Only after the canonical trials for her beatification were completed, was it possible for the Pope to officially pronounced that Teresa of the Andes had practiced the virtues heroically and merited the title Servant of God. This meant that she could be called "Venerable Teresa of the Andes." This step signaled that the way was open to the next stage of the journey to beatification.

At least one proved miracle must be submitted in support of a beatification. The miracle approved for Teresa's beatification is the amazing cure of Hector Richard Carrasco, a young Santiago volunteer firefighter. The account of that event is best related by Olga Carrasco, his mother:

*On December 4, 1963, my son went (as a volunteer fireman) to a fire. During the course of fighting the fire his leg accidentally touched an electricity cable and he was electrocuted. He fell to the ground with a heart attack and was quickly rushed to the Central Headquarters. There he was diag-*

*nosed as having cerebral and pulmonary edema. When they called me to Central Headquarters I was told he was very ill and the doctor told me that there was no hope. Then on the 8th of December I went to Los Andes (where Teresa's tomb was then located) and I asked her to intercede for him so he would live, even if he were only a vegetable. When I returned to Central Headquarters, the doors where usually no one is allowed entrance were open. The doctor called me and said there was no hope. I asked permission to see him and when I entered I found him on machines. He was unconscious. I approached and began speaking to him, and begged him to keep on fighting, then I kissed him on the forehead. All at once he moved very abruptly. I called the nurse and they made me leave.*

*During the night the captain of the firemen called me to notify me that they had disconnected the respirator. They went back connecting and disconnecting it, and the next day he was breathing on his own.*

*On December 19th he returned home totally cured. We then made a pilgrimage with the firemen. He led the way and we walked from Huechuraba to Los Andes. Now, he is feeling fine and every December 8th we gather to give thanks.*

## Beatification

Once the miracle was approved by the medical board at the Vatican, it was only a matter of time before the next step was taken and a date and place determined for the beatification of Sister Teresa de los Andes. Within only a matter of weeks it was publicly announced that

97

Pope John Paul II planned to beatify the young cloistered Carmelite from the Carmel of Los Andes during his forthcoming trip to Chile. On April 3, 1987, during a memorable pastoral visit to Chile, Pope John Paul II officiated at her beatification during an outdoor ceremony held at O'Higgins Park in Santiago. Several hundred thousand people attended this memorable ceremony. The Pope stated that with this solemn act we may now call her Blessed Sister Teresa of Jesus or Blessed Sister Teresa of Los Andes.

## Papal Homily During the Mass of Beatification

During his homily for the solemn beatification of Juanita Fernández Solar, more popularly known in Chile as Sor Teresa de Los Andes, the Pope stressed that the young woman had been favored by God with the fullness of charity. This statement coincides with the celebrated chapter on the universal call to holiness in the *Dogmatic Constitution on the Church* of the Second Vatican Council. That decree states that all the faithful, without exception, are called to the fullness of holiness, which essentially consists in practicing divine charity perfectly. The Lord clearly enjoins all His followers to love God with all their hearts, with all their minds and with all their strength, and to love their neighbor as themselves. His love-command is the yardstick to measure Christian holiness or the process of progressive consecration to God.

Papal homilies for beatifications or canonizations are very rich, documents or veritable gold mines for insights into the holiness God infuses into His special servants. These documents are precious for their reflections on the beauty and fullness of the life Christ came to bring to the church and to all humankind. They open for us vistas on the greatness of human life which is all too seldom considered or even thought possible.

In his homily the Pope highlighted many important features of the holiness of the teenage Carmelite nun he had just beatified. Several of these points deserve comment:

## Life of Holiness:

The Pope stressed that:

*Ever since she was a child, Teresa of Los Andes experienced the grace of communion with Christ. It developed within her with the charm of her youth. She was full of vitality and cheerfulness, never lacking a sense of healthy amusement and play, and contact with nature, just as a true daughter of her time. She was a happy and dynamic young girl, open to God. And God made Christian love blossom in her, an open love, profoundly sensitive to the problems of her country and the aspirations of the Church.*

The Pontiff continued:

*The secret of her perfection could be none other than love, a great love of Christ, who fascinates her and moves her to consecrate herself to him forever, and to participate in the mystery of his passion and resurrection. At the same time she feels a filial love for the Virgin Mary, who drew her to imitate her virtues.*

## Distinctive Experience that God Is Infinite Joy:

The Pope emphasized the central point of Teresa of the Andes' spiritual message. He did so with these magnificent and immortal words:

*For her, God is infinite joy. This is the new hymn of Christian love that arises spontaneously from the soul of this young Chilean girl, in whose glorified face we can sense the grace of her transformation in Christ. In her we see the virtue of an understanding, serving, humble and patient love, which never destroys human values, but rather elevates and transfigures them.*

## Jesus Is Our Infinite Happiness:

The Pontiff's homily moved to another important point: Christ was the center of Blessed Teresa's life; she was truly, in name and deed, Teresa of Jesus.

*Yes, as Teresa of the Andes says, 'Jesus is our infinite happiness'. That is why this new Blessed is a model of the Gospel life for the young people of Chile. Teresa, who heroically practiced the Christian virtues, spent the years of her adolescence and youth in the normal environment of a young girl of her time. In her daily life we see her piety as she collaborated with the Church as a catechist, at school with her friends, or in the works of mercy and in the times of recreation and rest. Her exemplary life evidenced a Christian humanism, but always accompanied with the unmistakable seal of a lively intelligence, sensitive awareness, and the creative capacity typical of the Chilean people. In her we see an expression of the soul and character of your country as well as the perennial youth of Christ's Gospel, which enthused and attracted Sister Teresa of Los Andes.*

## First Fruits of Holiness
## of the Teresian Carmel in Latin America:

A touching and timely facet of the beatification shone forth when the Pope solemnly declared:

*At the beginning we heard a brief biographical profile of Sister Teresa of Los Andes, a young Chilean girl, symbol of the faith and goodness of this people; a Discalced Carmelite, captivated by the heavenly Kingdom in the springtime of her life; the first fruits of the holiness of the Teresian Carmelites in Latin America.*

This point addresses a special lesson of the new Carmelite for her Order and for our new world. Previously, it may have seemed that holiness in Carmel was reserved to Europeans, since all the canonized and beatified in the Teresian Carmel were of European ancestry. Now we see the grace of God working in the Carmel of the new world, and it is interesting that the first recognized fruits of outstanding holiness are to be found in a young, teenage Carmelite. God's ways, ever marvelous and admirable, can only fill us with wonder.

## An Ugly Moment

While the faithful by the thousands were filled with deep emotion and wrapped in profound prayer throughout the ceremony, it happened. Just when the readings of the Mass and especially the Gospel on the Beatitudes was about to be read things went bad. A group of young protestors and demonstrators had planned to take advantage of this solemn ceremony, the presence of the Pope and the throngs of people in attendance to draw attention to their political cause. The police had to move in quickly. Tear gas was discharged to quell the demonstrators lest severe damage be inflicted on the innocent. Fortunately, no one was killed, but many were overcome by the teargas. Newspaper pictures showed the Pope with a handkerchief in hand, protecting himself against the harmful fumes.

At the end of his Homily the Pope repeated the Scriptural words, words that clearly referred to Teresa of the Andes and the spirit that motivated her whole life. The Pope proclaimed to the crowd, *"El Amor Es Mas Fuerte,"* which means Love Is Stronger Than All Things. At that moment of the beatification of a young girl from Santiago, there were in evidence two opposing groups joined in conflict. One group was filled with bitterness and hatred, the other, with the spirit of the gospel. But the message of the latter group was upheld very clearly at the outset of the Papal homily. The Pope said:

> *Blessed Teresa gives us a message of reconciliation; "There are three things that last: faith, hope and charity; and the greatest of these is love." These words of St. Paul, the culmination of his hymn to charity resound with new tones in this eucharistic celebration. Yes, the greatest of these is love.*

The words of the Pope profoundly inspired the people in attendance and are still remembered today. These words adorn her simple tomb. Probably never before have political demonstrations been staged or tear gas used at a beatification ceremony, but in modern times such things are possible. Providentially, however, the Word of God prevailed. It was a scriptural text dear to the heart and spirit of Sister Teresa of the Andes. Yes, "Love is greater than all things." Today when people come to her National Shrine to pray, some still recall that ugly incident, but more importantly they remember the message their little saint learned from Saint John of The Cross that, "where there is no love, put love and you will draw out love." Yes, God's love is the greatest thing in the world.

## Teresa of the Andes, Role Model for Our Times

Teresita, as the new Saint is affectionately referred to in South America, has a special mission of renewing, deepening and transmitting the beauty of the holiness of Christ to others. This young Carmelite mystic, from her own immediate and direct awareness of God and divine things, can offer witness and help to all.

## Her Direct and Immediate Experience of God

Why is the intimacy and partnership of a mystical soul with God so powerful and precious? Romano Guardini offers this assessment of the witness-value of a mystic. He wrote: "It enables the one who has been blessed to bear witness: 'I know that God lives'; to counter every doubt or objection with the words: 'It is so, I have experienced it,' thus by bearing personal witness to God he or she may give others great support."

Teresa of the Andes bears witness to the God she knows in with and through Christ. Her experience of God is Christocentric. She only wants to know God and divine things in Christ. This is an important point in her spirituality and in all spirituality that claims to be Christian.

The new saintly Carmelite's true love of Christ admirably stands the test of Christocentric spirituality, which Guardini, in harmony with the tradition of many saints, claims to be important for a sound and authentic Christian spirituality. The former celebrated professor and lecturer at the University of Munich wisely wrote:

*The true Christian judges everything only in the light of Christ. He will hold "only what stands the test before God in Christ and is true. We must first bring our experience to Christ; we should say to ourselves: 'All this is what I want only if Christ is*

103

there, if it is in the Spirit, if it can hold its own before Him. Christ's name and His Cross is my standard, and anything that is incompatible with that I do not want.' It may be tempting to abandon oneself to the 'divine in itself' or to seek God as He is 'beyond all words and ways,' but there is great danger in this. At all times must we put the person of Christ in the center, refer to Him, think of Him and commit everything into His hands."

## Charm and Simplicity

Precisely because people find her so normal, so natural and attractive is Juanita Fernández Solar immensely popular in her Chile and in adjacent countries of South America. There is nothing forbidding about her. She is warm and human, a beautiful human expression of the life of Christ and the values of the Gospel. But she is also seen to be a true child of our 20th century, and she makes the truths she learned in life and in prayer accessible to us with a special sweetness and tenderness. Her charm and simplicity appeal to all.

In the trials for her beatification and even in the Papal homily in Santiago, frequent mention was made of the great charm and simplicity of this young contemplative. Charm can accomplish much and is a great and precious gift. This attribute is real but elusive. The power it exerts over hearts is irresistible.

Her charm is always delightful because it is truly feminine. Even though she had many enviable achievements, especially in sports and academics, she was never proud or aggressively competitive. Her virtues as well as her virtue pattern remained strong, appealing and attractive.

## Canonization

With deep joy and enthusiasm the faithful demonstrated their veneration for the first Chilean ever beatified. Immediately after she was officially called Blessed Teresa, something very special became clearly evident to all. Everywhere one went in Chile, a picture of the young Carmelite could be seen. Sor Teresa had become a real spiritual force in her own country. Now people became increasingly anxious to see the Church bestow the full honors of sainthood on her.

But the Church in its wisdom will not proceed to the final step until and unless at least one miracle is adduced as evidence of divine intervention. Fortunately, the needed miracle was not long in coming. On December 8, 1988 a young girl of twelve, Marcella Antúnez went swimming during a school picnic at the Las Condes section of Santiago, and was found at the bottom of the pool, having been there more than five minutes. The Emergency Squad was called and Marcella was taken to the hospital. The other girls of the school were in a state of panic when one of them said, "Let's pray to Teresa of the Andes for Marcella." Everyone got down on her knees and began to pray.

When Marcella arrived at the emergency room, one of the attendants remarked, "her condition is such, it's too bad she didn't die in that pool, for she'll forever be a vegetable." Hospital records confirm that the staff held out little or no hope for the twelve year old girl.

Still, the prayers continued. After a while Marcella awakened. To the amazement of the hospital staff, she was able to move about. Marcella was given a thorough medical examination and it was learned she had suffered no psychic or physical damage, despite the fact the girl had been without oxygen so long. There is no medical explanation for this, was the unanimous conclusion of the doctors.

When the case was reviewed by Medical Teams at the Vatican, it was declared an official miracle. Shortly afterward, on July 11, 1992 Pope John Paul 11 signed the decree stating the miracle was authentic and stated that the canonization would soon take place. The news was warmly greeted by all.

## Solemn Canonization in Rome

When news came from high ranking sources in Rome that the first American Discalced Carmelite was scheduled to be canonized, it was rumored that the great event would take place in Santo Domingo of the Dominican Republic. The Pope planned to travel to that Caribbean country to assist at the festivities planned for the fifth centenary of Christopher Columbus' discovery of and the subsequent christianization of the new world. The date given for the canonization was Columbus Day 1992. The Pope's visit was also to coincide with the meeting of the bishops in their Latin American Episcopal Conference, whose topic was to be the new evangelization needs of our times.

But in only a matter of days, the Papal Trip had to be cancelled. The Pope became ill and had to be taken to the Gemelli Clinic in Rome for surgery. The canonization would have to be postponed and held in Rome at a later date. Within a few months, news came from the Eternal City that the Cardinal Secretary of State had officially announced to the world that the Holy Father had signed the decree permitting the canonization of Teresa of the Andes together with Sister Mary of Saint Ignatius (Claudine Thénevet), foundress of the Congregation of Jesus and Mary. The canonization at the Vatican was scheduled to take place on March 21, 1993.

If this announcement of the official ceremony brought great joy, attendance at the canonization made all ecstatic with loving joy. Who could possibly explain this priceless event? Who could find words appropriate enough to describe this celebration? One man. And he did it felicitously. Combining both elegance and eloquence, Angelo Cardinal Sodano described the sacred event that took place beneath the awesome cupola of the Basilica designed by Michelangelo Buonaroti.

These are the Cardinal's words.

*In this basilica, on March 21, of the year of the Lord, 1993, just when springtime was beginning in this northern hemisphere and when the grape season was beginning in the Alcongagua region of Chile, His Holiness Pope John Paul II canonized the first Chilean Saint, Sister Teresa of Los Andes.*

Then, with great fervor, he fervently implored:

*Saint Teresa, Carmelite, take us by the hand to climb the mountain of Christ, and to safeguard the summits of hope the horizon of the Most Holy Trinity."*

Could there be finer words to describe the spirit of the canonization of one who loved Christ with the fullness of her springtime fervor and love and who would like us to love Him in the same way?

Pope John Paul II preached a memorable homily in Saint Peter's at the canonization. Among other things, he said: "Sister Teresa de los Andes, Teresa of Jesus, is the light of Christ for the whole Chilean Church; this Discalced Carmelite, the first fruit of holiness of the Teresian Carmel of Latin America, today is enrolled

107

among the Saints of the universal Church." And on the following day, in the Paul V Audience Hall, the Pope delivered a Discourse which was entitled, *We Rejoice to Have Saints Praying For Us in Heaven.* In that talk the Pope affirmed, "Beloved daughter of the Chilean Church! St. Teresa of Los Andes (Juanita Fernández Solar) is a choice and mature fruit of the presence of the Gospel in America, precisely at the time when we are commemorating the fifth centenary of the arrival of the faith on this Continent of Hope."

The Pope presented Saint Teresa of Jesus of the Andes to us as a true role-model, saying, "Dear brothers and sisters, the new Saint must be for all of you an exceptional witness of woman at prayer and a model of Christian life which can never be separated from love of neighbor." Continuing, the Pope affirmed, "The charism of the contemplative life, of which St. Teresa of the Andes is a special example, must be seen as especially timely and necessary in the Church, which is called to the urgent task of the new evangelization."

### Those Who Helped Teresa to the Altar

While the young Beata had much charm and goodness, was filled with grace and virtue, this should not however make us overlook the significant help she received in her life from other persons. At every canonization ceremony, great praise is heaped on the Servant of God. Implicitly but importantly, Popes of necessity likewise assign deep tribute to those who providentially were instrumental in the formation and education of the sainted person.

In the Fernández family we see that Lucía, her mother, played an outstanding role in the human and spiritual development of her daughter. She and Aunt

Juana took the little girl to Mass each day and were solicitous for her religious formation and education. Clearly, the Religious of the Sacred Heart were outstanding and providential in the role they played in the young girl's life. Her father and brothers and sisters did not at first understand Juanita's vocation, but they made the sacrifice of allowing her to leave home and supported her decision. Nor can we overlook Mother Angélica, the Prioress of the Carmel of Los Andes, who offered great love, wise guidance and help as she assisted the young novice. The priests who ministered to her through retreats and in the confessional played significant roles. None of these nor even some of her important friends should be overlooked. They merited her gratitude and deserve our admiration.

### Evangelizing Her Own Family

Teresa, however, after being helped by others, extends her heart and hand to assist others. Of particular note is the way she helped her own family, especially in a human and spiritual way. She was a great source of comfort to her mother, who could see her daughter growing in wisdom and age. And we have already seen that Juanita wrote many beautiful and tender letters to her father when he was away from the family hearth. They were letters of comfort and love, letters to encourage him in his loneliness when he was far from home and the family celebrations.

But Juanita was particularly helpful to her sister Rebecca, encouraging and sharing religious experiences with her. When Rebecca was only 14, Juanita wrote to her, telling her that "my thought is taken up with Him alone, He is my ideal, He is my infinite ideal. I long for the day when I can go to Carmel, to concern myself only with Him, to abase myself in Him and so to live His life alone: to love and suffer to save souls." Then in her great love for Rebecca, Juanita adds, *I wish I could inflame you with that love. How happy would I be if I could give you to Him!*

Later Rebecca, influenced by Juanita, did follow her sister's example and sought admission in the Carmel of Los Andes and there made her profession in the Order of our Lady of Mount Carmel. Like Juanita's life, Rebecca's was brief. Sister Teresa of the Divine Heart, as she was known in Carmel, died in 1942 in the odor of sanctity. She was forty years old at the time.

### Don't You Feel Closer to God When I Am With You?

Juanita's brother Luís publicly acknowledged how much his sister helped him spiritually, especially in the recovery of his faith. When he was in high school, Luís began reading philosophical books, unaware of the serious implications of such injudicious reading for his faith. As a result he began to experience difficulties concerning his faith and grew slack in the practice of his religion. Fortunately, he always found Juanita ever willing to listen and help. He liked talking with Juanita about religious matters, he says, because he felt safe when he confided in her concerning his inner religious difficulties.

Once after Luís had told his sister of his religious doubts, he reports that she just put her arm around his shoulder and said, "How can you doubt God? Don't you feel close to God when I am with you?" On another occasion when he and Juanita were out in the country on vacation they were looking up at the stars and admiring the heavens at night. All of a sudden during that unforgettable dialogue, he asked Juanita: "Don't you feel terror in the presence of the infinite spaces that Pascal speaks of?" She replied: "Why should I feel afraid? Isn't this world the house of God? Instead of frightening me, they move me to take flight into my soul with the confidence of a creature of God."

This was her way. She never ventured into futile arguments that would have served no purpose; instead, from her inner life she brought strength and comfort to others. Her method was the method of an educated heart, which relies on the wisdom of love.

## Joy and the Passion of Christ

In reading her *Diary* or *Letters*, one is struck with her frequent use of the word "joy." Juanita often speaks of finding joy or taking her joy or delight in God. Elsewhere she states that Jesus is her source of joy. She not infrequently says she'd like to influence others to find this same joy, for joy was the climate of her life. And yet, Sister Teresa of the Andes was no stranger to suffering and pain in her life, nor did she pretend that life is free of problems, as Pollyanna does in the Eleanor Porter novel. In that novel, we remember that Pollyanna's father was a preacher, but his daughter explains that he didn't want to preach the whole Gospel, but only "the glad texts of the Bible," presumably leaving out the rest. Teresa of the Andes was never guided by empty optimism in her religion but meditates at great length, deeply and lovingly, on the sufferings of Christ. That Christ suffered "for us" puts great demands on each of us and requires personal involvement. Because she was lovingly involved, she found joy, because the sufferings of Christ brought her the fullness of God's love. She tells us that she's so proud to be associated with Christ her Spouse in all His mysteries.

### The God Who Is Infinite Joy

A most appealing and distinctive feature of the spirituality of this young Chilean girl is the special way she was inwardly drawn to relate to God. For Teresa of the Andes, God is loving and merciful but above all, her infinite joy. The Pope stressed this very point in his homily for her beatification, saying "This is the new hymn of Christian love that rises spontaneously from the soul of this young girl."

Because she so often speaks of joy, it is imperative to define the term as accurately as possible. In *Webster's Dictionary of Synonyms,* we read that joy is often the word that must be used in place of pleasure and still more often in the place of delight. It is the preferred and often the necessary term, however, when a deep rooted rapturous emotion is implied, or when the happiness is so great as to be almost painful in its intensity."

What does Teresita mean when she says that God is infinite joy? Does she have a message here for the men and women of our times? Yes, but the key is to explain that the deepest joy comes from God and that He alone is the origin and source of this joy. The bible confirms this. In the fifth chapter of Paul's letter to the Galatians he lists joy as one of the precious fruits infused by the Holy Spirit to make our life to be blessed with overflowing joy, even in this life.

Saint Thomas Aquinas in his *Commentary on Galatians* offers his brilliance when he clarifies for us that joy is basically a form of love, but insists that it is a very special kind of love. It is a love, he says, that is experienced only when the beloved is present. A mother, for example, may love all her children wherever they may be. Whether they be in Tokyo or Buenos Aires or Paris she will love them just as much as ever across the distance of thousands of miles.

But she can only have the very special joy of love when they come through the front door and are with her. The presence of the beloved is the cause of the mother's joy.

Joy is often associated with happiness. But in precise and meaningful language, joy is not the same as happiness, since happiness distinctively signifies the fulfillment of one's life and goals. Thus one will never have full happiness until the trials and cares of this life are finally over. But in this life one can have joy, even intense joy, despite the trials or difficulties of life, provided the beloved is present, even if we only know of this presence through faith. That is the way we generally know of God's presence. We are assured of divine joy through the words of Jesus: "Behold, I will be with you always."

For Saint Teresa of Jesus of the Andes, the true meaning of her life and the source of all her happiness was grounded in and based on God's presence to her in Christ. She was certain that no one else could satisfy the deepest and infinite longings of her heart.

## To Suffer With Joy

One of the paradoxes of Christianity is the presence of suffering and joy in the christian. How often we find christians rejoicing to be found worthy to suffer for Christ as He suffered for them. This paradox played itself out also in the life of Teresa of the Andes, for even when she suffered, she was never unaware that God was close and near to her. Therefore she was never without joy. Nothing could separate her from the joy of the living God who, like a vessel overflowing with oil, was ever present and surrounding her with His love.

113

With characteristic frankness the 15-year-old Juanita writes: "Today, ever since I got up, I am very sad. It seems that suddenly my heart is breaking. Jesus told me He wants me to suffer with joy." And then she continues: "He told me that He joyfully ascended Calvary and laid His head on the cross for the salvation of humankind. Is it possible that you are seeking Me and you want to be like Me? Then come with Me and take up the cross with love and joy." Notice that she can still have joy because she is told to "come with Me;" being close to Jesus will enable her to suffer with Him and for Him, but always with joy.

The modern world enjoys material possessions and comforts undreamed of in previous ages. And yet, there are more people suffering from depression and loneliness than ever before. This state of mind and soul come from sadness, which is the opposite of joy. Hence the Chilean saint's timely message for all and especially for today's youth is: only in Christ can one find the true source of joy happiness, for He alone can lead us to the discovery that our lives are bathed in the joyful presence of God.

Saint Teresa of the Andes still speaks to us and recalls to our minds the teaching of Jesus in His priestly prayer recorded in John's Gospel, where the Lord told His apostles and tells us still: "You are sad for a time, but I shall see you again; then your hearts will rejoice with a joy no one can take from you." Christ lives in our hearts by faith and there He is present fulfilling His promise: "All this I tell you, that My joy may be yours and that your joy may be complete."

The recently canonized Teresa of the Andes is rightly classified as a young saint, and young saints are very special. In the fullness of their youth the saints were able to love with purity and intensity, accompanied by the great strength and vitality of that blessed season of life. They show, as only the young can, a wonderful spirit of generosity and sacrifice, as well as a willingness to undertake anything in the name of love and for great and noble causes. The young saints had heartfelt dreams of working for the good of others and for the transformation of the world. They have a delightful and infectious way of inflaming others, especially the young, and even those of us a bit longer in the tooth, with their exciting dreams of bringing the fullness of the good news of the Gospel to all.

Young saints, in the generous and attractive years of their lives, when their souls still have the charm and sincerity of the springtime of life can rejuvenate us, can help us recall the many, many graces God gave in the greener years of our youth which now may unfortunately have become a bit jaded or practically forgotten. Young saints can elevate and ennoble us, by recalling to our minds the joys and blessings of our youth.

## Presence and Absence of God Today

Father Marino Purroy Remon, O.C.D., the outstanding biographer of the new saint, offers us unending optimism when he writes that Saint Teresa of the Andes has the special gift of writing and writes in a way that modern men and women can easily understand. She speaks of the nearness as well as the frightening absence of God with its consequences in human life. That message needs to be heard more frequently today, and more insistently. Better still, it needs to be heard from those who have been captivated by the nearness and joy of God. The same message can and must be gently conveyed to those who are hurting deeply, those numerous souls who are experiencing the painful and tortuous absence of God in their souls. This beautiful young Carmelite can assure them as she assured her

115

brother Luís so many years ago. To them she lovingly says: "Yes, it is true. You are loved by the God who is the God of Infinite Joy! My life proves this. When I am near you, don't you feel the presence of God?" St Teresa of the Andes has a mission of sharing this joyful message of the Gospel with everyone. From her place in heaven our saints longs to infect souls with the exuberance of her charism. She would especially love us to imitate her charism of bringing this joy to all.

## With Us Still

The young virginal saint of the Andes is still present with us and her spiritual message has abiding value for everyone. Her importance - and indeed the importance of all the saints - has been admirably captured in the following passage of the Second Vatican Council:

*When we look at the lives of those who have faithfully followed Christ, we are inspired with a new reason for seeking the city which is to come (Heb. 13:14; 11:10). At the same time we are shown a most safe path by which, among the vicissitudes of this world and in keeping with the state in life and condition proper to each of us, we will be able to arrive at perfect union with Christ, which is holiness. In the lives of those who shared in our humanity and yet were transformed into especially successful images of Christ (cf. 2 Cor. 3:18), God vividly manifests to us His presence and His face. He speaks to us in them, and gives us a sign of His kingdom, to which we are powerfully drawn, surrounded as we are by so many witnesses (cf Heb. 12:1) and having such an argument for the truth of the Gospel.*

# Part Three

## Relevance of Her Joyful Message for Our Times

Having reviewed the earthly career of Teresa of the Andes and having considered her heavenly life, it is now time to examine the relevance of her life and message of joy in God for men and women living today. It may be asked whether her life and message retain a special and abiding relevance today? Is her influence limited only to her native Chile? Or is it a truly universal spiritual message?

Those who have read the *Intimate Diary* and *Letters* of Teresa of the Andes for the first time have expressed amazement at the depth and originality of thought in this young Carmelite sister's writings. They wonder how she was able to achieve such profundity at so early an age. More than that, they are impressed that this young sister has not only an original and true message but one that is so relevant for the last decade of this century. We are referring, more precisely, to her message of joy, a message that seems particularly helpful to these times.

## God Is Infinite Joy

Though all love and serve the one true God, we find that different men and women feel a particular attraction to various mysteries or aspects of the mystery of Christ. Some feel a particular attraction to imitate the saving activity of Christ, perhaps by caring for the poor and needy or teaching the young. Others, such as the more distinctly contemplative saints, seem drawn to spend their existence imitating the mystery of the

117

praying Christ of the Gospel: the Christ who spent long nights in the most profound intimacy and union with His Father, the Christ who prays for the needs of humankind in the Garden and on the Cross.

Those who live a contemplative way of life are more deeply drawn to experience the nearness, the closeness of God. Those drawn by God to a more active imitation of the ministry of Jesus are more directly available to all God's people, as Jesus Himself was. Others drawn by God to an exclusively contemplative vocation, as was the cloistered Teresa of the Andes, make themselves totally and directly available to God as they pursue their hidden quest for divine intimacy, but are chiefly available to the needs of God's people through their life of prayer and reparation.

All saints have one thing in common, the fact that they are striving to live for God alone, the compelling concern to make God the deepest and most profound center of their personal life. Saint Paul is a splendid example of what it means to live for God alone. After he met the Risen Lord on the way to Damascus and was subsequently baptized, his whole life was radically changed. Christ had taken possession of him and he could in all truth say to the Galatians: "I live no longer I, but Christ lives in me." Paul knows too that despite his weakness, he can do all things because of his union with the Risen Lord.

God's love for every person is unique, and it is not surprising that each person has a very special and a personal relationship with God. While He is the God of all, He is the God of each in a very special way. No individual person can understand all the attributes or perfections of God, but we find individual saints especially drawn toward a particular divine attribute and take their delight in a specific divine perfection manifested in the life of Christ. Thus we see Saint Francis and his compelling love for the poor Christ of the Gospel; he loved to contemplate the poverty of the Christ who became needy so we can be filled with the richness of God. Saint Dominic, on the other hand, feels driven to bring the wisdom of God to those in ignorance about God and His holiness. Saint Thérèse of the Child Jesus felt especially drawn to the Divine Mercy and experienced that despite her littleness God stooped down to raise her up to His divine heights. The little Chilean Carmelite, Teresa of the Andes, felt irresistibly drawn to the mystery of the joy of God's presence. She longs that Christ's words will be fulfilled in each one that we may have His joy and that no one will take this joy from us. She would also like us to go out and share our divine joy with others.

Spiritual joy is one of the most precious gifts of the Holy Spirit and its fullness is an unmistakable sign of holiness. Joy indicates very intense pleasure as well as a sense of exceptional good fortune. True spiritual joy emanates from the presence of God in our life, and especially from our awareness of His loving and abiding presence. In the New Testament we see that tidings of great joy filled the world when it was announced that God the Savior was born. Under the guidance of the Holy Spirit, men and women in Luke's Gospel are filled with joy at His appearance and are unshakably assured that the Savior will be with His people forever.

Because spiritual joy does not depend on our emotions or on material well-being, it cannot be lost as long as God is present and as long as we believe in His presence and love. In fact, as we can see in the lives of the martyrs, not even suffering, hardship or sickness deprived them of the joy of God's presence. When God is the loving Guest of a Soul, nothing can interfere with the joy He brings.

## Sadness

The feelings and emotions directly opposed to joy are sadness and despondency. Sadness is the great enemy of spiritual joy. When we are aware of the presence of God in our lives, we are eager to serve Him fervently, practice the virtues and spread goodness everywhere. When we are spiritually sad, we feel and act in just the opposite way. Our souls are troubled and disheartened, unable to find inner peace; we avoid prayer and our good resolutions are weakened and diminished. Deprived of the delight of the nearness and closeness of God in our lives, we feel helpless and disinclined to do good. With wisdom that is both human and divine, Saint James writes: "If anyone among you is sad, let him pray" (James 5:13), thus reminding those who are suffering sadness because of hardship or tribulation that if they pray, their hearts will be strengthened and the awareness of the goodness and presence of God will lift their spirits and fill them with confidence.

## Unimagined Influence

Sister Teresa of the Andes never dreamed she would influence anyone after her death. She lived what she considered a simple, ordinary Christian life. She strove to center her life in the mystery of Christ and the depth of her response to Christ was the divine faith and love given to every Christian by the Holy Spirit. But she strongly and urgently longed for every Christian to find the fullness of life and joy in Christ.

It is true, of course, that during her lifetime she did strive to help and influence others, that she wanted to become holy so she could be effective in gaining souls for Christ. She fervently wanted to aid priests to be ardent but gentle ministers of the Gospel and exercise an apostolic ministry that is fruitful. Was there a special way that God related to her and that He wanted her to relate to us? Was her special mission the mystery of how God showed forth His glory in her life by drawing her to take her delight in Him who wants all to be enriched with His own life and beauty? The attractive way this Chilean girl responded to God's loving presence has made her a convincing witness, leading others to experience and enjoy union with the God who is infinite joy. Simply but powerfully she has been able to articulate the sublime mystery of how this awareness of the goodness of God and joy in His presence is attained through daily prayer and the Eucharist. She has become a powerful friend to many because with them she shares her secret: in constant prayer you too can find strength and the awareness of God's joyful presence in your life and you can find the peace for which your heart longs.

## Rejoice in the Lord

A sound grasp of the meaning and importance of spiritual joy is outlined in *Rejoice In The Lord*, an insightful Apostolic Letter of Pope Paul VI that is a veritable treasure on the nature and practice of true Christian joy in life. In that celebrated letter, dated May 5, 1975, the Pope prophetically dealt with the subject of Christian joy or the gift of joy in the Holy Spirit for our contemporary technological society. He maintains that while modern society has succeeded in multiplying opportunities for pleasure, it has great difficulty in generating joy because joy comes from a source other than material goods, financial prosperity, technological advances or future promises.

The pontifical document issued for the 1975 Holy Year also gives strong encouragement to teach people or to teach them anew how to savor the simple joys the Creator has placed in their path. Making his letter more concrete and practical, the Pope gave these examples of true joy: "the elating joy of existence and of life; the joy of chaste and sanctified love; the peaceful joy of nature and silence; the sometimes austere joy of work well done; the joy and satisfaction of duty performed; the transparent joy of purity, service and sharing; the demanding joy of sacrifice."

It might be useful at this point to explore the foundation and relevance of Sister Teresa's inspired message that God is infinite joy. Taking as our starting point the pontifical document already referred to, we discover that spiritual Joy is an important characteristic of the Old Testament as well as the New, for God sincerely desires to fill His people with joy.

## Biblical Teaching on Joy

There is a great deal of stress in the Bible on the joy God brings His people. It is the joy experienced by every man or woman who is wholeheartedly seeking God. It is the special blessing of those who seek to have a right relationship with God, to walk in His ways and fulfill His commandments. Such people have light and glad hearts and are able to sing the praises of God with joy and happiness.

But it is in the New Testament that we have the greatest evidence of joy and of the God who brings the fullness of joy. Because one has joy or can rejoice when

122

in the presence of a cherished and loved one, we find the angel announcing to Mary that she has been overshadowed by the Holy Spirit and thus she can rejoice because God is with her and she has found the exceeding favor of the Lord. This overshadowing filled her soul with such overwhelming love and joy that Christian piety has always honored Mary as the cause of our joy. Thus the joy of Mary, who is the dawn of our salvation, is also the source of our joy.

Throughout the Gospel of Luke and in the Acts of the Apostles are found innumerable instances of people who are filled with joy because of the presence of God in Christ. Luke stresses that all these men and women were led by the Holy Spirit to take their joy in the Incarnate Son of God, especially aging Simeon who was able to hold the Child in his arms and Anna who was privileged to see the Messiah before her eyes were closed in death.

Saint Paul in his Epistles urges Christians to be always filled with joy, even in suffering, because Christ, the source and cause of joy, is always with them and conforming them to His likeness. Paul expresses in very simple words a formula he used and one that is helpful to all Christians. The holy Apostle tells us to do three things: rejoice in the Lord always, pray without ceasing, and give thanks to God unremittingly. This is a good summation of the life of Teresa of the Andes and explains her secret and her message. She too would like to exhort us to constant joy through attentiveness to daily prayer or attentiveness to the presence and nearness of God in our lives and she would urge us to be constantly pouring out our gratitude to God for His marvelous love bestowed on us in Christ. With the holy Apostle, the young Saint Teresa of Chile urges all to rejoice in the Lord always. How fitting it was that this attractive Saint from Chile was canonized on Laetare Sunday, which is so called because the entrance antiphon of the Mass begins with the words, "Rejoice, Jerusalem! Be glad for her, you who love her. Rejoice!"

Strange as it may seem, it is only in the last book of the Bible, the Apocalypse, that we come to find untold numbers of men and women singing and rejoicing because they are eternally with God and with the Lamb. The heavenly inhabitants are all blissfully joyful and will remain so eternally because they have the assurance that nothing will ever interfere with or separate them from their union with God, who is the source or fountain of love, joy and happiness. This final book of the Bible has special relevance to the life of Teresa of the Andes, who desired to live here on earth as the joyful angels and saints live in heaven, unceasingly adoring and singing the praises of God.

## Joy, Fruit of the Holy Spirit

In the fifth chapter of his Letter to the Galatians, Paul gives a powerful exhortation on Christian living and tells us how we can attain the liberty of the children of God, the freedom to enjoy God's love fully and to love Him with our whole hearts, minds and souls. Paul does not deceive us into thinking that by our own efforts we can bring this about in our lives. Instead, he assures us that through th presence and power of the Holy Spirit we can attain the glorious freedom Christ merited for us. One can be sure that the Holy Spirit is working lovingly in his or her life when the Spirit produces the fruits enumerated in that chapter. Then one truly possesses the freedom of the children of God and is assured of being liberated from all that is opposed to the love of God. The love of God that has been poured into our hearts by the Holy Spirit is the proof and assurance that takes away all contrary fear and anxiety.

It is especially interesting that Paul speaks of the "fruit" (singular!) of the Holy Spirit, which is another way of saying that the Holy Spirit works in our souls in such a way that an integral pattern of life is produced, or, to put it another way, that the Christian is given the perfect form of the life of Christ. Essential characteristics of the true and complete Christian life are described as a the sum total of rich blessings which the Holy Spirit, the divine Artist who fashions Christ's image in souls, produces in the souls of men and women who are in the state of sanctifying grace. Paul enumerates the blessings that make us a "perfect copy of Christ," which Teresa of the Andes ardently longed to become.

The infused fruits come from the same source and have the same foundation, the presence of the Holy Spirit. The work of the Holy Spirit is twofold: to enlighten our minds and to inflame our wills. In his letter to the Galatians, Paul enumerates twelve fruits of the Holy Spirit: "love, joy, peace, patient endurance, kindness, generosity, faith, mildness and chastity." Through these spiritual fruits or blessings, the soul is totally ordered to God and is able to say with the bride of the Canticle, "I to my beloved and my beloved to me."

## Love, Joy, Peace

The first three spiritual fruits of the Holy Spirit directly deal with the presence of God in our hearts. Paul insists that love or charity is the first of the fruits because it deals with the ability to maturely appreciate the love God's presence brings us as well as our ability to fittingly express our love for God. From love proceeds divine joy, which is always grounded in charity. In fact, love and joy are always inseparable. We possess God through charity and have the assurance of being one with Christ through charity, the source and fount of our joy. Perfect love casts out all fear, removes all sadness and above all fills the soul with delight and joy. Joy is that happiness or the happy consciousness we have of the infinite goodness of God and His presence in ourlives. Paul then goes on to speak of the next fruit, peace, which is the confident assurance that nothing will separate us from our union with God and the joy His presence produces in our lives. These first three fruits of the Spirit are directed to possessing God and give us the assurance that we will constantly have the presence of God so that no trial or difficulty or temptation can interfere with this gift.

It would be hard to surpass the excellent summary of the first three fruits of the Holy Spirit given by Bishop Luís Martinez in his famous book, *The Sanctifier.* He writes, "Here then, are the three fruits of the Holy Spirit which, by ordering the soul, give it a true experience of heaven: the delight of loving, the joy of union, the tranquillity of peace. Without doubt, in order to possess these three completely it is necessary to attain the heights. But God has willed that we shall find, all along the road of the spiritual life, some measure of these precious things that satisfy the longing for happiness we have in our soul. Thanks be to Him, at every stage of the journey toward Him there are charity, joy, and peace, even though they may not be in their fullest perfection."

## Fun and Pleasure

Adrian van Kaam has written a very helpful book, *The Roots of Christian Joy,* which easily enables us to distinguish true joy from its counterfeits. The book was written because of the author's heartfelt conviction that today many people are devoid of joy. Father van Kaam tells us that in his lectures at Duquesne University he constantly stresses that frequently the humanistic and existential promises of self-actualization, fulfillment, and happiness so often stressed in modern literature are deceptive because they neglect the roots of lasting Christian joy.

Father van Kaam laments that too few people today link spiritual living with joyfulness, even though the New Testament describes joy as the central aspect of Christian life. The Bible is accurately characterized as the most joyful book ever written and the Christian life can be described as the most joyful ever known, hence the Christian must ever be a joyful person.

Modern life, the distinguished professor argues, has become too "functional" and neither emphasizes the need to devote time to joy nor reminds us of the need to strive for true joyful living. This, of course, may seem surprising, especially when so many movies and television programs stress fun and pleasure. But fun and pleasure are not the same thing as Christian joy. Father van Kaam notes the profound difference between fun and pleasure and true joy. He argues that living in the dimension of vital pleasure and gratification can give us fun but will not make us joyful in the deep and transcendent sense. It does not lead to lasting happiness. Instead we become people always hunting for more occasions of fun and pleasure. This helps us temporarily, momentarily lifting our spirits, but we soon find we are not satisfied and begin to look for more and more ways of fulfilling ourselves.

Unfortunately, the circle never closes with lasting happiness. In fact, van Kaam reminds us that modern people even find it difficult to find that gentle, loving humor that is so helpful to our perfection. Gentle humor unites and never separates. It is inspired by love and joy.

The solution to our quest for joy comes from an honest recognition of and a loving surrender to the true meaning of life that was expressed by Augustine when he wrote: "Our hearts are restless and will remain restless until they find their repose in God."

Just as the people of the New Testament were led to see and appreciate that Christ is infinite joy, so the little sister in the Carmel of Los Andes was led by God through her prayerful life to understand and to communicate to us this time-honored Christian truth that God is the infinite joy that all are craving for. She is able to see and to tell us that the love and presence of the all-loving God is the source of all Christian joy. Her mission in heaven seems to be to show us the way to the infinite joy that comes from God and is found in Christ.

This is not to assert that she is the first one who discovered this truth; clearly all the saints did. But divine joy was the dominant motif of her life, and her witness of divine joy is especially relevant today.

## The Joy of Christ

The tenth chapter of Luke's Gospel presents an event in the life of Christ that is only recorded in the third Gospel, namely, the scene of "Christ rejoicing in the Holy Spirit" because God has hidden wisdom from the wise and proud of this world and revealed it to the merest of children. The heavenly wisdom that was infused into the heart of this little Carmelite is something that cannot be learned in school since the infinite joy of God can only be learned from God's actual presence and under the guidance of the Holy Spirit, who filled the heart of Christ with joy and floods our hearts with joy. This is how Teresa learned and experienced the joy that she describes and teaches. How often in her letters from Carmel she writes, "I feel like the happiest girl in the world."

This does not mean that Sister Teresa worked out a whole theology of Christian joy or that she was ready to hold classes on this theme. No, she was too young for that; she did not have that kind of maturity. But this gifted young woman was led by God and experienced the joyful presence of God in her own life in a way hidden to the wise and clever but revealed to little ones. This is the simple but powerful, authoritative witness that shines forth in her life and writings. And we can easily learn this eternal truth from her because her life remained so simple, normal, yet filled with the wisdom that God withholds from the wise and powerful of this world and reveals to those who are open to and totally appreciative of God's love and live in His presence.

Saint Teresita of the Andes did not wait until she arrived in heaven to communicate this doctrine to others. During her life, we are told, she loved to listen to others talk of the love of God and she herself loved to talk of the love of God and of the joy He brought into her life. Her brother Luís, who was several years older than Juanita but very close to her, assures us he personally enjoyed listening to her speaking of the love of God. In a little book he wrote in honor of his favorite sister, he notes that she loved to talk of the love of God and hated to be interrupted when speaking about God and His love. It was her favorite subject, her all-embracing concern.

This is evidence that there was a pattern to her life. God was central to her. We have already seen that when she was only a postulant in Carmel she wrote a letter to her mother, asserting that when she began to write about God she could hardly put her pen down. And when her brother Luís was having difficulties with his faith, she did not argue with him but instead drew closer to him, put her arm around his shoulder and just asked very softly, "When I'm with you, don't you feel close to God?" In this simple but helpful way Juanita lovingly and effectively shared her joy with him. She can do the same for all who approach her for help.

But it is her infectious way of showing us how to take our joy and delight in God that constitutes her important spiritual mission. She knows how to awaken a hunger and thirst for God in souls. She invites all to "taste and see how good the Lord is." This is what makes her message perennially relevant and universal.

## Her Irresistible Urge to Communicate God's Joy

God makes each of His servants out of a special mold. They are incapable of keeping the love of God to themselves. All were simply driven by an irresistible urge to share their spiritual gifts and treasures with others. So, too, Teresita was able to and even has a holy compulsion to proclaim, praise and glorify God and share her overflowing joy with others. She did this when she taught catechism; when she wrote her affectionate letters; as she shared her love with her own family; and as she continues to spread the same good news of the joy of the Gospel with us today.

What is very distinctive about her is that she did this as a teenager. Because of this she is a special model to the youth of today. She did not do this to upstage others or to draw undue attention to herself; she did it because her love for God was so profound and heart-felt that it had to express itself. In the words of the Second Vatican

130

Council, she is a good role-model to our youth, whom the Church exhorts "to infuse a Christian spirit into the mentality, customs, laws and structures of our own day." The young can do this with great effectiveness if they themselves have found God in prayer and have tasted His sweetness and discovered for themselves that He is infinitely good, the source of their infinite joy.

## Prayer and Joy

Unfortunately there are still too many today who have not learned the secret of discovering enjoyment in prayer, too many who think of prayer as drudgery or boredom. The unusual joyfulness of the little Chilean Carmelite was not due to a naturally bubbly spirit, but was rooted in and nourished by her deep life of prayer. In prayer she took her delight in God, rejoiced in God and longed to have the whole world enjoy her grace-filled secret.

Perhaps we should say more about joyful prayer. Taking our delight and joy in the Lord is an excellent definition of Christian prayer or meditation. Father John Catoir, the current director of the Christopher Movement, has written a book titled *Enjoy the Lord: A Path to Contemplation*. This book can be recommended to all searching for growth in prayer.

In the Preface Father Catoir tell us the reason he wrote this book: "After counseling priests, sisters, mothers, fathers and teenagers, I came to realize how difficult it is for most people to be joyful. Life isn't easy and there are always problems to weigh us down. On the other hand, we were made for joy and there is in us a human faculty tuned to God's inner life of total joyfulness. It is called the soul."

Father Catoir says no one ever taught him that he was to enjoy God in prayer. Possibly his teachers thought this was self-evident, but it did not become evident to him for many years. Gradually he was able to solve this problem, becoming aware that God is the God of joy and wants His children to be happy. And then he knew that prayer is not just a duty, but a joy.

Needless to say, many can identify with Father Catoir's experience and can testify that they were never promised great joy in prayer. And many find their lives changed when they discover that God wants us to find joy in prayer, for God is then present to us as the God of love and joy, the God who satisfies the needs of our hearts. What a refreshing discovery this would be for many souls.

Saint Teresa of Avila in the *Interior Castle* observes that in books about prayer she found that there is a great deal of information offered to beginners about what they are to do in prayer, the rules they are to keep, the things they are to avoid. But, she shrewdly observes, such books tell us very little about what God does for us in prayer. In all her writings the wonderful saint from Avila again and again stresses the way God offers Himself and His love and joy or delight to us in prayer. From her own experience she can testify that the more she progressed, the more her own prayer became a prayer of praise to the Lord who was filling her with his graces and favors. At one point in her prayer life she became so inflamed because of her union and joy with God that she wished she could be all tongues in singing His praises and desired that all souls would join her in this endeavor.

All the saints emphasize prayer and write beautifully about its practice. But if there is one single point that Teresa of the Andes stresses it is that joy comes from prayer and that prayer can be the source of constant joy in our lives. To keep in mind this one point of her doctrine, could become the all-important starting point for which so many men and women have been craving. Another point worth remembering is that she experienced so much joy when she was before Jesus in the Blessed Sacrament.

## Her Joyful Letters

The active way she spread the joy of the Lord to others stands out in her letters. This young twentieth century Carmelite carried on a very fruitful apostolate of the pen. She took time to write to her loved ones and willingly opened the deep secrets of her heart to those she loved. Though this kind of apostolate of sharing our love of God with others is open to all, Teresa of the Andes excelled in demonstrating how this can be done, and how it can be done with special effectiveness.

Let us examine some of her correspondence aided by the penetrating observations of Father Robert Moretti. After careful study of her letters, the Roman Carmelite describes the beauty and spirituality of her correspondence in these words:

*Both her Diary and Letters give us a candid human and spiritual picture of the Chilean Carmelite.*

*One day after entering the Monastery she wrote to her little brother: 'My soul is always united to yours; the two form one. Now I am already immersed in God. His love is the life of my soul. I want to raise you up to Him. I want to share with you, my brother, a little of the fire that*

133

*burns in me. I want to warm you in this infinite fire so that you may have life. I feel wrapped in a divine atmosphere of peace, of love, of light, and of infinite joy.'*

*And to her own mother she wrote, 'I assure you, Madrecita, that I feel an insatiable hunger and thirst that souls may seek God, but that they seek Him not out of fear but out of a limitless confidence in divine love.' And thus Juanita was able to say to her mother: 'Madrecita, I'd like to be able to let you read my soul so that you might see all that the Lord has written there these days. He makes me understand, He makes me see things unknown and wonders never before seen. You can't imagine, Madrecita, the change which I already feel in myself. He has transformed me. He's opening the veils that have hidden Him. Each time He seems more beautiful to me, more tender, and more crazy.... I don't want to continue writing, because when I begin to speak of the Lord, I can't restrain my pen'.*

*That is how the young Carmelite of Los Andes writes,* continues Father Moretti. *She has pages vibrating with humanity, shining, fiery pages that set us ablaze with an enthusiasm that leads to the heights, pages that fill us with joy. Here is how she writes to a friend: 'I'm happy, in fact, the happiest creature in the world. I'm beginning a heavenly life of adoration, of praise and continuing love: God is infinite joy'.*

Father Moretti concludes that this is "the spiritual experience of this young Carmelite. We can also say that this is her spirituality. We can further say that it is a message that is particularly relevant to our times. We can quickly read her message, a message that seems particularly helpful to those of us who are advancing in years."

## Wonderworker?

There are reports from the Shrine in Los Andes that many physical miracles have been wrought through the intercession of Saint Teresa of the Andes. There are even more reports of greater spiritual graces obtained by those who have visited her tomb to express their affection and confidence. When such miracles are true and not imaginary, we can only say "Blessed be God in His mighty works."

The wider subject of inordinately seeking miracles, of course, raises very delicate spiritual problems, and the rules for discerning the workings of God becomes very important. True, Jesus did work miracles to help the afflicted and to manifest the power and goodness of His Father. He performed miracles, but not to seek the acclaim of men.

First of all, we notice in the Gospel that Jesus was hesitant and even discouraged the spread of his reputation as a wonderworker. He complained that many who eagerly followed Him did so only because He gave them bread to eat, not because they had faith in Him. Jesus' only desire was to be recognized as God's Son, the One who brings life to the world.

The same law applies to the saints. Teresita of the Andes does not seek to be admired primarily as a wonderworker or a miracle worker, but wants only to be acknowledged as Teresa who was transformed into Jesus here on earth and who was "mad with love for Him." Today in heaven she wants to share with all her life of love and joyful union with God. The greatness of any person stems from their degree of union with God in love. This counts for more than everything, even the working of miracles. The saints in heaven do not perform miracles on their own, for them God "is all in all"and they seek only His glory. They plead with God on behalf of those who seek their help, but it is God alone who can work the miracle.

True miracles are the voice of God and show the love of God. Father Purroy, the vice-postulator of her Cause, recently spoke on this important aspect of popular piety. He cautioned against promoting her as a miracle worker and strongly emphasized that there is too much stress by some on her miracles. What should rather be stressed and how she should be thought of is as a "a gift of God," he said. She is like an angel or messenger of God, reminding us of how to draw closer to God in our daily prayer and how to dialogue with God intimately in prayer. Blessing God for His saints, for these perfect messengers of love and holiness, is the proper way to honor God in His saints. Let us not fear that our prayers through their intercession will not be heard, provided this be the will of God. In the First Letter of John we read: "Our prayer will be heard, if this be the will of God."

In her lifetime Teresa of the Andes did not seek extraordinary things or miracles; her constant and sincere prayer was to do God's will in all things. To understand her secret of sanctity it suffices to recall the words she wrote when she was 17 years old: "My Jesus, I love you. I am totally yours. I give myself completely to Your divine Will. It doesn't matter whether you give me the abandonment of Calvary or the delight of Nazareth. I only want to live to please You."

The simple inscription on her tombstone reads "El amor es mas fuerte" (Love is stronger than all things). These words were chosen as a fitting epitaph because they were used by Pope John Paul II in his beatification homily; they beautifully sum up what she has to say to us. She wants us to come to her with the awareness that the love of God is stronger than all things, and with the assurance that her own life on earth was dominated by her love for God and this brought her boundless love, joy and peace.

This is her message, this is her plea: Seek the will of God above all things because God is love.

## The Joyful Living of Her Vocation

In the last analysis, the way one lives one's vocation determines the fullness of one's life. It is more important than working miracles. Sister Teresa of the Andes was convinced that our vocation is God's greatest gift to us. There are many ways in which one can serve God, in the single or married life, in the religious life or in the priesthood. The all-important thing is that our life be lived with the fullness of love and dedication and that it be crowned with the unmistakable sign of divine love and joy flowing from our union with God.

In all vocations there are features that are by their nature joyful and easy; there are aspects that afford the greatest comfort and consolation. At such times it seems easy to find God and serving Him is a delight. But experience teaches us that life is not all pleasure and things are not always easy. There are to be sure hardships in every life and the cross will always be part of the Christian experience.

But even in the most difficult aspects of our lives it is always possible to have joy, though it may not be possible to always experience happiness. We have happiness when all sorrow is removed, when all pain is taken away; but joy can still be present even when there is suffering and pain, because joy is occasioned by the presence of the beloved. When we are aware of the divine presence in our lives we can always be confident and experience the Holy Spirit's joy.

The *Diary* and *Letters* of Teresa of the Andes offer abundant proof that she knew how to struggle and be faithful to Christ, her Spouse, and knew how to welcome the sufferings and pains that enabled her to be conformed to the Christ who suffered in the Garden, walked the way to Calvary and there became a perfect sacrifice for the glory of the Father and the salvation of all mankind.

Sister Teresa was extremely faithful to her vocation when she lived at home and when she was in boarding school, and was just as generous and faithful to her Carmelite calling. Her example is a fresh and original expression of the teaching of Christ to His companions on the road to Emmaeus, when He taught them the meaning of suffering, telling them that "it was fitting for Him to undergo His sufferings so He could enter into His glory."

Like the disciples on the way to Emmaeus, Teresa stayed close to Christ in her vocation, allowed herself to listen to and be taught by Christ in prayer each day and as a result had the same experience of those disciples of long ago who exclaimed, "Was not our heart burning within us as He spoke and explained the Scriptures?" That is the secret of it all: to remain with and listen to Jesus. Then our hearts will burn with joy and no trial or difficulty in our vocation will ever overpower us.

The joy of living with Christ for the good of others is the most mature stage of any vocation. The young Chilean saint longed to enter Carmel because she was convinced that there she would be able fully to spend herself for the good of the Church and for the good of priests. She wanted others to know more and more about the greatest discovery she had made in her life, that in God alone can true and lasting happiness be found and that He is the source of all joy. She was willing to sacrifice herself totally for priests so they could overcome the obstacles to divine joy that are part of human history and could teach people what they long for most deeply, the joy of intimacy with God in Christ.

## The Happiness of Being a Discalced Carmelite

As we come to the conclusion of this introduction to the life and vocation of Blessed Teresa of Jesus, I think it fitting to give the last word to the Superior General of the Discalced Carmelite Order. Describing how Teresita found the fullness of happiness in her Carmelite vocation, Father Felipe Sainz de Baranda, O.C.D., wrote to his Order: "The testimony and message of Teresa of the Andes is not only valid for young postulants and novices. She offers a lesson and experience to all Discalced Carmelite nuns precisely because of the testimony given to a clear vocational identity, and the message of joy and happiness in a vocation taken on in all truth and lived with utter consistency."

"Happiness in anyone's life is the fruit of fidelity, fidelity to something, to someone, with all the renunciation that such happiness imposes everyday in certain moments and circumstances. This is also the law of happiness for the Discalced Carmelite nun: the happiness of a contemplative and Teresian vocation shouldered without that compromise which diminishes its radicality, and without projects that evade the demands of community, prayer, abnegation, and solitude.

"Happiness, as is joy, will always be the fruit of the Spirit (cfr. Gal. 5:22). Vocational happiness grows day by day as love for one's vocation with all its demands increases. But joy has an intimate relation with that fraternity to which every consecrated soul is called, fraternity which is spiritual communion and friendship with the whole community. Teresa de los Andes lived in the happiness of a community which was simple, fraternal, joyful.

"To live always joyfully. God is infinite joy" (May 14, 1919). "When one loves, everything is joy. The cross doesn't weigh down. Martyrdom isn't felt. One lives more in heaven than on earth. The life of Carmel is to love. This is our vocation" (May, 1919).

# Part Four:
# Teresa, Model For Youth

## Heavenly Mission

"From heaven the true mission of Saint Teresa of the Andes is beginning,"declared Pope John Paul II as he canonized the Chilean saint. The Holy Father expressed his sincere hope that the young may discover in her the joy of living the Christian faith to its ultimate consequences. He urged young men and women of our time "to take her as your model!"

Emulating Saint Teresa is an inspiring thought. But what does this mean in practical terms? What does it involve? I wish to address these questions and offer some reflections on how young people may discover Saint Teresa of the Andes as an accessible model of holiness.

Educators have long known the value of setting before their students models whose lives are especially attractive, helpful, and worthy of imitation. Paul exhorts his followers to imitate Christ; to "put on the Lord Jesus Christ," because He alone is the perfect reflection of the Father's glory. But the holy ones or saints who have been taken into the life of Christ and have been filled with His goodness are a true reflection of God's perfections, hence can and should be imitated. Saints are worthy of our imitation because they faithfully walked in the footsteps of the Master, molded themselves in His image and above everything else sought God's glory and the good of others. The benefit of imitating the saints, the Second Vatican Council assures us, is that in this way "the People of God will grow into an abundant harvest of good, as is brilliantly proved by the lives of so many saints in Church history."

Not without good reason, successful preachers and teachers are constantly pointing out personalities capable of inspiring heroic deeds, dissuading people from wrong deeds or encouraging people to overcome selfish interests. While the primary aim of teaching must be the transmission of truth, it is also true that religious truths need to be clarified and demonstrated with flesh and blood examples of men and women who successfully imitated Christ. Noted psychiatrist, Karl Stern, told priests and religious that they are making a serious mistake if they overlook the lives of the saints who lived such successful spiritual lives. The Church keeps our gaze on the saints because they practiced heroic virtue and are excellent models and helpers for all who wish to walk in the footsteps of the Master.

## Admired By Youth

Our new saint has captured the minds and hearts of the youth in Chile. They are thrilled to have one of their own as a canonized saint. It is reported that young boys and girls were at first especially impressed by St Teresa's attractive and appealing human qualities. They felt drawn to her, proud of her. At the same time they were particularly aware of something special and sacred about this teenage young woman. They were especially pleased to know how much she loved her country, its people, its beauties and natural assets. It made them feel close to her when they were told she swam in the same ocean they swim in, looked at and loved the same skies and stars that cover them, and rode horses on their hills and mountains. They were especially delighted to learn that she found God amid the beauties of nature and was able to confess, "All that I see brings me to God. The sea with its immensity makes me think of God in His infinite grandeur. It is then that I feel a thirst for the infinite."

## The Pedagogy Of Christ

From a pedagogical standpoint, the first thing we must do when considering a saint to be as a model is to look at the individual's physical appearance, external activities and special accomplishments. After that, we can go deeper still and examine their inner spiritual qualities. The Gospel assures us that this was the method Jesus used. Viewing Christ as a teacher in the Gospels, it is both interesting and instructive to see how Jesus first looked at and then **carefully observed** each one who approached to become His disciples and followers. What eyes Jesus had! His was not a casual glance. He read the heart of each one and ascertained the future accomplishments of these men. Looking at each one individually, Jesus noted that all were not alike nor did they have the same life experiences.

Peter and his brother Andrew, for example, were rough fishermen, but their love and enthusiasm could be read in their eyes as soon as the Master met them. Jesus easily envisioned them as successful fishers of men.

Nicodemus presented a somewhat different case. When the Master saw Nicodemus begging permission to enter His dwelling place that important night, He welcomed an elderly man, a timid and very frightened man. Nicodemus was, after all, a doctor of the law. It showed in his speech and manners, in everything he did. He was a cautious man, too, and came to Jesus only after the sun had gone down. He feared others might see him associating with Jesus. Jesus at once understood this complicated man, but saw that he had to be given more time. But, by the end of the Gospel we are, in fact, told that Nicodemus had overcome his fears and openly and officially acknowledged his belief in Jesus.

Jesus' first meeting with Martha and Mary was special. Again, as was His method, Jesus carefully observed them outwardly and learned of their background. Jesus at once became aware of the inner goodness of these two women, but He also noticed how different each woman was. Martha's great love expressed itself in being carefully attentive to details when serving and entertaining guests who came to her home. Mary, on the other hand, preferred to listen to and converse with the guests. Jesus accepted their differences and welcomed them appropriately.

All who were to become future helpers and followers were joyfully welcomed by Jesus. He rejoiced that they wanted to become His disciples and could readily envision them as models for others as well. Observation was the first law Jesus practiced. Then He offered a warm welcome and helped them through His love and instructions.

### Application to Our Saint

How does all this, it may be asked, apply to St. Teresa of the Andes? Let's go to her *Diary* for our answer. The saint from Chile tells of her first deep encounter with Jesus. "It was shortly after the earthquake in 1906 that Jesus began to take my heart to be His own,." she reports. In other words, this was the time when Jesus became the Heart of her heart and the true living center of her life. From that time on Jesus claimed her to be His own and never left her go, and, on her part, she became aware of belonging entirely to Him.

When Jesus looked lovingly at this six year old girl and gave Himself completely to her, did He see anything special? What did He see in her? Could He have foresee greatness in her the way He foresaw greatness in Martha and Mary? And, if so, what kind of greatness?

Teresa's life demonstrates that Jesus could see her growing to become the perfect bride of His heart; He could see her as another St. Teresa of Avila: an outstanding lover of prayer, the Eucharist and His Cross. Jesus could in addition foresee the day when she would lead other young women to share her love of prayer and intimacy with God and who would inspire many to consecrate themselves to the religious life for the glory of God and the good of His Church. He saw farther and was pleased to take cognizance of her ardent longing to save souls together with Him, and to live her cloistered prayerful life for the sanctification of His priests. In a word, the marvelous eyes of Jesus saw that she would be a precious vessel of goodness for the Church and for the world.

## Juanita's Appearance

Let us further apply the Master's helpful method of observation to our young Chilean saint. While all saints are models of Christ, each one brings a different background and a different history. In Juanita's case, all her pictures and the testimony of her friends describe her as a beautiful girl, with fair skin, light hair, blue eyes and a bearing that was graceful and pleasing. Her fine manners were evidence of the education she received at home and in school. She had appendicitis and diphtheria when she was young, we are told. For many years she suffered from anemia, but this condition did not prevent her from growing to become five feet ten inches tall. Her first biographer aptly described her as "tall among the tall."

Juanita truly loved sports. Her athletic accomplishments are legendary. This gives us a lot of insight into this young woman's courage, dedication, discipline and determination. Juanita was long remembered for having won many swimming meets. They say she loved to play tennis and was reported to have played the game furiously. But, above all else, she excelled in and loved horseback riding. "I loved the horse more than anything," is the way she describes this aspect of her personality. But, today's reader should not overlook the fact that she enjoyed and practiced these sports virtuously. Her charming feminine graces were never compromised or diminished by these activities.

Juanita Fernández was described by her contemporaries as a happy girl who enjoyed life like other girls her own age. She knew how to laugh, love, play and serve. Her merit was not in having done extraordinary things but in having done everything extraordinarily well. Abandonment to God, giving of herself to others and acquiring dominion over herself were the keys she used to fulfill the supreme commandment of love of God, self and others.

Additions to this portrait of the future saint can easily be added. While there was general agreement that she was just like all the other girls, there was a stronger consensus about her being different, outstanding. Her mother wrote to her spiritual director, "I don't understand why God wanted to make me mother of such an angelic creature, because from the time she was little she was more angelic than human." Mother Angelica Teresa, her Superior at the Monastery of Los Andes, also noted there was something special about this girl and that she never tired of attentively observing this in her, but without making it obvious. We are told that others were aware of this, too.

### Newspaper Interview of Juanita's Cousin

From an exceptionally important interview given by Anita Rucker and reported in the Sunday Arts And Letters section of *El Mercurio* on the day of the canonization, we are able to garner many precious details of the saint's life. Anita Rucker, lived with Juanita at the Sacred Heart Schools for eleven years, and thus is able to offer us priceless reminiscences of her cousin.

Anita tells us she often saw Juanita in the chapel, both at the Alameda and the Maestranza schools. It was in the chapel that her cousin stood out from the other girls. Juanita was oblivious of everything else but the

146

God with whom she was in communion. However, in all the other daily events of life, Juanita was perfectly normal. Anita describes her cousin as a girl who physically was beautiful, vivacious and friendly towards everyone. She was especially sympathetic towards the young. Anita stressed that Juanita truly loved little children, liked to work with them and enjoyed teaching them, as she did when she taught catechism during her free time or when she was on vacation.

## Patroness of Children

Anita's was careful to describe the feelings of the children towards Juanita. Children liked Juanita and enjoyed being with her. Juanita, she tells us, could be very playful at recreation time. She also liked to tease and play jokes, but Anita added, the children liked to tease her and play little jokes on her even more. Children perceived Juanita as good tempered, kind, generous and helpful.

It is now official. Soon after the canonization, Chile very fittingly and solemnly proclaimed Saint Teresa of Jesus of the Andes to be the patroness of the young. Archbishop Carlos Oviedo of Santiago declared Teresa "to be the patroness of all children, especially those who are homeless, or lack families and have not received an adequate education." He declared with great feeling: "I am thinking of minors, those in orientation centers, or in prisons for minors. **Teresa, to you I confide all these children.**"

In declaring St. Teresa patroness of numerous homeless children, the Chilean bishops took this solemn step because of the saint's devotion to children, and especailly to a homeless orphan boy whose name was Juanito. In the twenty sixth entry of her *Diary* Juanita

147

speaks of how she was moved to compassion to care for this young child with her own hands. Often she saved her desserts for him. She permanently cared for him, using money from her own allowance. To raise funds to help him, on one occasion Juanita even pawned her watch. When she entered Carmel she asked her family to care for him and, from the convent, showed her concern for him in various letters. "It is so rich to give to the poor," is the way whe sums up this entry in her *Diary*.

Regarding her class work, Anita Rucker describes her cousin as being careful and very conscientious about her studies. She admitted Juanita did not distinguish herself in sewing and embroidery classes. She recalls that Juanita progressed in her class assignments, and took first prizes only in the last years of high school.

After the canonization was over, Anita summed up her impressions of the glorious event:

*When I saw that great banner hanging from the facade of Saint Peter's, with Teresa's beautiful picture on it, I could only ask myself, is it true that I'm really seeing a cousin of mine and a companion at the Sacred Heart boarding school on Maestranza Street being raised to the altar? And then she slowly added: We didn't know the treasure we had so close to us, one we sometimes failed to understand. Detachment and devotion to God's will were her aim. All her joys and sorrows were transformed by this single ideal.*

## Friendships

Blessed with a rich, warm personality and many gifts, Juanita developed all the sides of her personality and became a blessing to her many friends. Several girls testified that she made a stupendous friend and that she brought them closer to God. In examining her as a role model for the young, her friendships are especially noteworthy, because friendships formed in youth can make or mar one's life.

True friendship can exist only between virtuous people. Among all the gifts God gives human beings, it is universally admitted that friendship ranks as one of life's greatest blessings. We have no less an authority than Saint Thomas Aquinas to confirm that friendship is a truly great good, but is only successful if each partner is rich in virtues. When friendship is rooted in goodness and grounded in Christ it is a blessing beyond compare. Let us listen to St. Teresa as she extols the blessings of the friendship that Christ offers to all:

*I feel a need to bring Him to you. I want Jesus to be your intimate friend, to whom you may entrust your heart, tired and filled with sorrow. Who, Daddy darling, can fathom the intensity, the torrent of worries pouring over you as can Our Lord who delves into our deepest hearts and with delicate touch can touch those painful wounds whose depths even we ourselves don't understand. Oh, Daddy, how your life would change if you went to Him often as a Friend. Can you be thinking Jesus won't want to welcome you as a friend? If that's what you thought, it would be a sign that you don't know Him. Jesus is all tenderness, all love for his sinful creatures. He lives in the tabernacle with His Heart open to receive us, waiting for our arrival that He may console us. (Letter 150).*

### Truth And Freedom

The lives of saints are shining examples of human goodness because their lives were governed by truth and lived in full human freedom. This is one of the basic reasons why the saints can be such helpful models, especially to the young. Above everything else, the human heart yearns to know the truth and craves to live it fully and freely. That's why it is so valuable to associate with people and have friends who respect our freedom and not violate our conscience.

Today, *truth* and *freedom* are the words of the hour. Many meanings can be assigned to these words; but, unfortunately, many of these interpretations are far removed from Jesus' teachings. The full radiant meaning of these life giving words is found in John's Gospel where we read the words: "If you continue in my word, you are truly my disciples, and you will know the truth, and the truth will make you free."

The text tells us that abiding in or remaining in the words of Jesus is what makes someone His true disciple. These alone are the ones who truly believe, who move completely into the sphere of  influence and action of Christ's words. They take the words of the Master to heart and are led to that deep and authentic union with Christ which brings the soul divine life. It is such as these who can know the truth and enjoy true freedom.

Jesus declares that these men and women will know the truth and that the truth will make them free. But what kind of truth does Jesus mean? What kind of freedom is He speaking about? Regarding the former question, Jesus means divine truth. He does not mean mere academic knowledge or love of truth; instead, He means the true believer will fully come to know the Father and His love; he or she will also inwardly know the boundless love of God's Son and remain faithful to His words. Another way of saying this is to say that true disciples of Jesus go from death to life, from darkness to light. In the words of Paul, "They are alive to God in Christ Jesus."

Concerning the question of freedom, Jesus teaches that if we personally internalize His words and carry them out, we will no longer be in bondage. We will be freed from living as strangers, and at a distance from God. We will possess the glorious liberty of the children of God, which means the freedom to live like true children of God. In this way, here on earth we will experience the joy of being the dearly beloved children of God.

St. Teresa of the Andes received the words of Christ with a loving heart. She made Christ the center of her life. She disciplined herself to be perfectly submissive to the Lord's teachings, and was eager to resist any indifference or influences contrary to the Gospel. She is therefore a luminous model of selfless love and devotion for the young, who need to let Christ bring His truth and goodness to their lives. Her example shows us how to make sure our freedom is always used in the right way and to be followers of Christ in sincerity and in truth.

That Teresa of the Andes perfectly understood and lived the words of Jesus perfectly is repeatedly brought out in her famous declaration: "He is my Captain, I am His soldier. Let Him give the orders and I will follow Him."

The opposite of the freedom God wills for His children is a freedom which implies license and absence of restraint. This is a spurious and harmful use of freedom. It can only lead to destruction.

Juanita cherished the glorious liberty enjoyed by the children of God, and this is what enabled her to give her heart fully to God and to others. She also possessed that very important inner freedom of being sincere with her friends. She always felt free to speak her true inner convictions. She explains this clearly when she wrote to one of her friends:

*Never let yourselves be guided by the other girls'
opinions but rather have your own convictions, as a
child of Mary should. And don't worry about what
others may think when you express your own
convictions. For example, if you go to a theater and
don't like the picture because you don't think it's
wholesome, even though the other girls may enjoy it,
tell them that you don't like it. And be that way in
everything.*

In his canonization Homily Pope John Paul II
eulogized Teresa "as one who welcomed Christ, the Light
of the world and who opened her eyes to the inner vision
of truth that Christ brings." The Pontiff also declared
that it was with great joy that he could present the
beloved young Carmelite to the Church:

*God made shine forth in her in an admirable way
the light of His Son Jesus Christ so that she could be
a beacon and guide to a world which seems to be
blind to the splendor of the divine. In a secularized
society which turns its back on God, this Chilean
Carmelite whom to my great joy I present as a model
of the perennial youth of the Gospel, gives the
shining witness of a life which proclaims to the men
and women of our day that it is in living, adoring
and serving God that the human person finds
greatness and joy, freedom and fulfillment. The life
of Blessed Teresa cries out continually from within
her cloister, "God alone suffices."*

The Holy Father, who takes such a sincere interest in
and who and has demonstrated such paternal love for
today's youth, continued with these words:

*She shouts it out particularly to the young people
who hunger for the truth and seek a light which will
give direction to their lives. Today young people*

*who are being allured by the continuous messages and stimuli of an erotic culture, a society which mistakes the hedonistic exploitation of another for genuine love, which is self-giving, this young virgin of the Andes today proclaims the beauty and happiness that comes from a pure heart.*

## Family

On the day of St. Teresa's canonization, the Vatican distributed a handsome little booklet for use at the Mass and as a reminder of the occasion. It contains a short biography of the new saint which states that "during adolescence she reached perfect psychic and spiritual equilibrium." This was obviously attributable to her family and wholesome school background. A good and well adjusted family provides its children with proper and healthy surroundings for the development of a well-integrated and healthy personality. Such families afford a healthy environment for acquiring Christian and family virtues.

Family virtues are important for successful relationships with others. These same family virtues are especially important for those aspiring to the priestly or religious vocation in the Church. Popes have taught that while marriage is the common vocation of mankind, it does not follow that to be happy and attain perfection everyone must marry. What is required, however, these same Popes repeat, is that no adult can attain true maturity without also acquiring the capacity to become a good spouse or parent. Should that capacity be lacking, then those men must not to be admitted to the altar or those women should not to be allowed to enter convents. A careful examination of the life of St. Teresa of the Andes reveals that she was exceptional in her practice habitual of family virtues and possessed the maturity and skill to help others. She was neither egotistical or inordinately self-centered. She was fully capable of entering into mature social relationships with others.

In the light of what we have just said, is it any wonder that after her beatification people who visit the National Shrine of Our Lady of Mount Carmel in Chile where her body is buried, began bringing their deeply felt petitions to St. Teresa of the Andes and asked her to intercede with God for their many intentions? They beseech her to intercede for a variety of intentions, but what do the petition boxes reveal to be the number one intention of numerous pilgrims? Precisely this: that God grant them peace, love and harmony in their homes. Love in the home and the living out of family values is without question the **greatest need of our times**. And isn't it surprising how many people are praying to this young saint to be granted love in their homes? But, it is quite evident they do so only because of their awareness that every member of the Fernández family unanimously testified that Teresita was "the treasure of the household, the sunshine of the family."

In this world, every life is filled with both joy as well as sorrow. Teresa's life also had these characteristics. So strongly did she love her family and so much love did she receive from them that St. Teresa repeatedly said in her letters that the greatest sacrifice she had to make in order to enter Carmel was to leave her family. Though the Gospels might be silent on the point, we instinctively believe that Jesus was not without regret at leaving the home of Nazareth where he had received so much love from Mary and Joseph, the ones who were nearest and dearest to Him.

In a beautiful collection of 164 letters that St. Teresa

154

wrote before and after entering Carmel, 53 warm and affectionate letters to her immediate family have come down to us. Fittingly, this young girl who was so loving and affectionate wrote her last letters to her parents, the ones "I love most in this world." Her correspondence reveals a great deal about her soul and tells us much about her spirituality. While these letters show how God blessed her with deep love for her Christian family, they also make us aware of how much she owed to her family. Good homes are a great blessing because they offer a favorable climate where that personal relationship with God which is the source of authentic individual and community love can take root and develop. A good home is a garden where many important virtues are born and develop.

## Vocation

In high school our newly canonized saint's most important decision concerned her vocation. She kept asking herself how she was to serve God? What vocation is He calling me to? In the Gospel, a young man came to the Lord asking what he should do to be perfect? Christ replied, "If you will be perfect," "go, sell what you have...and come, follow Me." Well, after having consecrated herself to Jesus with a vow of perfect virginity at the age of fifteen, the Lord drew close to her told her He wanted her to become His bride. He wished her to sacrifice everything and live a cloistered contemplative life in Carmel. After that time, whenever she discussed her vocation with her spiritual director, she always asked him, "which convent should I enter so that I can become holy as soon as possible? No wonder she summed up her conviction succinctly when she wrote, "The vocation is the greatest gift God gives to a person." Once she made up her mind, nothing could ever shake her in this conviction. Her desire to enter Carmel was validated interiorly by the love, joy and peace that filled her soul.

In a letter to her sister, Rebecca, she explains how she arrived at certitude regarding her religious calling. "You hear a voice and a light shows you the path of your life," is the way she describes her own experience of the divine invitation that confirmed her in her own conviction. But, prudently, she did not act on the Lord's invitation until she received the approval of her spiritual director.

## Discipline

When reading the *Diary*, one is struck by the number of spiritual retreats she made. This tells us that even when living in the world, she was living a very disciplined life. The retreats she made were often preached by Jesuits, who may have come from nearby Saint Ignatius Church. And when these priests preached the *Spiritual Exercises of Saint Ignatius* to the students, it was not done to entertain but to make the girls take the life of Christ as well as the great truths of their faith to heart. The exercises were made especially effective because, at the end of the conferences, each student was invited to make spiritual resolutions on the central truths of the faith and to make a promise to keep them.

This is one of the very important ways in which St. Teresa of the Andes learned discipline in her spiritual life. It is also an important way in which she learned to keep Christ as the central focus of her life and all her activities. In her *Diary* she diligently recorded the resolutions drawn from the retreats, and she then seriously and systematically examined her conscience on how sincerely she was carrying out her resolves. Holiness did not come to her automatically or with the wave of a wand. Instead, she had to discipline herself and exert herself to acquire the virtues or habitual dispositions of mind and heart that would fit her for life of union with God. Her diligence is apparent in her *Diary*, which, at times resembles a work-book where we can observe her as she studiously tries to climb the mountain of perfection.

## Spiritual Direction

Before discerning whether she was called to the religious life, she spent long hours in prayer. The *Diary* reveals a young girl who took her vocation seriously and dedicated much time and effort to discerning if her vocation had a divine origin. She was utterly sincere and honest with herself. This means she was living a very fervent prayer life and was trying to put into practice the virtues needed for a cloistered vocation; and, as a result, she was clear in her own mind about her privileged vocation to follow the praying Christ of the Gospel in an exclusively contemplative vocation.

She always sought spiritual direction and guidance; in fact, it has been mentioned that St. Teresa had a spiritual director from the time she was very young. Being humble and sincere enough to seek spiritual direction is the description of a very prudent spiritual person; it tells of one who wants to live her life fully and completely. Both knowing how to get wholesome guidance and knowing how to cooperate with wise directors or counselor is a sure sign of great maturity.

## Generosity and Fortitude

Everything worked out so very well in discerning her vocation because Juanita was clearly determined to give herself totally to God. She also endeavored to do everything God had requested. Saint Francis de Sales said that he always felt confident when he had a very spirited person to direct. Such people are prepared to make decisions when their goals are clear, are willing to make any sacrifice, and once they put their hand to the plow they never look back.

And, in this matter, St. Teresa is such a splendid model for the young. She was courageous and generous with her God. So determined about and enamored of her vocation was she that she could write to her cousin: "If I had to walk through fire to consecrate myself to Him, I would not waver in doing it; for every sacrifice fades from sight before the joy of possessing God alone."

## Good Influence On Other Girls

Saint Teresa of Avila, the great patron of Saint Teresa of the Andes, has much to say about determination. *In The Way of Perfection* she assures her sisters that determined souls always make progress because they are decisive. The Saint of Avila says that determined souls are like captains. They will never go to heaven alone. They will always lead a multitude of souls with them. History assures us that our young Chilean lover of Christ, whose sole desire in life was to become the Spouse of Jesus was such a leader. In her lifetime she actually influenced ten other girls to become religious. She also inspired her own mother to become a Third Order Discalced Carmelite, whose members are an integral part of the Order and live its full spirituality.

158

Interestingly enough, in the interview given by Anita Rucker, who is a Religious of the Sacred Heart and now 93 years of age, Anita was asked whether she herself was influenced by her cousin to become a religious. To this interesting question, she gave an interesting answer. She simply said:

> *Juanita became a religious before I did. The reason is because in our family there were only two girls, and so my father absolutely forbade either of us to enter religious life. Juanita died some time later and her death had a great impact on many people, including my own father. As a result, shortly after Sister Teresa's death my father allowed me to become a Religious of the Sacred Heart. In this way, Anita Rucker said, my cousin helped my vocation.*

**The Diary**

Thanks to the direction Madre Ríos was giving Juanita, the young girl was encouraged to start keeping a diary to write down the graces and favors God was granting her. A second purpose was that she might learn more about herself so that she could serve God better. A careful reading of her *Diary* reveals that she was fully aware of how much she was loved and favored by God. This filled her with joy but also increased her humility as she pondered how undeserving she was of God's love. Knowing how much you are loved and how much you have been favored by God is, without question, one of the most important lessons we can learn in life. It is the foundation stone of unlimited spiritual progress.

In addition, Juanita possessed exceptional self-knowledge, which in turn, facilitated her maturity and spiritual growth. She had deep knowledge and understanding of self. Both are important qualities for human and spiritual growth.  In the *Soliloquies*, Saint Augustine prays, "Lord, give me the grace to know myself so that I might know You." They both go together, one leading to the other.  True knowledge of God always leads to knowledge of self; whereas, all true knowledge of self leads us to a better understanding of our relationship with and our total dependence on God.  I am convinced that if Teresita had not learned to know herself as well as she did through keeping a spiritual diary, she would never have been able to write such effective and insightful letters.

### What Governed St. Teresa of the Andes' Life?

Questions that concern the guiding principle of Juanita's life can be answered with one word: *Jesus*, her Spouse.  By examining her spiritual life when she was a high school student,  we can assess the controlling features of her life.  All her determination, feelings and emotions were increasingly governed by her love for Christ.  He alone became her true and vital center. Because there are many people today who have no center in their lives, how blessed this young Latin American was to have found and experienced Christ as the living center of her life and existence.  In Christ, she found herself to be at the heart of her destiny and her mystery.

The important secret of St. Teresa's young life is that it was through constant prayer that she grew in intimacy with Jesus.  Hence she became bonded to Him in intimate friendship and was transformed by Him from one degree of love and intimacy to another, from one degree of love to another on the ladder of love.  Jesus gradually brought this young Chilean girl to live a life fully worthy of the Gospel and totally pleasing to God.

160

According to her own writings, she was actively guided and directed by Jesus. At times He told her how much He loved her. When she was discouraged by her weakness, He gave her confidence in His love. It is from Him that she drew the right criteria for direction and discernment in every situation. Sometimes Jesus encouraged her to do more for His honor and glory. Then there were times when He scolded her for her slightest faults, but He did so only to encourage her to return His love more fully. He inspired her to make a vow to strive to be most perfect. Above all, in prayer Jesus was her Teacher and Companion, the One who enlightened her concerning His own divine attributes and perfections. She experienced Him in prayer both as her dearest Friend and as her true Spouse.

Gradually, Christ became her all, or as she put it, "my adored Everything." Jesus taught her that He wanted her entire life and love. She followed His guidance and strove to bring her heart into conformity with the divine wishes. She summed up her blessings in a letter to Rebecca when she wrote: "Oh, if you but knew how I love Him! He is my God, my Father, Mother, Brother, Spouse, my Jesus!"

It can be stated unhesitatingly that her religious life was chosen and lived as an espousal with Jesus Christ. This is the specific form her relationship with Christ took. This bridal relationship with Christ dominated her spiritual life.

## Divine Attributes

God's divine attributes played a most important role in the prayer life and spirituality of Carmel's youngest Saint. In her *Diary And Letters* Teresa tells us that Jesus explained His divine attributes to her. "He explained them to me," she reports, "in a practical way one by one." What are divine attributes and what is their importance? Divine attributes denote those perfections which God possesses and which distinguish Him from all His creatures. They are often mentioned in the Bible. By means of this knowledge and the love that flowed from it, Jesus immersed her in His perfections and led her to an ever deeper appreciation and transforming love of Himself.

Because these divine attributes played such an important part in her prayer life, it is important to emphasize that when Juanita speaks of God's attributes, she is not resorting to lofty literary adjectives. She frequently and advisedly invoked God's divine attributes or perfections, such as, His beauty or goodness, truth or compassion, wisdom or power. She did this because she felt their richness deeply within her soul and because through them God became much more personal to her. Saint John of the Cross in *The Living Flame of Love*, when speaking of souls who are experiencing high perfection and transforming union with God, observed that "This is love's trait: to examine all the goods of the Beloved." Sister Teresa of Jesus, being a contemplative, loved to consider the ways in which her Beloved was special and different and absolutely superior to and infinitely above all others. But she states that all His perfections flow from His goodness and awaken our love. Let's take just one example from a letter she wrote on September 30, 1919:

*In the measure in which the God man is known we go on loving Him with madness. I would like you to know this so that you may truly fall in love with Him. How can we not love that Jesus with all our soul? He who is uncreated Beauty; He is eternal Wisdom; He is Goodness, Life, and Love.*

Saints are led to follow Christ and are centered on Him in specific and special ways. The framework of our Carmelite's love for Christ her Spouse is found in her devotion to the Eucharist and to the Sacred Heart of Jesus. Devotion to the Sacred Heart led her to devotion to the Lord's Sacred Passion and death, where the love of Christ is most powerfully and forcefully experienced. In a letter to her mother, to whom the young religious was able to express herself so completely, she wrote:

*Believe me, it is Jesus' Passion that does the most for my soul, increases love in me. I see how much my Redeemer suffered, as well as His love of sacrifice and self-forgetfulness. It helps me to be less proud. It excites in me a trust in that Divine Savior who suffered so much out of love for me. Trust is what most pleases Jesus.*

While still living in the world and later in Carmel, this young woman's intense love for Christ and her union with Him made her fully aware that sanctity does not consist in sensible religious feelings but in doing God's will and in being guided by faith. Her life is a reminder to us that to achieve the perfection of the gospel, we must bring our wills into conformity with the will of the Father through constant living of the central petition of the Lord's prayer, which is, "Thy Will be done." Of this petition of the Lord's prayer, Padre Pio said, "Thy Will be done is the most effective and transforming prayer we can ever say."

## Mary

Saint Teresa's greatest desire in life was to become a perfect copy of Jesus. She strove to walk in His footsteps and to pattern her life according to His, in order to resemble Him as closely as possible. In keeping with the spirit of one Preface of the Mass, her greatest desire was to have "the Father to see and love in her what He sees and loves in Christ."

Closely intertwined with her devotion to Jesus was a tender devotion to Mary. From early childhood, devotion to Mary was paramount in Teresa's life. She related to Mary deeply for two reasons. First, because of Mary's close relationship with the humanity of Christ. By the power of the Holy Spirit, Mary clothed the Son of God with His humanity. No one was closer to Christ and no one understood or loved Him more than did His mother. Secondly, devotion to Mary is simply carrying out the Lord's command of taking Mary to be our loving Mother. St. Teresa knew that these are not just words of the Bible but that Jesus spoke these words personally in her soul and graced her with the power to live them. Thus Mary became so important to her that she wrote, "after Jesus, She is my Mother and my all."

In high school she wrote, "I found written in a copybook something called: My Mirror. The statement reads, My mirror must be Mary. Given that I am her child, I must resemble Her and thus I will resemble Jesus." In Mary she contemplated the virtues and perfections that delighted the Heart of Christ, and, from Mary, she sought to learn the science of perfection. Every Saturday she did what Father Cea counselled her to do, namely "to think about the virtues of Mary and every day seek something new so that I won't grow tired." Even before entering Carmel, she asked a friend to "Pray to the Mother of Sorrows for me that I will never descend from Calvary, for I must be there at every moment of my crucified life."

The young teenage girl longed to share her love of Mary with others. This can be seen in the advice she gave her father in a letter:

*When you are suffering, gaze at your Sorrowful Mother holding the dead Jesus in her arms. Try to share her pain. There is nothing that compares with it. It is her only Son, dead, destroyed by sinners. And at the sight of the bloodied body of your God, and the tears of your Mother, learn to suffer by being resigned, and learn to console the most Holy Virgin by weeping for your sins.*

## Life in Carmel

St. Teresa lived in Carmel of Los Andes only eleven months. She was given the habit of Carmel and from that time on was called Sister Teresa of Jesus. She took this name in honor of the incomparable Carmelite saint of Avila. Being called Teresa after the Foundress of the Teresian Carmel, prompted her to write to her confessor: "I took the name of a great saint, and now I will have to become a great saint." Before she lived her Carmelite life one full year she was stricken by a deadly attack of typhus. She was allowed to make her religious vows on her death bed. This solemn consecration to God officially made her a full-fledged member of the Carmelite Order, something she had longed for from the time she was fifteen.

After her death, when it was time for the Mother Prioress to write a customary circular letter to all the other Carmels, people began to ask: what can Mother Prioress say that is important about this young novice? After all, what did she do? What did she accomplish in her short life? But, aren't these the very same questions that were raised immediately after the death of Saint Thérèse of the Child Jesus and after the death of many other young saints?

165

At first, people find these questions to be rather hard to answer. In reality they are quite natural. Comparing the lives of Saint Thérèse and Saint Teresa of the Andes, two very young Carmelite Sisters, *from an outsider's point of view*, it does appear that in their lives very little was accomplished. But when we look at the intensely heroic and generous interior lives these two saints lived and evaluate their lives from the standpoint of God's providence, we come away with a totally different impression. We see their lives as nothing less than moral miracles of extraordinary proportions.

### Testimony Of Mother Angelica Teresa

Outstanding or exceptional are the only words that do justice in describing the Circular Letter Mother Angelica Teresa of the Blessed Sacrament wrote about the spirit and life of this young girl after her death. It is evident that no one was more qualified than she to write this letter, which is now recognized to be a spiritual classic. Because Mother Angelica Teresa had corresponded with Juanita for several years before her entrance into Carmel and because she had guided Sister Teresita's soul during her months in Carmel and understood her so well, Mother Angelica was uniquely qualified to evaluate the exceeding greatness of this privileged soul's inner life.

In her outstanding Circular Letter, Mother Angelica describes Sister Teresa of Jesus as "an angelic child," an "angelic Sister." Twice she calls her a "privileged soul," and notes "that even in death she did not lose her angelic beauty. "She was a privileged creature in whose soul God, when creating her, had placed the treasures of his love," wrote Mother Angelica in her letter.

Regarding her many virtues, the Prioress wrote, "Our little sister, who from her earliest years exercised herself in acquiring and practicing virtue impelled by her love of Jesus, appeared to have mastered them all." Attention is drawn in the letter to Saint Teresa's desire to live a hidden Carmelite life, a hidden life to be with Christ, her Spouse. In this vein Mother Angelica wrote:

*She was affable and joyful. She always strove to hide her intelligence and evident talents, the solid instruction she had received, and the enlightenment on the highest matters which God's grace had given her. She made a concentrated effort in this matter." More remarkable still, is the superior's observation, "She did not display knowledge of anything in matters of prayer, virtue, etc., although she had received instructions in them from God Himself."*

The Circular Letter closes with the words: "The deep impression of the sanctity of our angelic Sister remains with us. These thoughts are based on having seen her practice virtue in the form already described and in her manner of being." Clearly Mother Angelica knew of Sister Teresa's holiness. Did the others? Addressing these questions, we are told, "Except for one or two in the community *(Mother Angelica and possibly one other Sister)*, the others remained ignorant that she had extraordinary gifts from the Lord and that she was such a privileged soul."

With feeling and poetic insight, the Prioress depicts the lasting impression the angelic young novice left on the community:

*We watched her pass as a ray of light, like a vision, and her absence has left a most profound sorrow in our hearts. But we have thanked the Lord for having drawn her to our Monastery and for having*

167

*permitted us to contemplate sanctity in such a young girl.*

## Days of Joy and Happiness

As she had hoped, her days in Carmel were days of incredible joy and happiness, though pain and suffering were not lacking. Her sole purpose in entering Carmel was to be united as closely as possible with Jesus and to be transformed into His divine likeness. She also desired to immolate and sacrifice herself for the sins of others and the sanctification of priests.

Reciting or singing the Divine Office in choir with the other Sisters thrilled her. She felt she was reciting the prayers that were inspired by God and that she was joining herself to the choirs of angels who unceasingly praise and adore God.

From Carmel, Sister Teresa of Jesus wrote 71 extremely beautiful and important letters. And there is scarcely a letter in which she does not describe her joy and happiness in her vocation. Eight days after entering the Carmel of Los Andes she wrote home telling them, "I am in heaven." In yet another letter she wrote, "I am the most happy of all people. I no longer desire anything, because my whole being is filled with God who is Love."

Characteristic of her personality was her tendency to think of the good of others. While she herself experienced the fullness of joy in Carmel, she wishes this same blessing for others. That's why she penned the beautiful words:

*Oh, if I could but make you feel the happiness that is felt when one has no other occupation in life than loving and contemplating. Then the soul engulfed in the ocean of the divinity loses sight of the shores of this world, which is the homeland of sorrow and wickedness.*

Six months after entrance into Carmel, in a letter written to her mother, Sister Teresa describes how happy she was in her Carmelite vocation because her dream of being so close to Jesus had been fulfilled. Because she was so close to and so deeply understood by her mother, she found it easy to open her filial heart to her with these memorable words:

*Right now I look at my Jesus and laugh with Him at the whole world. Let me weep in His arms all day long, while the rest laugh and amuse themselves. How little I mind weeping, gazing upon infinite joy and taste bitterness with the divine sweetness of my Jesus. I am happy and I shall never cease to be so, for I belong to my God. In Him I find my heaven and my eternal, unchanging love. I want nothing but Him. I love no one more than Him. And this love continues to grow in my soul to the extent that I am brought into His divine Heart of love and adorable perfections.*

## Her Spiritual Message and Mission

God blesses the world and the Church through His saints, for they are the praise and radiance of His glory. Each canonized saint has been chosen by the Holy Spirit and given a special divine mission for building up the Church. Holiness is essentially the same in each saint, but the gifts and charisms of each may differ. Not every saint, for example, has been granted a special doctrinal spiritual mission in the Church and for the world. Teresa of the Andes has received such a mission and is acknowledged by the Vatican as "a prophet of God for the men and women of today."

Father Simeone de la Sagrada Familia, O.C.D. the Postulator General of her Cause for Canonization, dealt with the special mission of this teenage saint when he spoke to the press in Santiago:

*Her words are filled with great energy and offer security. She will have an impact upon the faithful because they know that she has passed into the universal history of the Church. The beautiful but now faded pages of her original Diary and Letters which contain her spiritual legacy have now become part of the select literature of the Church and of her spirituality and holiness. Her writings will now be consciously placed alongside the immortal works of Saint Teresa of Jesus of Avila, Saint John of the Cross, Saint Thérèse of Lisieux and Blessed Elizabeth of the Trinity.*

And what is her precise mission? Father Marino Purroy, O.C.D. of Chile formulates the mission of Saint Teresa of the Andes in these simple words: "Teresa of the Andes is fulfilling her mission which was recognized a short time after her death: *to create a hunger and a thirst for God in our materialized world.*" It is evident that our dear saint has been given this special charism. A charism can rightly be described as a special gift given by the Holy Spirit for the benefit of others. In the case of Teresita, she was granted the special charism of attracting others to know, love and serve God. Her credentials are found in her life and its influence on others. One of her favorite phrases in her letters is, "I wish I could make you love Him the way I do."

### What You Keep Doing, Is What You Become

Saint Teresita's message came from her own life. Philosophers say that one can only give what one has acquired. Behavioral psychologists formulate this principle in different words. They would explain that her gift is understandable to a certain extent, but would insist on adding the following principle: namely, what a person keeps doing, that is what the person becomes. Applying this principle to the case at hand, it is evident that her power and influence came from daily fidelity to the Lord in prayer. We see that if one prays day after day, one will draw ever nearer to God. On the other hand, if one never prays one cannot draw close to God and cannot, therefore, gain the many blessings and spiritual fruits God can give. One of the most important benefits of prayer is the joyful awareness of God's nearness, love and goodness.

Research indicates that many men and women suffer from sadness and depression today. They are devoid of joy, despite repeated protestations they seek joy and happiness above everything else. If that be the case, one is led to ask, what is modern man doing wrong? On the other hand, one can and must ask what did this young Chilean do that made her find joy in such abundance? What was her secret? We can safely assume that if people are looking for joy in all the wrong places, they are bound to come up short and fail in their quest. But if a person is moving in the right direction, living in a constant state of the love, joy and peace which only the Holy Spirit can bring to the human heart, then that person is living in a way that is conducive to such blessings.

All the official documents we have on this saint tell us that Saint Teresa of Los Andes found so much divine

171

joy and happiness, that she was able to share her joy and happiness with others. This leads one to conclude that she was doing the right things in her life. She was both experiencing divine joy herself and able to share it with those around her.

What did Teresa of the Andes do so successfully? This saintly young woman devoted her whole life to one purpose: union with God. Union with God is the secret formula of her beautiful life. We know that God alone is the source of all love and joy. We also know that the saint of the Andes consciously chose a way and program of life whereby God became the joy of her life. To those who decide for Christ, Jesus says, "your heart will rejoice and no one will take your joy from you. Ask, and you will receive, that your joy may be complete." Commenting on this text, William Barclay writes:

> *There are two precious things about this Christian joy. a) **It will never be taken away.** The joy the world gives is at the mercy of the world. The joy which Christ gives is independent from anything the world can do. b) **It will be complete.** In life's greatest joy there is always something lacking. In Christian joy, the joy of the presence of Christ, there is no tinge of imperfection. It is perfect and complete."*

### Holiness For All

Teresa of the Andes offers everyone a vision of Christian life filled with love and joy. Like Augustine of the fourth century and Teresa of Avila in the sixteenth, Teresa of the Andes knows that our restless twentieth century hearts crave the love and joy God alone can give us. She explicitly teaches that everyone can experience endless divine love and joy in their own heart, if they

172

seek it. But this joy, this pearl of great price can only be purchased, as she wrote, by "giving God the throne of our hearts." One must strive for this joy. How? "Ask, and it shall be given," answers the Gospel. This means one must seek to fulfill the commandment of love: that is, by striving to love God with our whole heart, our whole mind and our whole strength. We must likewise strive to love our neighbor as ourselves. The Carmelite saint of the Andes found divine joy because she looked for it in the right places; she especially looked for and found it in the Eucharist and in the Heart of Jesus. After finding God's love, she fully reciprocated that love.

The most direct and the surest way to divine joy is found in frequent daily prayer. Prayer is the opening of our mind and heart and character to the influence of God's love. If one does not lose heart and keeps praying day after day, one will become a close friend of God. Then God will not just make the praying person joyful or happy, but will fill the praying heart with His own joy and His own happiness. When Jesus said, "I no longer call you servants but I call you my friends," he was praising friendship's basic law, namely, that the goods of one friend become the goods of the other, and then all things are held in common. That God wants the fullness of His own love and perfections to become ours is a mystery that forever enraptures the Christian heart.

Saints are models because they went before us, lived the gospel fully, and show us the road to holiness. The central aim of this Chilean young woman's life was union with God through constant prayer and the heroic practice of the virtues. Prayer, in the words of Saint Augustine, is the affectionate raising of our minds and hearts to God. This practice denotes a tender attachment to God, and a desire to be affected, changed or transformed by God, by His love, goodness, and perfections. Getting back to our basic law of behavioral psychology we see that if one prays daily he or she will be deeply influenced by God's love and goodness. Such prayerful men and women will draw closer to God, causing them to increasingly experience the joy of God's friendship and presence.

## Make My Joy Complete

Those who constantly enjoy God's presence and friendship are most anxious to have others taste the Lord's goodness and sweetness. They desire no one to be deprived of this joy. Saint Paul is an excellent teacher in this matter. Writing to the Phillipians Paul opens his heart to these Christians and begs them, "make my joy complete!" You will make my joy complete, he writes, if you put on the mind and heart of Christ. Filled with God's love and joy and peace, Teresita wrote, "I wish you could love Jesus as I do." Obviously, it would make her joy complete if she could see many striving to follow her example of constantly raising their minds and hearts to God, begging the Sacred Heart of Jesus to make their hearts like unto His.

Saint Teresa of the Andes chose a very simple and direct way to God. It is clearly based on the gospel and is attainable by all. Saint Thérèse of the Child Jesus, popularly known as the Little Flower, proposed a spirituality of going to God by knowing that He is infinitely merciful and will make his goodness and power available to everyone. She lived in the nineteenth century when people were afraid of God, afraid to draw near to Him. Her simple way of holiness has helped millions of souls. Her Carmelite sister in Chile in this century repeats the same message, but St. Teresa of the

174

Andes would draw attention to the fact that in God alone can one find the infinite love and joy they seek. This message of divine joy has special importance and relevance for the people of our century who are afflicted with sadness, depression and loneliness.

Speaking of depression, this writer recalls the time he attended a seminar given by the well known Dr. William Glasser, famous for his Reality Therapy books. Someone asked how to help people escape from depression. I was at first startled by the lecturer's answer. He simply said, "when a depressed person finds something that brings him more enjoyment, he will get over his depression." Obviously, Dr. Glasser didn't mean a person can be healed overnight, but he did mean that as darkness is dispelled by light, as the cold is replaced by heat, as fear is casts out by love, so joy will drive away all sadness, loneliness and depression. And, it can be added, when the joy comes from the conviction of God's loving closeness to us and His presence in our lives, that joy will bring a peace and assurance that no one can ever take from us.

Through charity Teresa was able to love God, but through the gift of wisdom and understanding she was granted to know God's infinite goodness because she tasted and experienced it. Her spiritual message is based on this experience. Her message is this: everyone can experience God's love and joy and no one need ever be deprived of it. But our charming young saint would add, the royal road to divine joy is faithful and constant daily prayer. She learned this from her own experience. Essentially, she was instructed by God. But she worked at it, too, using all her courage to remain faithful to her Spouse. Her life is a shining example of a young woman who met life and all its challenges head-on and relied on the loving presence and strength of her Spouse dwelling within.

175

## Summary

It is now time to sum up her important and fruitful message. There is no doubt but that the Lord wants to tell us something special and important through this beautiful saint. The Holy Spirit lighted up her mind and heart with such a deep loving insight into His divine love and perfections in order that she can help souls who are hungering and thirsting for God. From personal experience and from divine illumination, this newly canonized Saint will bring enlightenment to many through the power of her life and teaching. Pope John Paul II framed and immortalized her spiritual mission and message with these words:

*For her, God is infinite joy. This is the new hymn of Christian love which rises spontaneously from this young Chilean girl, in whose glorified face we can sense the grace of her transformation in Christ."*

At the Shrine at Auco Rinconada de Los Andes people with anguished hearts come to pray at her tomb. Large numbers of pilgrims are heavy with grief that loved ones have fallen away from their faith. People coming to her tomb, are mindful that the saint's favorite brother lost his Christian faith and didn't recover it until shortly before his sister's beatification in 1987. After his return to the faith, he testified that his conversion was due to her prayers. It is well known that our saint suffered terribly in knowing that the brother whom she called "Luís of my heart," had seemingly drifted far from God. Parents and relatives who pray for loved ones who no longer practice their religion bear one of the most terrible burdens the human heart can know. Knowing that St. Teresa awakened in her brother a hunger and thirst for God and thus enabled him to return to the full

176

practice of his faith prompts many to turn to this saint for help. Such prayers have frequently been answered.

## Look for Jesus and You Will Always Find Me

The saints in heaven are filled with the perfection of light and love. They unceasingly glorify God with a fullness we can only dimly perceive. In heaven they are deeply concerned for those on earth who are journeying towards Christ and eternal glory. "There is more joy in heaven," says the Scripture, "over one repentant sinner." The faith of the Church has always maintained the mystery of the communion of saints, that there is a living bond between those on earth, and those in heaven. Heaven rejoices to see men and women of earth rejoice in God.

The Church continually pays honor to the saints and encourages us to do the same. She implores us to seek their intercession that we may fulfill the grand work of walking courageously in the footsteps of Christ and of serving Him in this land of exile. The Church offers us the example of their lives to give us the help, inspiration and encouragement we need. In the Mass, the Church continually reminds us to turn to them with confidence, urging us to go to them with needs.

"When I love it is forever," is one of this Saint Teresa of the Andes' most quoted sayings. If when she was on earth it was our Saint's greatest desire to glorify God and to love everyone, now from her place in heaven she hasn't forgotten us: she loves us still. Today, she understands with greater clarity all our spiritual and material needs and the dangers we face as we journey towards Christ and eternal glory. Feeling a deep bond of love for all who have been redeemed and sanctified by Christ, she now pleads with Christ for all our needs, but does so with, in and through the Risen Christ who is ever interceding for us at the right hand of the Father. St. Teresa of Los Andes can do this most effectively now that she has become what she always longed for, that is, "a perfect praise" of God's glory. Certain words bring comfort that remains forever. When it was time for Christ to speak to His disciples for the last time before He ascended to heaven, His deep love for them prompted Him to give them assurance by saying: "I will be with you forever." These comforting words brought the apostles (and the Church) lasting encouragement. Jesus was going away, true, but now the apostles were assured He would always be with them and never leave them. "Presence through absence," is the way Paul Claudel describes the mystery of Christ's ascension. Because Christ spoke those few words, sadness has never dominated the Church, instead, it has always relied on and found comfort and joy because with Christ ever present, it is filled with His abiding presence.

Those she held deeply in her heart, Saint Teresa of the Andes loved to be with and loved to help. But, while she sojourned on earth, it was not always possible for her to be with her loved ones. She had to leave them from time to time and, of course, she had to leave them all forever when her Master called her to enter into the eternal joys of the Father's kingdom. While she lived, however, she assured her sister Rebecca and other friends that she always wanted to be close to them. She wanted nothing to break or interfere with the bond of love and friendship that made them one. Her comforting and inspiring words were meant not for her friends alone, but for all of us. These are the immortal words of her heart:

*Be without fear, my dear little sister. There will*

*never be any separation between our souls. Search for Jesus and in Him you will find me and there we three will carry on these intimate conversations that we must always carry on there for all eternity.*

In other words, we can never really be separated. Through the Risen Jesus I will always be with you, always ready to help you in any need. The solution is so simple and so easy. All you need do is search for Jesus, and in Him I can always be present to you and help you!

## Model For Chile

I can think of no more fitting way to conclude this section than to point to the way the young Chilean Carmelite Saint has become a luminous model of holiness for her native land. Her actual spiritual impact in Chile is nothing short of phenomenal. This was brought out dramatically when the bishops of Chile gathered at her Shrine on Sunday, April 18, 1993 to thank God for her canonization and to pledge to remain faithful to the saint's legacy. What follows in a report of that event.

After a thanksgiving Mass for the canonization of Teresa de Los Andes, with Cardinal Fresno presiding, there was a solemn ceremony of the enthronement of the canonization picture of Saint Teresa de los Andes at the Shrine of Our Lady of Mount Carmel in Auco, Chile.

In his homily, Bishop Manuel Camilo Vila underlined the importance of the new saint as a model for Chile. He stated that she was a three-fold gift of the living God to the Church and our country.

First of all, Saint Teresa de los Andes signifies a deeper incarnation of the Gospel in Chilean culture, he said. Her canonization is achieving an inculturation of sanctity among us. We can comprehend how all the saints are brothers and sisters and that every one of them can become part of our story.

According to Bishop Manual Camilo Vila, the canonization of St. Teresa was also for the Chileans a gift of intercession, and he pointed out in his homily that "this elder daughter" of Chile had shown herself to be an indefatigable intercessor before the majesty of the merciful God. This experience is an immense consolation that has swept through the country, fortifying it in its inmost being. What good it has done us to have a solicitous and powerful sister in heaven!."

The third gift implied in this canonization, said the prelate, is a "gift of encouragement", and he explained that when Chile finds itself at a decisive crossroads, because of a new, emerging culture; because of the journey to full democracy and because of the need for renewal, conversion and reconciliation, Teresa is there to keep us from bring carried away by mirages."

After the Mass, the picture of the saint was brought down by the bishops to the crypt of the Church in Auco, where it was placed at the head of the tomb containing the remains of the first Chilean Saint.

People came away from that ceremony with new confidence and courage. Above all, they went back to their homes with the vivid awareness and renewed conviction that the days of the saints are far from over. They know they have a special friend watching over them before the throne of God's mercy.

# DIARY
# 1900-1914

## 1. Summary And Division of My Life

Dear Mother: You believe you are going to find an interesting story, but I don't want you to be deceived; the story you are going to read is not the story of my life, but the intimate life of a poor soul who, without any merit on her part, Jesus Christ loved in a special way and filled abundantly with His favors and graces. *(Juanita began her diary when she was 15 years old. These first paragraphs were written in ink in 1917, when she dedicated it to her beloved teacher Madre Julia Ríos, a Religious of the Sacred Heart, and titled it* **THE STORY OF THE LIFE OF ONE OF YOUR DAUGHTERS.** *Mother Ríos, the spiritual director of the students at the Sacred Heart school in Santiago, was greatly loved by all because of her virtues and sympathy).*

The story of my soul is summed up in two words: "To suffer and to love." Here is the whole of my life from the time I became aware of everything, that is to say from 6 years of age or before. I used to suffer, and the good Jesus taught me to suffer in silence and to unburden my poor little heart to Him.

You know, Mother, the way Jesus showed me from the time I was little was the same way He traveled, the way He loved; and because He loved me, He sought to nourish my poor soul in suffering. My life is divided into two periods: the first, more or less from the age of reason until my First Communion. Jesus filled me with favors both in the first period as well as in the second: from my

First Communion till now. Or better still, until my soul enters the harbor of Carmel.


## 2. Spoiled By All. My Family

I was born in 1900 on the 13th day of July. My mother is Lucía Solar de  Fernández and my father is Michael Fernández Jaraquemada. *(Juanita was born and lived 7 years in the house of her maternal Grandfather at 1352 Rosas Street in Santiago, Chile. The house has since been demolished).*

We lived with my grandfather, who was already quite old. You can say that he was a saint, since one could see him praying his rosary all day long. His name was Eulogio Solar.

Jesus did not desire me to be born poor like Himself; I was born in the midst of riches, spoiled by all.

I was the fourth child in the family. The first was named Lucía, who was 7 years old; Miguel, the second, was 6 years old and Luís, the third, was 3. My aunt Juanita Solar lived in my grandfather's house with her four children. My uncle, Luís Albert Domínguez, had already died. The eldest of my cousins was 13 years old and the youngest was 5. My aunt Teresa Vicuña also lived there with her two children. One of her boys died in childhood. Her older child was called Thomas Bernardo (the name of my uncle). And Teresita, her second, was 8 years old. My uncle Francis, *(Francisco Solar Armstrong)* who was a bachelor, also lived there. He was 23 years old.

A short time later Rebecca was born, and there was a difference of 1 year and 8 months between us. *(In 1910 her last brother, Ignacio, came into the world. He died at Santiago November 2, 1976.)* Though quite spoiled, I was very timid. Rebecca was the opposite. We were both very spoiled. We could do whatever we pleased with my Granddaddy and we used to trick him with our kisses and caresses.

From the time I was small they used to say that I was the prettiest of my brothers and sisters but I paid no attention to this. But they kept repeating these same words to me as I grew older, unbeknown to my mother, since she didn't like this. God alone knows what it cost me to overcome this pride or vanity that took possession of my heart as I grew older. My character was timid, my heart sensitive. I used to cry for any reason, but my disposition was extremely gentle; I never used to get mad at anyone.

### 3. Desires To Receive Holy Communion. School.

It was shortly after the earthquake in1906 when Jesus began to take my heart to be His own.

I recall how my mother and my aunt Juanita took us to Mass and always explained everything to us. During Mass, when it was Communion time, I was inflamed with desires to receive Our Lord. I used to ask my mother for this favor, but thanks be to God she didn't find me ready for this sublime act. I remember my mother and my aunt Juanita sitting me down at table and asking me about the Eucharist. I answered their questions, but because they saw I was very young, they didn't allow me to receive Communion.

When I was 7 years old I went to Confession. We were prepared for this by the Sisters.

But first I want to describe my starting school. My Granddaddy in no way wanted us *(Juanita and Rebecca)* to start school, but my mother finally prevailed and placed me with the Teresianist Sisters. I was to go there after lunch and leave at five, but I hardly ever really went. After one month they took me out. I observed that the teachers didn't sufficiently supervise us at recess time and one of the little girls was not very nice. I told my mother what was happening.

My mother went to complain. As a result, the Mother Superior became angry. They put me in a room by myself on examination day and gave me bad marks. Then the Superior scolded me, saying that these things should not be told. I was surprised because I had always been told that I should tell my mother everything. They punished me. I cried a great deal, and when I got home my mother wrote a letter to the Superior telling her that I would not return to the school. I was happy because some of those little girls were very mischievous. There was one from whom I suffered because she was always trying to hurt me. When we went to Chapel she always pulled my veil off. And I, being little, didn't know how to defend myself. I had a cousin whom they attacked very often and I had to defend her. The others loved me. Finally, I don't remember that school with affection, even though I learned to read when I was there. *(This school, conducted by the Carmelite Sisters of Saint Teresa, was located on Saint Dominic Street, very close to Juanita's home).*


## 4. My GRANDDADDY DIED.

In 1907, my dear grandfather died as a saint. I remember very well that when we went to our summer home - at Chacabuco - he was all right. My aunt Teresa went there with her two little ones and him and us, from whom she was inseparable.

Every evening he made us mount a horse, flipping a

coin heads or tails to see who would be first. Rebecca always won. He was in good health until one night he was stricken with an attack of paralysis. My aunt immediately took him by land to Santiago and then they said that there was no hope for him. They made him suffer by giving him the most horrible medicines. Finally my poor little old man did not know how he felt. On the 13th of May, the day of his death, he received the Sacraments. He called his children and counseled them. By the side of his room there was an oratory. They began to say Mass when they saw that his face was filled with great fear, and he kept saying "take him away" while he covered his face with his hands. There were terrible temptations from the devil. My mother threw holy water on him and the devil left. The devil then tempted him another time and left so that his death was like his life: in peace. At the moment of the Consecration of the Mass, when the Sacred Host was elevated, his soul took flight for heaven, without anyone taking notice. It seemed that he was sleeping. His death was that of a saint, as was his life.

We were immediately notified at Chacabuco. I remember that I was in bed sleeping and they came to notify us. They didn't pay much attention to us little ones. We didn't cry because my brother Luís was very sick and had barely escaped death, so they didn't want to inform him. Thus it was that without any effort we remained very quiet. After a while they began to dress us and Luís began to shout and cry bitterly. They went to see him and he began to say: "Why did they deceive me? Why didn't they tell me? My grandfather is dead." He cried oceans of tears. No one knew how he came to know of this, because no one had told him. My grandfather told him while he was sleeping. A few days later my uncle Francis arrived crying and saying the saddest things. This caused me to cry oceans and I couldn't be consoled. They took us to Santiago and seeing Granddaddy's empty room made such a great impression on me that it seemed that everything was finished. It's impossible to imagine how sad I became.

A short time later they auctioned off the house and the farm, dividing it in perpetuity into three little estates. Don Salvador Huidobro inherited the middle estate; my uncle Francis inherited the one on the hill and my mother inherited the one at Baños. My uncle Eugene inherited the house in Santiago. *(Till the death of her grandfather, Juanita and her brothers and sisters alternated between living in Santiago and spending long periods of time at the summer house at Chacabuco, also the property of Don Eulogio).*

We moved to Saint Dominic Street to a house that, like the other one, was full of very pleasant memories for me. Here something happened that is worth relating. At night, when we put out the light in my room, there was still light from my mamita's room. *(Juanita's mamita, the servant who took care of her from birth, is Ofelia Miranda, a very religious woman and a very good person. Juanita sends greetings to her in numerous letters).* I used to see my dead grandfather appear at the foot of Rebecca's bed, but I didn't see more than half of his body. He appeared to me eight consecutive days. I was scared to death and went to Rebecca's bed. From that time, I no longer saw him.

## 5. My Devotion To The Virgin.
### Preparation For My First Communion.

When we went to Chacabuco for the last time, my

aunt Juanita gave me a porcelain statue of the Virgin of Lourdes to keep by the side of my bed, provided I would drink my medicine. I used to drink it and so she gave me the statue. This is the Virgin who has never ceased to console me and to listen to me. *(Till his death her brother, Luís Fernández (Lucho) had this statue in his possession).*

My devotion to the Virgin began at this time. My brother Luís gave me this devotion, which I have kept and will keep, as I hope, until death. Every day Luís used to invite me to pray the rosary, and together we made a promise to recite it for the rest of our lives. This I have done till now. Only once, when I was a little child, did I forget.

Our Lord, from that time on, it can be said, took me by the hand with the Most Holy Virgin. At that time my character was very irate, since I had ferocious fits of anger, but they were far apart. After that time no one made me lose my patience; the children and my brothers deliberately did and said many things to make me angry, but I went on as if I didn't hear them. Because of this my mother spoiled me; but afterward whatever displeased me made me cry and break into hysterical sobbing.

When we went to Chacabuco, a cousin of my mother who could not stand me went with us, and Rebecca was the spoiled one. It's impossible to imagine how much I suffered as a result of this. I was terrible with her and I did not bear with her in any way. *(This is Rosenda Luco Solar. Juanita's mother assured us that Juanita acted very sweetly, despite what she says here).*

In 1907 we started school. *(This school, located on the Alameda, was run by the Religious of the Sacred Heart. These Sisters were referred to as the English Sisters).*

You, Mother, know how we upset you because of our character. How well I recall when my mother told you of the fights we had with my brothers, how you called us and made us put things right.

It was from that time on that Our Lord showed me suffering. My father lost part of his fortune and thus we had to live more modestly. Every day I asked my mother's permission to make my First Communion. Finally in 1910 it was granted and I began my preparation. It seemed to me that day would never come, dear Mother, and I wept with longing to receive Our Lord. For a year I prepared myself to receive Holy Communion. During this time the Virgin helped me to cleanse my heart of every imperfection.

In the month of the Sacred Heart I modified my character completely. I did this to such an extent that my mother was happy to see me preparing myself so well for my First Communion.

It was costly for me to obey, especially when I was ordered to do something, then out of negligence I took my time in going to do it. Then I told myself that, even though they did not order me to do so, I would hasten to comply before the others. I didn't fight with the children. Sometimes I had to bite my lips and hurry to get dressed. I performed acts of virtue, which I noted down in a little book. The book was full of my deeds. Oh, what a difference between then and now. Would that I could return to that period of my life. But have I not received more favors from our Lord?

## 6. My First Communion.

My First Communion day was a cloudless day.

My general confession. I remember that afterward,

when I had left the confessional, they put a white veil on me. In the evening I asked for everyones' forgiveness. I remember the impression it made on my father. I went to ask his forgiveness and he kissed me. Then afterward I knelt down and, shedding tears, I begged him to pardon me for all the pain I had caused him by my conduct. Tears streamed down from my father's eyes as he picked me up and, kissing me, said there was nothing I had to beg his pardon for because I had never displeased him, and he was very happy to see me be so good. Oh, yes, dear father, it was because you were so indulgent and good to me. I begged pardon of my mother, who was crying. I did the same to all my brothers and, finally, my mamita and the rest of the servants. All were deeply touched when they answered me. And, since I was on retreat, I stayed apart and so did not eat at the family table.

The 11th of September, 1910, the centenary year of my country, was a year of happiness and one of the purest recollections I shall have in my whole life. That was a happy day for me, and a beautiful day for nature as well. The sun gave off its rays and filled my soul with happiness and thanksgiving for the Creator.

I got up early. My mother helped me put on my dress. *(On other days Juanita's mamita dressed her.)* She combed my hair. She did everything for me, but I wasn't thinking of anything. I was completely indifferent to everything, except to my soul and God. When we arrived, we began praying the rosary for First Communion. Instead of the Hail Mary, we kept reciting "Come, my Jesus, come. Oh, my Savior, come Yourself to prepare my heart."

The moment finally arrived. Two by two we made our entrance into the Chapel. You, my Mother, were at the head of the procession and Monsignor Jara - who would give us the Sacred Communion - was at the end. We all entered the chapel with our eyes downcast, without looking at anyone. We knelt down on the kneelers which were covered with a very fine white cloth, with a white lily and a candle on each side.

Monsignor Jara spoke such tender and beautiful words to us that we were all crying. I recall one thing he told us: "Ask Jesus Christ that, if you will ever commit a mortal sin, that He take you today, since your souls are as pure as the snow on the mountains. Pray to Him for your parents, the authors of your existence. For those who have lost their parents, this is the moment to seek to be united with them. Yes, you are approaching to become witnesses of the intimate union of your souls with Jesus Christ. Look at the angels of the altar, dear little girls. Look at them, they envy you. All heaven is present." I was crying. Finally he told us that he didn't want to delay any further our union with Jesus because we were already hungering for Him, Jesus Christ Himself.

While we were approaching the altar they were singing that beautiful hymn, "Happy the Soul," which I shall never forget.

It's impossible to describe what took place between my soul and Jesus. I asked him a thousand times that He would take me, and I experienced His dear voice for the first time. "Oh Jesus I love You, I adore You!" I prayed to Him for everybody. And I felt the Virgin near me. Oh, how my heart expanded! For the first time I experienced a delicious peace. After making our thanksgiving we went to the patio to share things with the poor, and each girl went to embrace her family. My Daddy kept kissing me and, being so happy, lifting me up in his arms. Many little girls came to the house that day. What can I say of the gifts they gave me? The bureau and my bed were filled.

That very happy day ended, which will be the unique day of my life. Shortly after that time we moved from that house *(at 475 Ejercito Street)*. Since that first embrace, Jesus did not let me go but took me for Himself.

Every day I went to Communion and talked with Jesus for a long time, but my special devotion was the Virgin. I told her everything. From that day on the earth no longer held any attraction for me. I wanted to die and begged Jesus that He'd take me on the 8th of December.

## 7. On December 8th I Was Always Sick.
### The Virgin And Jesus Spoke To Me.

Every year I used to become sick on the eighth of December, so much so that they believed I was going to die. When I was 12, I came down with diphtheria on the same eighth day of December; I was near death and my mother believed that I was dying because an aunt *(Maria del Carmen Solar Armstrong)* died of this same illness, and I had a worse case of the disease than she had. This aunt died when she was 12 years old. She was a saint from her childhood. To do penance she used to put stones in her shoes; she scourged herself using branches with thorns until she was covered with blood. In her last illness, when the doctors tried to remove the membranes from her throat, she took the instruments and kissed them, saying: "These are the instruments that will bring me to heaven." Then she took her crucifix and said: "Doctors, now do to me what you want." When the hour of her death came, she begged pardon of my grandparents and then from all, and asked that they excuse her because of the inconveniences of her illness. Then she remained in ecstasy and said: "How great, how immense God is!" In death a smile remained on her lips. I never compared myself to her; I still did not deserve heaven and Our Lord did not take me.

In 1913 I had a dreadful fever. At this time Our Lord was calling me to Himself but I didn't take notice of His voice. Then last year *(1914)* I got appendicitis, and this made me hear His dear voice that was calling me to make me His spouse later on in Carmel.

My devotion to the Virgin was very great. One day when I was very troubled by something, I told this to the Virgin and asked Her for the conversion of a sinner. Then She answered me. After that, when I called Her the Virgin spoke to me. Once, I asked Her about a doubt I had. Then, a voice answered me. I said to it: "This is not the voice of my Mother, because She can't be telling me this." I called Her and She said that the devil had answered me. I became fearful. Then She told me that whenever I heard the voice I should ask: "Are you my Mother?" And this is what I always do. Every time I wanted to know something I asked Her and what She told me gave me certainty. My attack of appendicitis was getting worse and I had to remain in bed. They took me out of school and for this I was very happy.

One day I was alone in my room. Because of my illness they spoiled me so that I couldn't remain alone. I want to relate that one day Lucita *(Lucía, her older sister)* was sick and Elisea - a servant who took care of my dear grandfather - went to be with her. Then I became envious and troubled and began to cry. My tearful eyes began to fix themselves on a picture of the

Sacred Heart, and I heard a very sweet voice say to me: "What! I, Juanita, am alone on the altar for your love, and you can't even suffer for a moment?" From that time, the dear Jesus spoke to me, and I spent entire hours conversing with Him. That's the reason I enjoyed being alone. He went on teaching me how I should suffer and not complain, and about intimate union with Himself. Then He told me that He wanted me for Himself, that He would like me to become a Carmelite. Ah! Mother, you can't imagine what Jesus was doing in my soul. At that time I didn't live in myself, it was Jesus who was living in me. I used to get up at seven o'clock, at the time Rebecca was going to school. I kept to a schedule for the whole day and I was doing all things with Jesus and for Jesus.

Our Lord showed me the goal of sanctity. I was to attain this by doing all things as well as I possibly could. Just shortly after that, the priest, my confessor, repeated the very same words to me. Then I told him what Our Lord had told me.

## 8. Appendicitis Operation.

Every day my pains and illness became worse. On the eighth of December I felt I was going to die. From that day I remained in bed until I was able to get up after my operation. My mother began a novena to Saint Thérèse of the Child Jesus (the Carmelite), because I'm very devoted to her. I became better, but on the 24th my mother forgot to recite the novena at night and the next day I got up feeling much worse. At noon on that day I became so weak they believed I was about to die, but Our Lord wanted to spare me. Oh, how good God is to me!

It was decided that I had to have the operation. On

Monday the 28th they rented a room in Saint Vincent's. Only God knows what I suffered. It gave me great pain to think of dying outside my home. On the other hand, I felt such great repugnance to sleeping in beds where other sick people have been.... Thus it is that I felt horrible in going.

Little Ignacio came into my room, his little eyes filled with tears, but hardly had he seen me than he dried the tears and began to be playful. I didn't see him cry for even a moment, an admirable thing in a little boy who was scarcely 4 years old. On Monday I went by car with my mother and my mamita to the hospital. I was almost dead from fatigue when I arrived at my room in Saint Vincent's, but then I recovered. At 5 o'clock in the morning I went to Communion. How beautiful that Communion was! I believed it was to be my last. With all my soul I asked our Lord that He would give me courage and serenity. What would have become of me without the help of Jesus? Oh, my most sweet Jesus, I love You!

The young girls came to see me. I calmly played cards with them. Later the nurse came to prepare me. Then the doctors, etc. After lunch my nerves were so bad that I didn't know what was happening to me and I began to cry and to laugh. My mother gave me some medicine and I remained very calm. The little girls came at two o'clock with aunt Juanita and I asked her if she might stay for the operation. She promised me that she would. Later my uncle Eulogio, my mother's brother, arrived, and also Juanita Ossa de Valdés, but they carried on such a different kind of conversation from the one I was expecting. They tried to amuse me, but I was preparing to die. We were in the midst of this when the *(hospital)* Sister came looking for me. I can't say how good the Sisters were to me. When they could, they always kept me company. They prepared flowers for me in my room so it would look cheerful.

I took my statue of the Virgin and embraced my crucifix; I kissed them and said to them: "Soon I'll contemplate you face to face. Farewell." They placed a quantity of relics on me and I got on my stretcher. My aunts took me, but my mother went by my side, and also Lucita and Rebecca. Each Sister I saw was asked to pray for me and I spoke with all of them. I went for two blocks before arriving at the clinic. I passed by the men's section. I had gotten to the point that I was unable to stop my tears, when I spied a very old servant who had undergone many operations. It gave me such pain to think that I wouldn't see her anymore and, further, it seemed to me that they were taking me as a lamb to the slaughterer to kill me. I began to cry. I gave out a shout. A sob escaped from me, but I told myself I must not cry. I dried my tears and appeared calm so I wouldn't give my mother pain. Afterward I begged Jesus that my mother wouldn't say goodbye and Jesus granted me this. My mother and my uncle Eulogio remained behind, but without my being aware of it. When I arrived at the clinic some of the servants took me up the stairs. Then Lucía and Rebecca said goodbye to me - for me, that goodbye was like a dart that tore my heart to pieces and my tears began to fall. But had I not promised Jesus that I wouldn't cry? Making a great effort I dried my tears and said goodbye to them.

The doctors came out. They began to converse with me calmly, but they seemed like butchers to me; however, Jesus conquered for me. Before receiving the chloroform, I kissed my medal and placed myself in the Heart of Jesus, bidding farewell to the world.

195

My father and my aunt Juanita should have been there, but my father didn't have the courage. When I awoke my head was aching and I didn't know where I was. I believed that I had come from another world, that's why I began to cry when I saw each person. The pain was terrible. The chloroform caused terrible aftereffects, but I remembered to offer myself to Our Lord, since my mother had reminded me to do so. For a single instant, but no longer, I was in despair, but I immediately repented.

On New Year's Day a letter arrived. That day the Sister who was taking care of me, who was so good, said to me after I had gone to Communion: "There is a letter for you." I was happy and thought that my friends had written to me. But imagine my surprise when I opened it and it was from Jesus, in French. The letter was precious and the Sister had sent it to me, with many beautiful holy cards.

This good Sister showed me a thousand kindnesses. Every day she arranged flowers so the room would be cheerful. A doctor from the clinic sent me orchids, an especially expensive flower. It was the first time anybody had sent me flowers and I remembered to give them to Jesus. This sacrifice cost me dearly, but I made it. *(The dramatics of her narration are explained by the danger of death that the operation entailed in those days).*

## YEARS 1915 - 1916

### 9. A Fit Of Temper I Had.

Soon after we left the clinic we went to a house my father had rented at Chacabuco. I was unable to go horseback riding, which was a great sacrifice for me because nothing pleased me more than the horse. We had a very good time. There were Missions. We often had Mass, and I was very happy.

For greater humiliation I will relate a fit of anger I had that was so great that it seemed that I was mad. The cause of it was that my sister and my cousin who was with us did not want to go bathing with us, because we were very small. It disgusted me that they called me "little" so I didn't want to go swimming, but they forced me. When we were getting dressed the little girls came to hurry us up, but I answered them that I wouldn't get dressed until they had left. But they didn't want to leave, and my mother told me that I should dress. I, obstinately, didn't want to. My mother punished me but it was all useless. I began to cry and so great was my anger that I wanted to throw myself into the bathtub. My mamita began to dress me, but I kept on being angry. When I was ready, I repented of what I had done and I went to ask my mother's pardon. She was very upset to see me this way and said that she was going to return to Santiago so she wouldn't be with a little girl who was so angry. She didn't want to forgive me; as a result, I was crying and inconsolable. She threw me out of her room and I went to hide so I could cry freely. When it was time to take tea I didn't want to go until I was forced to do so. I felt ashamed and didn't want to look at anyone, since I had given such bad example. I don't know how many times I begged pardon, until my mother told me that night that she would see what my conduct was like in the future.

I believe that I had perfect contrition for this sin; I don't know how many times I wept for it. And every time I remember it, I feel sorry for having been so

197

ungrateful with Our Lord who had so recently given me
back my life. *(Her mother later explained that Juanita's
anger was due to nervousness caused by the anesthetic).*

## 10. Today I Am 15 Years Old.

July 13. Today I'm 15 years old. Fifteen years old!
The age all would like to be; the younger ones, to be
considered as grownups, and the older ones and those
who have passed this age, even those who are 25 years
old, would like to return to this age because it is happiest
of all.

Yet I keep on thinking: 15 years, 15 years that God
has preserved my life. He gave it to me in 1900. In
creating me He preferred me to millions of beings.

In 1914, the year that just ended, I was sick and
nearly died, but He gave me life another time. On my
part, what have I done for so great a favor and because
God has twice given me life?

Fifteen years old! What have I been concerned with
in these 15 years? What have I done to please that
omnipotent King and most merciful Creator who created
me? Why did He prefer me to so many other creatures?

The future hasn't been revealed to me, yet Jesus has
pulled back the curtain and I have glimpsed the
beautiful shores of Carmel.

How many times have I not begged God to take me
from this world. And He almost deigned to grant my
pleas but has sent me illnesses from which they believed
He wouldn't save me. Yet Jesus has taught me that I
must not ask for this and has put as a limit for my
journey of life 9 more years in the blessed harbor of
Carmel. *(Juanita, filled with enthusiasm from reading
Saint Thérèse, had formed an idea that, like Thérèse, she*

*herself would die at the age of 24)*

Fifteen is the most dangerous age for a young girl because it marks her entrance into the tempestuous sea of the world. But now that I'm 15 years old, Jesus has taken command of my ship and has protected it from encountering other vessels. He has kept me in solitude with Himself. Consequently, my heart, by knowing this Captain, has fallen under the spell of His love, and here He keeps me captive. Oh, how I love this prison and this powerful King who keeps me captive; and how I love this Captain who amid the waves of the ocean doesn't allow me to suffer shipwreck.

Each day Jesus nourishes me with His adorable Body and, together with this delicate food, I hear a sweet and soft voice like the harmonious echoes of the angels of heaven. This is the voice that guides me, that loosens the sails of the ship of my soul so I will not perish, will not sink. I always hear that dear voice which is the voice of my Beloved, the voice of Jesus in the depths of my soul. And in my pains, in my temptations, He is my Consoler, He is my Captain.

May my Jesus always lead me by the way of the Cross. And then my soul will take flight, where it can encounter the air that gives life and where there is repose.

## 11. Boarding School.

During vacation time I wrote to you, Mother, giving you an understanding of my vocation which you had already guessed.

We came in March and I started school but you, my Mother, were already ill at the time. How I suffered and how I prayed for your recovery. But the Lord didn't want to make you better and made you drink the chalice of bitterness that He reserves for those He loves. They moved you to the school on Maestranza Street. *(This is the school of the Religious of the Sacred Heart on Maestranza Street - now Portugal Street - here Juanita and Rebecca entered as boarders during the last days of July, 1915).* What pain this separation caused me. But together with you it was offered to Our Lord. In seeing you so filled with strength and so heroic, I was filled with courage and asked myself: "Isn't Jesus the One who is her support and isn't He the One who is assisting her?"

I wrote you a letter in which I showed you my heart, and after a few days I went to see you, without realizing that very shortly I would also be there. During the semester my mother told us that we would enter as intern *(boarding)* students. Despite my pain, the least I could do was to thank the Lord, who was paving the way so I would become more separated from the things of the world. He was calling me to be with Him, so I'd become accustomed to live more apart from my family before my entrance into Carmel. *(From what Juanita writes here we see the immense sacrifice needed to adapt herself to the discipline of the boarding school; see also her letter to the Virgin. In her letters of February and March, 1916, she characterizes the boarding school as a jail or a dungeon. She gives us assurance that the thought of the school disturbed the happiness of her vacation and brought her to exclaim: "The boarding school should be reduced to ashes").*

What I suffered can be seen from the lines I wrote each day when I was getting ready for bed; they are a sort of diary. *(Juanita made several mistakes in dates; these have been corrected.)*

Thursday, 2 September 1915. It is 1 month and 2 days ago that they told us we would enter as boarding students.

I believe I shall never become accustomed to live far from my family: my father, my mother, those beings I love so much. Ah, if they knew how I suffer, they would sympathize with me! Nevertheless I must console myself. Will I live my whole life without being separated from them? This is what I would like: to repay them by taking care of them for all they've done for me. But the voice of God is demanding more and I must follow Jesus to the end of the world if He desires it. In Him I find everything. He alone takes up my thoughts. And all the rest, outside of Him, is shadow, affliction, and vanity. For Him I'd leave all things to go and hide behind the grilles of Carmel, if this is His will, and live for Him alone. What happiness, what joy! It's Heaven on earth.

But in the meantime, the years I'll have to wait before I give Him the most sweet name of Spouse seem like centuries. How sad are the days of this exile! Yet He's united to me and very often says to me: "My dearest friend." This infuses strength into me and I go on forcing myself to make myself a little less unworthy of the title that I'll bear. Where is the place where we'll celebrate our espousal and the place where we'll live united? He told me it will be Carmel. But each time I want to look at Him more closely, it seems that He covers Himself with a veil so that I see nothing, and without hope I retire sad and disconsolate. I see that my body will not resist and all those who are aware of this say to me that *(the Carmelite)* Order is very austere while your health is very delicate. But You, Jesus, are my Friend and as such You grant me your consolation. One day I went home for the day and found that the Mother Superior of Carmel *(of the Carmelite Monastery called Carmen Alto, then located across from Saint Lucy Hill on Carmel Street; today, it is at 3252 Pedro Valdivia Avenue),* without knowing me, had sent a picture of little Thérèse of the Child Jesus to me with my mother. It gave me great joy. I'll commend myself to little Thérèse so she may cure me and that I can become a Carmelite. But I only desire what fulfills the will of God. He knows best what is fitting for me. Oh, Jesus, I love You; I adore You with all my soul!

## 12. Toothache. Religious Vows. Visits.

First Friday. Last night Mother Izquierdo came to see me in my bedroom. I told her that I had a very bad toothache and had a headache all day. She spoke these words that Jesus had spoken to me in other trying circumstances: "My child, Jesus loves you very much. He surrounds you with His Cross. Offer this pain like a flower for your Communion tomorrow." I love this Sister very much. She's a true saint.

Wednesday the 8th. Today two novices took their vows; it made a great impression on me. They came forward and in the presence of the Sacred Host promised Him to be His brides. Oh, what sublime dignity! When will I be able to say my final farewells to the world? And one of the postulants received her habit. You can say that she's the bride of Jesus.

After that, young girls came from the day school and we were allowed to stay with them till 11:30.

I saw a great number of Sisters there, among them Mother Popelaire, who had been my teacher for 4 years. I love her very much and don't know why I felt sorry for myself and began to cry. This caused Rebecca to imitate me. Then I saw that it was necessary to be calm to console her, and this in effect is what happened.

We were with Mother Ríos. What pleasure could be greater! And as I do all that is possible to imagine I'm in Carmel, I sat on the ground at Mother's feet, an example the other girls followed.

On Sunday I shall be alone with Mother Ríos. This causes me fear since I'm thinking of telling her all the changes that have occurred in me since the operation, about my vocation to be a Carmelite, in short, everything. I don't know what I'll do, since it costs me so much to express all that's happening to me. I was happy all day long, but as always, Jesus sent me a little present: it was a cross, which pleased me very much.

Saturday the 11th. Even though I want to write in my diary every day, it's impossible for me. Today I went to Confession. What relief I felt, since I have sins that, even though they're involuntary, it doesn't please me to have since by them I'm separated from Jesus and I cause Him pain. And as I love Him, I would much rather die before offending Him. Yesterday and today I have not eaten caramels, since I have offered them to Jesus, which pleases Him more than me.

## 13. Decisive Interview.

Sunday the 12th. I have a lot to relate, and above all to give great thanks to Jesus because He allowed me to see Mother Ríos and tell her practically everything. We spoke a great deal. I told her that I was in no way used to this and she said the reason for this was the age in which I had entered. We rapidly passed over this, because she wanted to know what I had left her guessing about in my letter.

First, she made me begin to speak about my operation. She made me see the great goal to which God has destined me by restoring my life and the numerous favors He has granted me. I told her my resolution and she told me she had already guessed it, because God is planning something by giving me life for the second time.

I talked of my flirtation, and she asked me how I could have a boyfriend after so many calls from God. Even though it was not a sin, I should consider that the One who called me was the King of heaven and earth. Who was I to play in this way? Was I not a vile and miserable creature? Why should I give my love to a man when God was asking for it? If a man loved me and I paid attention to it, would I not be daring to divert myself? And why was I doing that with God? It is a very grave thing, it is much more serious than a marriage. She said I should consider that it was not for a day or for all of my life, but for eternity. Human love dies out, but divine love embraces everything. I should remember that many were called and few were chosen. Each time I go to Communion, she said, I should speak with dear Jesus about this and strive to become better each day by cultivating the virtues. I should make my prayer with my head on the ground, since I was speaking with the all-powerful One, the One who had abased Himself for me to choose me as His bride. *(Despite what Juanita wrote here, all who knew her unanimously affirmed that she never had any friendship with any particular young man; that she was very circumspect in her dealings with young men, even though she conducted herself spontaneously and joyfully with her brother's friends. This is a far cry from what we mean today by courtship. What she calls a courtship is reduced to not being rude, rewarding with a pleasant smile a young man who, manifesting his interest in her, sent her a bouquet of flowers or came to her house "walking up and down the block with her," as they then used to say).*

I also told her that I desired to enter Carmel. She asked me: And your health? Can you endure it? Oh, I'll not pay any attention to this miserable body. I'd like to fly but it won't let me. How much abhor you, vessel of corruption, because you oppose the desires of my soul. You are delicate. You don't take well to austerities, and you need to be spoiled. But my Jesus will do what He wants. May His holy will be fully accomplished. This cruel incertitude is like a torment for my soul. Because in this way it's better for me to unite myself to my Jesus in the Garden and console Him a little. It's the chalice that's approaching my lips, yet I believe He'll not force it on me.

Mother Ríos told me that she'd pray a great deal for me and my health, and that I should only think that I was to become the bride of Jesus. She recommended that I read the lives of Saint Teresa of Avila and of Saint Thérèse of the Child Jesus. I told her that I had read the latter many times and had drawn great profit from it since her soul had some points like mine. And also because I, like she, have received many favors from Our Lord, which made her come to perfection very quickly; while I repay Jesus so poorly. This moves me deeply and I promised Him to be better.

Rebecca arrived. I was sorry I had to leave.


## 14. September Vacation.

March 14. Today is the feast day of Mother Izquierdo. *(Mother Eugenia Izquierdo, the Sister in charge of the students, was distinguished for the solid formation she gave her pupils. After being Superior of*

*various houses, she died in September 1943).* We had a
free day and were very happy. We played a game of hide
and seek and afterward a game of catch the flags, and
our side won.

They read out the results of the handwriting contest.
I came out first. Fortunately there was not a single
mistake. Reverend Mother told us to come up to receive
a holy card, and when I went to receive it, Mother Ríos
smiled at me, which pleased me very much.

Today we went out. We were happy. We went to
Confession and afterward to the Alameda. I found
myself so distracted during this walk, since I was
mindful I should be thinking of Him. I tried to unite
myself to Him as much as possible; in this way I was
happy. We saw Miguel *(Juanita's older brother),* who
was doing military service. It was more than a month
since I had seen him. I love him so much. He was
promoted to corporal, the head of his squad. I'm very
happy.

Wednesday. Today I went to Mass and afterward to
the center with Lucía. In the afternoon we went to see
Inés and Maria Salas. After that the Zegers came and
later we went to see Salas Edwards, since Sylvia had
been operated on for appendicitis. From there I went to
see Carmen de Castro, but didn't find her. Only when
we were coming out did I see her for a moment on the
street. We embraced. We were happy; it had been such
a long time since we had seen one another. I love her so
much. She is very lovely.

Thursday 16. I find myself out in the country.
*(Juanita spent her vacation at Chacabuco, where her
Uncle Francisco Solar lived).* We arrived at 5 o'clock.
We walked all over. What happiness!

Friday 17. We went horseback riding. We went to see my uncle Francis and Maria Cáceres (a very old servant), and we also saw Juan Luís Domínguez, who is very sick and has been having fits of palsy. But here, thank God, he feels better.

Saturday 18. We went out early on horseback with my cousins. We enjoyed ourselves a great deal. Afterward, at 2, we flew kites, a game I greatly enjoy.

Sunday 19. We went to Mass. I was very distracted during it, since my cousins were in the presbytery looking at us. This was very trying. We sang, but I was not proud nor did I desire to draw attention to myself. Jesus helped me in this to overcome myself. I give Him thanks with all my heart.

Tuesday 21. Today I had the happiness of going to Communion. I felt I was so united to Him, I love Him so that it seems I'm in heaven and I continued in this union all day long. My Jesus, never separate Yourself from me!

Friday 24. Today we came back to school and I feel despondent and have crazy desires to cry. To You, my Jesus, I offer this pain, since I want to suffer to become like unto You, Jesus, my love.


## 15. To Suffer With Joy. Letter To The Virgin.

**Bride of Jesus, My Only Love.**

Today (*Sunday, October 24, 1915. She put Sunday 23*), ever since I got up, I feel very sad. It seems that suddenly my heart is breaking. Jesus told me that He wants me to suffer with joy. This costs me so, but it is sufficient that He asks this, so that I'll try to do it. Suffering pleases me for two reasons: first, because Jesus always preferred suffering, from His birth till His death on the cross. It must be something very great because He, the all-powerful One, seeks suffering in all things. Second, it pleases me because in the crucible of suffering souls are formed. And because Jesus sends this gift that was so pleasing to Him to the souls He loves most.

He told me that He joyfully ascended Calvary and laid His head on the cross for the salvation of humankind. "Is it possible that you are the one searching for Me and that you want to be like Me? Then, come with Me and take up the cross with love and joy."

I also found written in a copybook something entitled: "My Mirror." "My mirror must be Mary. Given that I'm her daughter, I must resemble her and thus I must resemble Jesus. I must love only Jesus. Hence my heart must hold the seal of God's love. My eyes must be fixed on Jesus Crucified. My ears must constantly attend to the voice of the Divine Crucified One.

"My tongue must tell Him my love. My feet must walk to Calvary. Consequently my pace must be slow and devout. My hands must embrace the Crucified, which is to say that the divine image must be impressed on my heart."

I also found a letter that I wrote one night when I could suffer no more:

"Dear Mother, Mother I almost idolize: I write you to unburden my heart that is being torn apart by pain. I do not wish, Mother of my soul, that you join its pieces but that my heart distill a little blood. The pain is choking me, my Mother. I'm suffering, but I'm happy suffering. I've taken the Cross from my Jesus. He is resting. What greater happiness could I have?

"I'm alone, my Mother. My mama is going to Viña today to see little Ignacio and we'll remain here. How long? I don't know. As long as Jesus wants. How does that seem so to you? I suffer...and I can do no more. I only ask that you heal the sick. You know who they are. You, Mother, can do this if you wish. My Mother, show that you are my Mother. Listen to the cry of my sinful but repentant soul, that suffers and consumes the chalice of pain to the dregs; but that does not matter. It gives me pain, but I love Jesus alone. I wish Him to be the Master of my heart. Tell Him that I love Him and that I adore Him. Tell Him that I want to suffer, that I want to die of love and suffering, that the world doesn't interest me, just He alone. Yes, Mother. I'm alone. I unite myself to your solitude. Console me, nourish me, counsel me, be my companion and bless me.

"You are my Mother and I tell you that I'm in pain. Previously my pain had a truce, a ray of light in my dark heart; but this ray of light no longer shines nor smiles for me. That smile of my mama made me live and I enjoyed it twice a week; but now I'll have it no longer. Tomorrow will be Wednesday and no one will call me to the parlor. Come with your Child, and my happiness will be complete.

"Help me to know my lessons, my reviews, my exams. Help me win prizes to make you and my Jesus and my parents happy. Mary, my Mother, hear me. Your child."

On the 7th of December I wrote: "Tomorrow is the greatest day of my life. I'm going to be the bride of Jesus. Who am I and Who is He? He, the all-powerful immense One, wisdom, goodness and purity itself is going to unite Himself to a poor sinner. Oh, Jesus, my love, my life, my comfort and joy, my everything! Tomorrow I will be Yours! Oh, Jesus, my love!

"My Mother, tomorrow I'll be doubly your child. I'm going to be the bride of Jesus. He'll place the nuptial ring on my finger. Oh, I'm happy, since I can truly say that He has been the only love of my heart."

My confessor gave me permission to make a vow of chastity for 9 days and afterward he will follow this up by telling me the dates when I can renew it. I'm happy. I have my formula written out: "Today, the 8th of December 1915, at 15 years of age, I make my vow before the most Holy Trinity and in the presence of the Virgin Mary and all the saints of Heaven, to not admit any other Spouse but my Lord Jesus Christ, whom I love with all my heart and whom I desire to serve till the last moment of my life. Vow taken for the novena of the Immaculate and to be renewed with the permission of my confessor."

This is the last entry I'm making this year. I didn't go back to write in my diary, but I do have my retreat notes and a letter I wrote to my sister Rebecca to tell her of my vocation to become a Carmelite and to ask her to help me. I wrote her on her birthday.

## 16. Letter To Rebecca.                 15 April, 1916

Dear Rebecca: I'm taking a few moments off from study to be able to wish you a thousand happinesses for your birthday, since one more year has been given to make you more serious and formal and this will be a motive to reflect on the vocation God has granted you.

Believe me, Rebecca, at 14 or 15 one understands one's vocation. You hear a voice and a light shows you the path of your life.

That beacon shone for me when I was 14 years old. I changed my course and planned the path that I had to follow, and today I come to share with you my secrets and the ideal projects I have forged.

210

Till today the same star has been shining on the two of us. But tomorrow perhaps we will no longer be united under its protective shadow. This star is our home, it is the family. It is necessary that we be separated and our hearts, which have been formed in the same way, will perhaps be separated tomorrow. Yesterday it seemed to me that you wouldn't understand my words, but today you are 14 years old, the age at which you can understand me. So I believe you'll put yourself in my place and you'll agree with me.

I will entrust to you the secret of my life in a few words. Very shortly we'll be separated and the desire we always cherished in our childhood to live together always is very quickly going to be shattered by another form of reality that is higher than our youth. We must follow different paths in life. To me has been given the better part, the same that was given to Magdalene. The Divine Master has taken pity on me. Drawing close to me, He said to me secretly: "Leave your father and mother and all that you possess, and follow Me."

Who can refuse the hand of the all-powerful One when He abases Himself to the most unworthy of His creatures? How happy I am, my dear sister! I've been captured in the loving nets of the Divine Fisherman. I'd like to make you understand this happiness. I can say with certainty that I am His promised one and that very soon we will celebrate our espousals in Carmel. I'm going to become a Carmelite. What do you think? I wouldn't want to keep anything in my soul hidden from you. But you know that I can't tell you in words all that I feel, and for this reason I've resolved to do it in writing.

I have handed myself over to Him. On the 8th of December I pledged myself to Him. It's impossible to say how much I love Him. My mind is taken up with Him alone. He is my ideal, an infinite ideal. I long for the day when I can go to Carmel to concern myself with Him alone, to abase myself in Him and so to live His life alone: To love and suffer to save souls. Yes, I thirst for souls because I know that is what my Jesus craves more than anything else. Oh, I love Him so!

I wish I could inflame you with that love. What happiness would be mine if I could give you to Him! Oh, I never have need of anything, because in Jesus I find all that I'm looking for! He never abandons me. His love never diminishes. He is so pure, so beautiful. He is goodness itself. Pray to Him for me, my Rebecca dear. I need prayers. I see that my vocation is very great: to save souls, to give workers to the vineyard of Christ. In comparison with the value of one soul, all the sacrifices we make are small in comparison. God gave His life for them and how we disregard their salvation. As one betrothed to Him, I must thirst for souls, and offer my Espoused the blood He shed for each of them. And what are the means for gaining these souls? Prayer, mortification and suffering.

He comes with His cross, and above it is written only one word that moves my heart to its innermost fibers: "Love." Oh how beautiful He appears with His tunic of blood! That blood is more precious to me than all the jewels and diamonds in the whole world.

Those who love one another on earth try, my Rebecca dear, as you see in Lucía and Chiro, to have one single soul and one single ideal, but their efforts are useless since creatures are so helpless. This doesn't happen in our union. Jesus already lives in my heart. I strive to unite myself, to become like Him and abase myself in Him. I'm a drop of water that must disappear in the Infinite Ocean. But there is an abyss that the drop cannot cross; and the ocean overflows in such a way that the drop of water remains in the most complete abandonment of itself and lives in a continuous whisper, calling to the Divine Ocean.

But I'm only a poor little bird without wings. Who will give me wings so I can go and build my nest so as to be always close to Him? Love. Oh, yes, I love Him and I want to die for Him. My love is so great that I'd like to be martyred so I can prove to Him that I love Him.

Doubtless your sisterly heart is torn apart on hearing me speak of separation, on hearing me murmur that word: farewell forever on earth in order to enclose myself in Carmel. But be not afraid, my dear little sister. There will never be any separation between our souls. I will live in Him. Search for Jesus and in Him you will find me and there we three will carry on these intimate conversations that we must always carry on there for all eternity. How happy I am! I invite you to spend time with Jesus in the depths of your soul. I have read in the life of Elizabeth of the Trinity how that little saint asked Our Lord to make her soul His little home. Let's make ours such. My dearest little one, let's live with Jesus within ourselves. He'll tell us things unknown. His lullaby of love is so sweet. Like Elizabeth, we'll find heaven on earth, because God is Heaven.

We'll ask Jesus in Communion that He build in our souls a little home; that we can arrange the material that must be our acts of overcoming self and of forgetfulness of ourselves, making our ego disappear, for these are the gods we adore interiorly. This is costly and will draw from us cries of pain. But Jesus asks for that throne and we must give it to Him. Charity must be the weapon to overcome those gods. Let's be concerned about our neighbors and serving them, even when it's

213

repugnant to do this. In that way we will obtain that the throne of our heart be occupied by its Master, by God our Creator.

Let's overcome ourselves. Let's be obedient in all things. Let's be humble. We are so miserable! Let's be patient and pure as the angels and we'll have the joy of seeing Jesus, who is a good architect, build a second house of Bethany, where you can concern yourself with serving Him in the person of your neighbors, as Martha did, and I, like Magdalene, will remain contemplating and listening to His word of life. While we are still in school it is impossible that He will demand of us the total union that consists of being occupied only with Him. But each hour we can offer Him a little bouquet of love.

Let's love the divine little Child who suffers so much without finding consolation in His creatures. May He find a refuge in our souls, a haven where He can heal in the midst of the hatred of His enemies and a garden of delights where He can forget the forgetfulness of His friends. I must bring my letter to a close. Farewell. Answer this letter of mine and keep it a complete secret. Your sister who loves you in Jesus,        Juana

## 17. Retreat Of 1916.

To make the spiritual exercises well, two things are necessary: 1) To be courageous and generous; 2) To place oneself into God's hands.

**FIRST MEDITATION:** For God, of God and unto God. This is the goal of every creature. We were created by God. How great is God's goodness, since He had us in His mind from eternity and afterward drew us forth from nothingness. I am a bit of mud but there is something

214

greater in me: my soul which God made to His image and likeness. The only thing I have that's valuable is my soul, because it's immortal. It's greater than the world, because the world has an end. My soul is not of the world. Consequently, it is of God, the only One capable of satisfying it because He's infinite. I am of God. He created me. He is my beginning and my end. To be entirely His, I must perfectly fulfill His divine Will. If He is my Father then He knows the present, the past and the future, so why shouldn't I abandon myself to Him with complete confidence?

COLLOQUY: About my particular examination of conscience: I should make it about a sin, or a capital defect or to acquire a virtue.

SECOND MEDITATION: Why were we created? To serve and love God above all things. God endowed us with reason so that we may grasp the benefit of creation. How should we serve God? As a slave serves his master, by doing what pleases Him. God has made His Will known to me. If I fulfill it, I glorify Him, but by always doing what is most perfect. To serve God we must be indifferent to all that doesn't give Him glory. We must hold God as the goal of our works and consider the love He has for us in every one of the events He sends us, and consider everything as stepping stones that bring us to Him. Our hearts must not be attached to the things of the world but to God alone. We must keep our heart pure of all disordered love, since everything is passing away. We must love only what brings us to God.

THIRD MEDITATION: Sin is monstrous. The first two sins. Lucifer in heaven, by only one sin of thought, was converted into a devil. How many sins have I committed in my life? God did not punish me; rather, on the contrary, He has overwhelmed me with His graces.

How many times has He pardoned me! He dismissed our first parents because of only one act of disobedience. With what will I repay You, my God. Depart, sin, from me. I abhor you with a terrible hatred. I want to belong to God. I'd prefer to die rather than commit sin. Forgive me, my God, pardon me, You who are goodness and infinite mercy. I'd rather die than offend You, even by the slightest fault. I love You but sin separates me from You.

**COLLOQUY:** About the vanity of life. Of the ordered love we must have for all things. Our heart must belong to the Most Holy Trinity. I want to live within my soul in such a way so I'll always contemplate God in it.

There are three classes of souls: First, those who are in mortal sin, who are attracted by sensuality and live in this way. Second, those who live in grace and experience peace, interior consolations and desires to be good. Third, those who feel no interior consolation, but experience the impulses of grace and follow them and resist nature. This is the best state because we live in humility.

**FOURTH MEDITATION:** The repentant Magdalene. Oh, Lord, how great You are in Your mercy! I prostrate myself at Your feet and wash them with my flood of tears. Yes, adored Jesus, I sinned; but You have saved me. I come to humiliate myself before Your minister who represents You. Yes, Jesus, You who pardoned Magdalene, pardon a greater sinner than she. All my life I have loved You and I hope to love You to the end. Forgive me, Jesus, because I didn't know what I was doing in offending You. Yes, Jesus; I'd sooner die than offend You. Like Magdalene I desire to retire and serve You, to be always joined to You. I love no one but

You. I'd like to unite myself to You always because happiness consists of loving only You.

**FIFTH MEDITATION:** The word of a king who invites his subjects to conquer the land of the infidels. Jesus invites us to the conquest of the kingdom of His Most Sacred Heart. For this reason we must: First, reform ourselves, be ready for all suffering so as to rejoice afterward with Him in heaven. Second, be disposed to follow Jesus wherever He desires. He chose poverty, humiliations, the cross and demands of me all these gifts. Should I not receive them joyfully since He created me, by preferring me to so many souls, since He spares my life and has preserved me from hell? Even more still, because He suffered all sorts of trials for 33 years and then died on a cross between two thieves as the most infamous of men, being considered a deceiver, a bewitcher, a traitor, a madman, a blasphemer? And I, shall I desire not to suffer anything for His love? I who am only a criminal nothingness, while He who suffers is a God who has the right to be adored and served by His creatures. Oh, Jesus, You keep me here prostrate before Your Divine Majesty, full of shame and confusion in seeing my littleness, my misery and my many sins. How long, my Jesus, will You have pity on this sinner? From now on, I am going to place myself into Your divine hands. Do with me what You wish. Yes, I am disposed to be humbled to chastise my pride. My adored Spouse, I want to live a hidden life, to disappear in You, to have no other life than Yours, to concern myself with You alone. Now that I am also purified, I desire that the Most Blessed Trinity may come and dwell in my soul so that I can adore You and live constantly in Your presence. Finally, I can tell You that I'm making my vow in the presence of the Most Blessed Trinity, and of the Most

Holy Virgin and Saint Joseph and the saints and angels of heaven; to have no other Spouse but Jesus, the only love of my soul.

## J. M. J.   RESOLUTIONS   A. M. D. G.

Mary, my Mother, bless me. (1) I'll make a particular examination of conscience. (2) I'll practice the third degree of humility, which consists of seeking, with joy, to be despised, dishonored, humiliated for love of Jesus Christ, considering myself unworthy to suffer anything for Him. (3) Each time I fall, I'll rise and impose a mortification on myself, if I'm allowed.

My Jesus, I have now seen that everything in the world is vanity, that only one thing is necessary: to love You and serve You with fidelity, to resemble and make myself entirely like unto You. This will be my sole ambition. I wish to travel with You joyfully through all disgrace. And if I fall because of my weakness, my dear Jesus, I will look at You in Your ascent of Calvary and helped by You I will rise again. Don't permit me to offend You even slightly. I would prefer a thousand deaths rather than give You the slightest pain.

My Mother, lily amid the thorns, teach me the way of Calvary. May your hand guide me along that path. Saint Joseph, guardian of virgins, protect me.

### Year 1917

## 18. Meditation, Mirror Of The Soul.

January first. One year closer to my homeland. How many benefits did I receive and how many graces did I squandered during this year that just ended? And the coming year, under its mysterious mantle, will perhaps contain all kinds of pain and happiness. Let's lean upon the cross. It is unchangeable. Neither centuries nor storms have broken it. Spes unica (*our only hope*).

January second. I am sad. My heart is bleeding. Oh, if I could, I'd offer up a thousand lives for Him; my God send me all sufferings, and give me the grace to bear them so that his soul may be converted!

My Jesus, I want to keep You company in the garden during Your agony. I want to console You and say with You: "Lord, if it be possible, let this bitter chalice pass from me; but not my will but Thine be done."

January 9. Every day I make my meditation and see what a great help it is to sanctify oneself. It is the mirror of the soul. How one comes to know self through meditation. Jesus has made me understand that to come to perfection three things are necessary: first, a love of prayer. Second, complete detachment from self, that is to say, forgetfulness of self which is acquired by uniting oneself to Jesus in such a way that one comes to form with Him only one person and always takes to heart what is pleasing to Jesus: that is, humiliations, pain, etc., and also charity toward neighbor. Third, perfect surrender of self, that is to say, the will to give oneself to God.

I read in the *Autobiography* of Saint Teresa that this Saint recommends to those who are beginning the practice of prayer to imagine their soul as a garden filled with weeds and harmful trees and all dry. Then, as they begin to grow in prayer, the Lord will place beautiful plants in it and we must care for them so they don't dry up. For this reason it is always necessary for beginners to draw water from the well. This is costly, since each one meets difficulties in the beginning of the practice of prayers. (*Life of Saint Teresa of Avila, chapter 11, n. 6 and following*).

For me it is human respect: others might see me meditating and might call me pious. Also there are times when I cannot hear the Lord's voice, and this separates me from Him. But now I'm resolved, cost what it may, to practice prayer each day. Everyday I'm going to write down the resolutions I draw from prayer.

January 24. Perfect obedience. To obey by taking into account that it is God to whom I submit my will. My obedience must be spiritual.

January 25. Today I promised my Jesus to fulfill His Divine Will by accepting with joy whatever He commands. The bride must unite her will to her groom's and submit herself to Him. With even much more reason, I who am His slave. Out of His great kindness He has made me His daughter and bride. How wicked and sinful I find myself!

## 19. Lourdes. Mary, Mother Full of Sweetness.

February 12. The day before and yesterday we went to Lourdes *(the Grotto of the Virgin of Lourdes in Santiago).* Lourdes! This word alone causes the deepest cords to vibrate in the Christian, the Catholic. Lourdes! Who doesn't feel moved when pronouncing that word! It means Heaven in this exile. The word bears under its mantle of mystery whatever great things the Catholic heart is capable of feeling. Her name causes past memories to be taken away and deeply touches the intimate feelings of our soul. It contains joy, superhuman peace, whence the pilgrim, fatigued by the sorrowful journey of life, can find rest; can without fear put down his baggage, which is our human miseries, and open his mouth to receive the water of consolation and comfort. It is where the tears of the poor are mixed with the tears of the rich, where they meet only a Mother who is gazing on them and smiling on them. And in that celestial gaze and smile there gush forth sobs from all breasts so that their hearts are filled with happiness and they cannot pull themselves away. It makes them hope and love the eternal and the divine.

Yes, Mother, you are the celestial Madonna who guides us. You allow heavenly rays to fall from your maternal hands. I didn't believe such happiness could exist on earth; yesterday my heart, while thirsting for it, found it. My sould was ecstatic at your virginal feet, listening to you. You were speaking and your maternal language was so tender. It was from heaven, almost divine.

In seeing You so pure, so tender, and so compassionate, who would not be encouraged to unburden his intimate suffereings to you? Who would not ask you to be his star on this stormy sea? Who is there who would not cry in your arms without instantly receiving your immaculate kisses of love and comfort? If he be a sinner, your caresses will soften him. If one of your devoted ones, your presence would enkindle the living flame of divine love. If he be poor, you with your powerful hand will aid him and show him his true homeland. If rich, you will sustain him with your breath against the dangers of his very agitated life. If one is in affliction, you with your tearful gaze will show him the cross and on it your Divine Son. Who will not find balm for his pains by considering the torments of Jesus and Mary? The sick man finds in your maternal heart the water of salvation that allows your enchanting smile to blossom forth, and makes him smile with love and happiness. Yes, Mary, you are Mother of the entire universe. Your heart is filled with sweetness. At your feet let the priest prostate himself with the same confidence as the virgin in order to find in your arms the fullness of your love. The rich as well as the poor can find in your heart their heaven. The afflicted as well as the happy can find on your mouth a celestial smile. The sick as well as the healthy can find caresses from your sweet hands. And, finally, sinners like myself find in you a protecting Mother who can crush beneath her immaculate feet the head of the dragon. And in your eyes I see mercy, pardon and a shining lamp to keep me from falling into the muddy waters of sin.

Yes, my Mother. At Lourdes I found heaven. God was on the altar surrounded by angels and you, from the concave of the rock, offered Him the cries of the multitude kneeling before your altar. You asked Him to hear the supplications of the people banished in this valley of tears, while at the same time, together with their hymns, they were offering you their hearts full of love and gratitude.

## 20. Resolutions For 1917.

1) To accept sacrifices interiorly without murmuring or being discouraged.

2) I must be more hidden.

3) I must strive to work for the happiness of others.

4) I will try to practice virtue in an amiable way for the sake of others.

5) I must forget myself: 1. by uniting myself to Jesus; 2. in being charitable to my neighbor; 3. in not giving my opinion unless asked; 4. in suffering humiliations with joy be being nice to those who cause me humiliations; 5. by living with Jesus in the depths of my soul, which must be His little home where He can repose. I will adore Him and offer Him mortifications, sufferings and humiliations. "To live with God, isn't this heaven on earth?

To live with Him in unity of thoughts, sentiments, and actions so that in looking at me the Father will find the image of His Son. And the Holy Spirit, in seeing the Father and Son residing in me, will make me His bride, and the three Persons will come to make their abode in me.

I must contemplate Jesus Crucified in my soul. I will imitate Him and receive the Blood of my Jesus at the foot of the cross, which I will preserve in my soul and which I must communicate to the souls of my neighbors so that, through the Blood of Christ, they may be washed clean. *(These resolutions were inspired by the book* **HISTORIA DE UN ALMA REPARADORA, by M.S.S.** *(Barcelona, 1912). On a loose sheet of paper from one of Juanita's letters we find these proposals: "J. M J.T. 1. I will make my particular examination of conscience. 2. If I fall, I will seek the help of the Virgin. 3. I will be all things to all people").*

## 21. Offering For Sinners. New Director.

My Jesus, You know the offering I have made You of myself for the conversion of the persons I have mentioned to You. From today on, I not only offer my life, but also my death the way it is most pleasing to You. I am yours, do unto me whatever is Your Holy Will. I will receive it with pleasure, whether it be the abandonment of Calvary or the paradise of Nazareth. Furthermore, if You want, give me sufferings, the cross, and humiliations. May I be trod underfoot as a punishment for my own pride as well as that of others. My Jesus, whatever You like. I am Yours, do unto me according to Your Holy Will. To you, O Mary, who have never left unheard the prayers I directed to you when I came to you as a child coming to her mother, I also place these souls in your maternal hands. Hear me. All through my life I have never ceased to petition you, my Mother. Listen to me, I ask you in the name of Jesus and through your spouse, Saint Joseph, that you intercede for this sinner.

I suffer. This expresses everything! Happiness! When I'm suffering I'm on the cross of my Jesus. What happiness could be greater than to tell Him: Jesus, my Spouse, remember I am your bride, give me Your cross.

April 1917. Thanks, my God, for you have given me a director *(Father José Blanch, C.M.F.)* who will direct my soul toward You.

He asked me about my state of prayer, was it empty or devout? I told him sometimes it is with devotion; but there were periods when I was unable to meditate and I remained tranquil with Our Lord. He said I must always strive to reflect, and to do the other only as a last resort. I should live constantly in the presence of God dwelling within my soul, and do this as frequently as possible. I should make this a subject of my examination of conscience. He told me to mark down the thoughts and affections of meditation that most move me to devotion. He permitted me to mortify myself by mortifications in eating and by sacrificing my taste, also to pray for a quarter of an hour with my arms extended in a cross or to pray three Our Fathers while kneeling on my hands. Later he will give me permission to wear the hair shirt. This is to be kept very secret. I should not speak about my vocation except with my mother and Mother Izquierdo because it is like perfume contained in a bottle that disappears entirely when it is opened. I should attract my friends to the service of God.

What gave me the greatest consolation and joy was when he told me I had a vocation to be a Carmelite. He asked me what virtue I preffered. I answered: humility. Then he gave me permission to renew my vow of virginity until the feast of the Assumption of the Virgin.

Resolution: a soul to be saved; a death to be feared; a life to be sanctified.

Silence. Celebration is found in silence. I feel I'm filled with Him. I love Him.


## 22. A Good Copy of Jesus? Child of Mary.

The feast of the Ascension of the Lord in the heaven of my soul. I'll do all things in union with Him, through Him and for Him. I'll console Him. I want to be crucified. And He left me His nails.

The more we unite ourselved to the Creator, the more we detach ourselves from creatures. My Jesus, Spouse of my soul, I love You. I am all Yours. I know You are all mine.

Tomorrow is the feast of the Trinity. *(The feast of the Ascension was on May 17, the feast of the Most Holy Trinity, June 3)*. Will the Father find the image of Christ in me? Oh, how much is lacking for me to be like Him! I haven't sufficient virtues. I at once become discouraged. Still, I'm more humble or I humble myself more and have more faith. The other day the little girls were misbehaving at table and I be came very impatient. Since I let them go on talking, I was told that I should have been stricter with them. I said they didn't listen to me. I became very angry, and when I saw the children I told them they were disagreeable. Would Jesus have acted in that way? Of course not! He would have scolded them and would not have excused them, but He would not have insulted them as I did. It's true that it took me a long time to get control of myself, but afterward I spoke of my anger, and the next day to humble myself I begged forgiveness from the children. These falls serve to make me aware that I'm still very imperfect.

June 15, 1917. Not only am I the spouse of Jesus, but today I have united myself even more to Him. I am His sister. I am the child of Mary. From today on, like the princesses bought to the palace of the betrothed to be formed like Him, I now also am going to enter into my soul, the house of God. There my Mother and my Jesus await me. Oh, how I love Him! *(Juanita received her medal as a Child of Mary on June 15, the feast of the Sacred Heart of Jesus. In nearly all the letters she writes from this time on, she adds H.M. to her signature. Translated from the Spanish these initials mean Child of Mary).*

I went to confession yesterday. The priest told me that three things are necessary to avoid impatience: 1) Never manifest my anger exteriorly; 2) Be lovable with the person who causes my anger; and 3) To be silent, to put down anger in my heart. The three essential parts of meditation are reflections, colloquy, petition.

## 23. More United With Jesus. Costly Victories.

June 19. Today I united myself to Our Lord. From the time I obtained that crucifix, I live more united with Him. Oh, how I love Him! I offered myself to Him for the conversion of those persons. How I suffer in thinking that there is the devil, not God, in these souls, that Jesus is calling them and He awaits them in the tabernacle and they remain insensitive. Oh, my God, how You love us and how ungrateful we are. My Jesus! Spouse of my soul, I offer myself to You. Do with me what You will.

Today I conquered myself greatly so I would not

become angry. My God, You have come to my aid. I give You thanks. In doing my chores and recreations I have done them perfectly. But this was not so in my classes.

Our Lord said to me that He would not accept my offering; but He would hear me and grant the conversion of those souls, but after a little more time. He said to me that I should unite myself to the crucified One, that He desired to see me crucified. I've suffered so much that I wept all during Mass this morning. But tomorrow I'll offer my tears for them.

Yesterday my meditation was good. I did what the priest told me to do. I made a very great act. I was studying in the garden when Rebecca came to give me a message from Mother Ríos for her and for me. I overcame my curiosity, even though I desired to know, and said I didn't want to hear anything, that she should go away. All day long my curiosity was piqued till supper time when she told us the message. This act which was so costly to me, I offered up for those souls.

June 20. I carried out my resolve to mortify myself as much as possible. I have denied Our Lord no deed.

Tomorrow is the feast of Saint Aloysius Gonzaga. I want to make a vow of never committing any voluntary sin. My Jesus, help me to fulfill this vow. My meditation was good. I did what the priest recommended. This morning my Jesus spoke to me for a long time. He took me to His heart and told me that He loved me. His voice was so sweet! I love Him so. I am all His. he told me I should count the acts I perform, but I forgot. he also told me to imitate Him.

## 24. To Be Humble. Not To Speak of Self.

June 22. I'm making a resolution of never speaking about myself, neither for good nor for evil. I'd like to shed tears of gratitude for the one intention He has already granted me: that gentleman is now reconciled with the Church. Oh, how good You are, my Jesus, how I love you! Oh, Virgin, my Mother, you have heard me! But I ask you for more: perseverance and even the conversion of the other person. Mother, I plead with You, for the sake of Jesus.

Today I accomplished two great acts of humility. How much they cost me, but the Virgin helped me. The other day in recreation we were sketching silent pictures. Then I said that we should dress up like the Mother Assistant. I didn't think it was a lack of charity, but one little girl told me she took it that way. Then I understood how wicked I am. Instead of giving good example, I incited others to sin. I'm unworthy to wear the medal of a Child of Mary. I finally asked forgiveness for the bad example I gave. I'll tell this to Mother Izquierdo so she can correct me and humble me before the Congregation. I want to be humble with Christ crucified.

I did what the good Jesus asked of me, thank God. I humbled myself for Him, although they cannot be called humiliations, since I am nothingness. More than that, I'm a criminal nothingness.

I tried not to mention myself, nor to speak of myself. It was very costly, but I'll do it for Jesus and to console Him. Last night He told me He was suffering greatly. He reclined on my heart and there He cried and I together with Him. A new persecution was beginning against Him, he told me, and said He loved us so much He was unable to live without us.

Every night I give Him a kiss in which I give Him my whole being. I'm so close to His altar that only a door separates us. Then I imagine He is a prisoner and I'm opening His prison and taking Him to my heart.

Today I tried to do all the good I possibly could. Nevertheless I have not been sufficiently silent, since I shouldn't speak, even to advise others.

## 25. Only God does Not Change. Incomprehension.
### First In History Class.

Tomorrow is my feast day. Perhaps it'll be the last one I'll spend in the world. Would that it were so. In the past I used to look forward to this day with so much ardor. Today I hate it.

June 24. Today I suffered much because my mother didn't embrace me until 10:30, even after much pleading. Nevertheless, I was very happy. Upon waking this morning, the Virgin, my Mother, congratulated me. She was the first. Jesus told me that He did not congratulate me because this was not customary between spouses. He only gave me presents. What an idea! Jesus! All day long I suffered because I wished them to treat me kindly, especially because it was my feastday. Human hearts love one day but are indifferent the next. God alone doesn't change.

June 25. I have known one thing and I'm at the point that I can suffer no more pain. It would have been better not to know anything. My God, I offer that to You. I know You are my protection. I beseech you for that person.

June 26. I felt distressed. I hardly dare look at Mother Izquierdo, because I think she'll think I'm a liar.

Finally, what can I do? I did it because I had reason. I saw what I started. May God pardon that person. I

229

prayed for her, so that she doesn't fall any lower. Yesterday my pain was so great that I became ill. During the night I was almost agonizing, but Jesus and my Mother consoled me. I'm suffering this for Him. Such was the impression I had on seeing people so deficient, that I doubted my vocation because I thought it was all hypocrisy. But Jesus said to me that I must not be surprised, since one of His apostles had fallen, and that I should pray for her. They *(the other girls at school)* told me all kinds of things that made me believe that all was lost. They even told me things that Mother Izquierdo was thinking about me. Then I became very upset, since I had said this to prevent a Nun from giving bad example. Finally, may God's will be done. I am what I am in the presence of God. What does the opinion of creatures matter?

June 27. I came out first in my history class. I'm happy. Never before did I have positions of honor, and now the Virgin is giving them to me. I also asked for them to please my father and mother and, above all, because this will be my last year in school and I want to leave a good impression so people see that, even though I'm thinking of becoming a Carmelite nun, I did apply myself to my studies. I find that I'm stupid and if I'm granted positions of honor they are due to Jesus and my Mother. I love her. She is so good!

June 28. Today I heard from Mother Ríos. She sent us her greetings. I so love that sister that I must overcome myself so I'll not love her too much and write to her. If she knew the sacrifices I made so I would not have to take time out from my studies. But, in the end, God knows those sacrifices and the fact that I offered them for her intentions so that He'd grant them.

June 29. Alleluia! Today, thank God, was a perfect

day to console Our Lord. I didn't speak at all. I overcame myself sufficiently, especially because I felt very strange. I had a desire to cry, to be angry, to speak and shout.

## 26. It Is So Rich To Give. Self Love.

June 30. Last night I cried when I saw Him on that cross, fastened with nails for my love. How good he is and how ungrateful I've been. Tomorrow I'm going to exercise my apostolate. May Our Lord and my Mother grant that I have happy results.

I collected 30 pesos on my feast day. I'm going to buy shoes for Juanito, and the rest I'll give to my mother to hold for me so it will be given to the poor. It is so rich to give to the poor. I gave my shoes to Juanito's nurse. *(Juanito was a very poor little boy whom she took care of permanently, using money from her own allowance. To raise funds to help him, Juanita even pawned her watch. When she entered Carmel she asked her family to care for him and, from the convent, showed her concern for him in various letters).*

Tuesday, July 3. Yesterday we went out. We had a good time with the girls. We thoroughly enjoyed ourselves, even though I had enough pain when I saw them teasing Rebecca and seeing that Lucía went with her and paid no attention to me. I'm happy they praise her, but I'd be more pleased if they could do the same for me. When they praise me, I praise her as well.

Furthermore, Lucía invited the nuns and Rebecca, but not me. And I really desired this, but I had to make the sacrifice, since Jesus has asked this of me. I played the piano when they asked me. All my pain was motivated by the self-love I have. I'm resolved to kill it in its roots. May Jesus and Mary help me.

I spoke with Carmen. *(Carmen de Castro Ortúzar, one of Juanita's best friends. She had been a Carmelite in the Monastery of Talca).* She told me that she had been with Mother Superior and had discussed her vocation. But, although she'd like to be a nun because she finds they are very happy, she is frightened. I spoke to the priest about this. He said perhaps it would be better if she lived as a religious in her own home. I'll tell her that when I see her.

Wednesday 4. Today I had a perfect day and I'm going to offer it for the intentions of Mother Ríos. I sacrificed my visit to the Blessed Sacrament to distribute the books; it was difficult but Jesus knows what I wanted to do.

The priest told me I should make my meditation in the morning, but the Virgin did not awaken me. Tomorrow I'll try for the last time. My Mother, why don't you hear me? Are you possible angry with me? You know that I love you always. Hear me and awaken me. I've forgotten the intention of my meditation. I don't know what to do.

## 27. I Am Very Proud. I Nearly Became Angry.

Thursday July 5. I must say nothing today. I haven't been perfect. I spoke in French class. Nevertheless, I conquered myself sufficiently. Tomorrow I'll make a day of retreat. I need it so badly. I unite myself to Our Lord but I don't imitate Him. I'm still very proud. I'm resolved to destroy the last germs of my self-love. I don't know on what I can base this proposal, since I'm a criminal nothingness. I'm pleased when I'm esteemed by people, but what use is this if God doesn't esteem me?

First Friday. Today I tried to make a retreat, though

it didn't work out. Still, I drew profit from my meditation, since I meditated on God and, when I think of Him, I remain submerged in love. I see His infinite greatness and my extreme misery, and I see what is sin and God's great love. Furthermore, I conversed with Jesus and He made me understand the insignificance of human esteem. One day they think I'm good; tomorrow they'll see a defect and at once find I'm wicked. What does it matter to be loved by creatures and be filled with honors, if God, the Infinite Being, despises one?

Today I made a vow not to commit a voluntary sin and thanks be to God I kept it. The priests preach very well. It seems that Jesus chose the sermon for me. The priest spoke about imitation of Jesus; "Learn of Me for I am gentle and humble of heart and thus you will find peace." Even though we may suffer persecutions etc., if we imitate Christ we'll be in peace. Birds like the Condor have wings and heavy feathers but they ascend to great heights even though it's raining, etc. In the same way the soul spreads its wings and is raised aloft. And those wings are the love of God.

Today I exercised my apostolate. I gave good advice. Jesus inspired me with it. I also made three young girls take their soup, encouraging them to perform little deeds for the good Jesus. Furthermore, we went to see a little sick girl. So, we had a chance to perform an act of charity. Jesus my dear, when will I be at Your side? I love you! I desire to unite myself to You eternally.

Saturday the 7th. I'm upset. I can do no more. My Jesus, I unite myself to You. Do as you wish and not my will. Today I asked Rebecca to beg pardon, but it was all useless. I asked this in honor of the Virgin but she didn't want to listen to me. All is lost. Afterward she said to me that just because I had asked her she didn't want to do it; that her concerns shouldn't matter to me. Nevertheless, to obtain her forgiveness I offered by bonbons for the whole week.

July 9. The little girls teased me so much in class that I finally began to cry. I had a headache and my back ached so that I didn't know what was happening to me. I didn't answer them because I didn't want to break the silence. I offered it to the good Jesus. But then, at recess time I told them they should go to the other side of the room, that they shouldn't tease me so much. Then I almost became angry, but afterward we made up very nicely and in the afternoon they sent me a holy card. It cost me dearly to put up with the teasing, but the little ones told me that I have a very good temperament and, because I don't get angry but go along with the teasing, they do it to me. Each day I feel that they love me more and this is because I give them good example.

## 28. In Bed. Surrender To The Will of God. Reading Sister Elizabeth of The Trinity.

July 10. I'm in bed with a cold. I haven't spoken sufficiently with Jesus. I feel Him within my soul. This morning I hungered for Jesus because I couldn't go to Communion. Since I returned from Chacabuco I have missed Communion only one day. I've received Communion 149 times.

July 13. Today I'm 17 years old; one year less of life. One less year separating me from death, from eternal union with God. Only one more year before I'll arrive at the harbor of Carmel. Oh, Carmel! When will you open your sacred portals? How many graces the Lord has granted me and how ill I've repaid Him. My Jesus, forgive me my ingratitude.

July 15. I was quite ill yesterday. They gave me some medicine that caused quite a bit of pain, but I didn't complain. I was happy because I was suffering; when I felt them giving me injections in my shoulders, I remembered my sweet Jesus when they scourged Him. I was happy and didn't betray my pain. Nevertheless, the last time I could hardly speak. Then I went to bed. Because of this they asked me if I was suffering. But I told them I was tired. I didn't lie, since that was true. Rebecca told me I was going to lose my grades, they weren't going to pass me and that I'd be leaving school. At first I was upset. But afterward I thought that it was the Virgin who had granted me those grades and honors and that now it was the will of God that I be sick. So, my Mother was happy in seeing me resigned. I was contented and said that was God's will, above all because I had asked the Virgin to obtain the prize for me, and I certainly hope it will be given to me. If not, the eternal prize will be given to me, since I'm doing this to fulfill my duty. Today I'm going to try to appear cheerful when they give me the medicine. For the sake of Jesus.

I'm reading Elizabeth of the Most Holy Trinity (*The Discalced Carmelite Nun of the Carmel of Dijon (France). She died in 1906 and was beatified by Pope John Paul II on November 25, 1984*) She enchants me. Her soul is like mine. Though she was a saint, I'll imitate her and become a saint. I want to live with Jesus in the intimate depths of my soul. I want to defend Him from His enemies. I want to live a life of heaven, as Elizabeth says, by being a praise of His glory: 1. By living a divine life. By loving God with pure love. By giving myself to Him without reserve. By living in intimate communion with the Spouse of my soul. 2. By fulfilling the will of God in all things. How? By fulfilling my obligations joyfully at every moment. Nothing must disturb me. All must be peace, like the peace that inundates the angels in heaven. 3. By living in silence, because in this way the Holy Spirit will draw forth from me harmonious sounds and the Father, together with the Spirit, will form the image of the Word in me. 4. By suffering, since Christ suffered His whole life long and was the praise of the glory of His Father. I'll suffer with joy for my sins and for sinners. 5. By living a life of faith. By considering all things from a supernatural point of view. By reflecting Christ as if in a mirror in our actions. 6. By living in a continual state of thanksgiving, that our thoughts, desires and acts may be a perpetual thanksgiving. 7. Living in continual adoration, like the angels, by repeating: "Holy, holy," etc. And since we can't be constantly in prayer, at least let's renew our intention before each exercise, and thus we'll be a praise of glory and we will live a life of Heaven. What is more, we must become more and more inflamed with zeal for the divine glory.

## 29. "We Are Going Into Solitude." (Retreat of 1917).

August 8. Today I'm going on retreat. I hear the voice of my Jesus who tells me, "We are going into solitude." "I'll lead her into solitude and there I'll speak to her heart" *(Hosea 2:14)*. I'll retire with Him into the intimate depths of my soul and there, as in another Nazareth, I'll live in His company with my Mother and Saint Joseph. Jesus told me He will search through His little house to see what's lacking so that He can purify it.

Oh, how great I consider myself to be after having seen my origin - all one God! - and my goal: an Infinite God! But there's a point between the beginning and the end, and that is life. What must I do then, while I'm living? Serve, honor, love and glorify my Creator. And how? Here is my will. If I'm generous, I'll give myself totally to my Jesus, who has given everything to me. The creatures and all that I possess God has given me. Consequently I must use them even though they don't belong to me. In short, then, I must fulfill the Will of God, who is my Creator, my Savior and my All. I belong to Him.

What are all things if not vanity.Everything passes away, everything dies. Then why attach myself to passing things that don't bring me to God who is my goal? Oh, my God, I don't know how to repay You for the many benefits You granted me. Lord, from now on I want to be faithful to You. I have given myself to You, I want to give myself completely to You. From now on I'll begin to reflect only You, since You alone are the Sovereign Being. I desire that all my actions be according to Your will. Poverty or disdain no longer bother me, because they bring me to You. I want to be indifferent to all things, except to God and my soul.

Oh, how ungrateful I see myself to be with my God! I'm filled with confusion and shame for the many sins I've committed. My God, pardon me. How I've offended You and how good You are, that You have not condemned me. From this moment on I hate sin because it separates me from You. It makes me the object of horror in Your sight. Lord, forgive me. From now on I want to be a saint. And to think that the root of all sin is pride, which is my dominant passion. What am I, Lord, but misery, a criminal? What do I have, Lord, that You haven't given me? Lord, I want to be humiliated, despised, abhorred, so I may draw closer to You, so I'll not love anyone but You. I want to suffer to make reparation for my sins. Pardon me, Lord, have pity on me!

I have understood that what most keeps me from God is my pride. From now on I desire and propose to be humble. Without humility, the rest of the virtues are hypocrisy. Without that the graces received from God are harmful and ruinous. Humility brings us the likeness of Christ, peace of soul, holiness and intimate union with God. Two things are the necessary means to obtain this: First, consideration of the motives we have to be humble. Second, frequent practice of acts of humiliation. These are the principal degrees of humility: 1. To feel abasement of self and to treat one's things as one does those one despises. 2. The truly humble person doesn't want to be esteemed. He doesn't consider himself to be great nor does he speak well of himself; above all, he considers himself the least of all. If others treat him this way, then he'll suffer this in silence. 3. To desire that they do so and to carefully seek those occasions. 4. To rejoice when they condemn your opinion or intention, and to give thanks to God for it.

I sometimes practice those first two. Humility must be voluntary; it must be sincere; it must be circumspect, that is, one must know when to practice it. Jesus, meek and humble of heart, make my heart like unto Yours.

Oh, Jesus, I'm confounded and frightened! I'd like to annihilate myself in Your presence. There are so many sins by which I have offended You. My God, pardon me. I see myself as a dark abyss, from which comes an unbearable stench. Yes, my Jesus, what pain I feel in having offended You, in having defiled y soul, and in having disfigured Your divine image in it! Not once, but possibly many times I've been the object of horror in Your sight. Lord, forgive me. I'd rather die before having sinned. I, a creature who am almost insignificant. I'm nothingness, better still, I'm a criminal nothingness who rises up against my Creator, that Being who is Wisdom itself, Power itself and Goodness itself, who has done nothing but fill me with favors and preserve me in life. Lord, my Father, my Spouse, forgive my iniquity and ingratitude! Lord, from now on I want to be a saint.

How different everything appears when considered in the light of death. Things appear in all their reality and then the soul exclaims: "Vanity of vanities and all is vanity." Everything is nothingness. Everything the world esteems is worth nothing. Jesus Christ despises it. Now I want to be poor, since on my deathbed what good will riches, money, clothing, comforts, good food, what good will these things bring me? Confusion, nothing more. Of what use is a great reputation, applause, honors, adulation and the esteem of creatures? At the hour of death, everything will disappear with that body which will soon become a vessel of decay and corrpution.

You, Jesus, Infinite Wisdom, You despise all this. Then Your ungrateful bride, with Your help, will despise it. Oh, Mary, my Mother, give me humility, give me true wisdom. I'll never let any day pass without remembering my death and the vanity of all human things. My heart, Jesus, must love You alone.

Oh, how it frightens my soul to see the full enormity of her faults, when my soul reviews her whole life in your sight and to see that I've disfigured the image of my Creator. What confusion will I have when Jesus Christ appears! What horror! My Jesus, have pity on me. Remember, Jesus, that during my whole life I've desired to be Yours. I don't know why the judgment doesn't cause me much fear, because I do (not) believe that souls that have taken and chosen Jesus as Master of their hearts can be rejected. A bridegroom has compassion on his birde. My Mother, "spes unica" *(my only hope)*, when I appear before my Judge, tell Him that I'm your child. Hell makes me freeze. But there's one thing which causes me more horror than all that, and it's what Saint Teresa of Avila said: "The condemned will never love." Oh, How the human heart will then suffer, since God created it for Himself! To hate God is the greatest torment. Dear Jesus, I just saw what hell is, how terrible it is. But I tell You that I'd prefer to be there for an eternity so that one soul, even though it be as miserable as mine, will love You. Yes, my Mother, let this be repeated to Jesus with each beat of my heart, even though I know that there would be no hell but heaven, since love is heaven.

Dear Jesus, I've dissipated the treasures of grace with which you've filled me. I've been ungrateful. I've abandoned You. My Father, I have sinned against You. Forgive me, dear Jesus. I'm not worthy of your celestial gaze. I don't want You to look at me, but only give me refuge in Your Divine Heart. There I want to live, by purifying myself through Your consuming Fire. Oh, Mary, I've despised Your Son by giving myself pleasure, by amusing myself. Pardon me! From today on I desire that my intelligence know Him alone; that my will be inclined only toward Him; that my heart and all my being belong to Him alone.

The retreat director spoke about imitating You, my Jesus. You grew in grace before God and men. You were obedient, a worker. My Mother, teach me to imitate my Divine Spouse.

## 30. You Never Committed Any Mortal Sin.
### I Want To Serve Others And Become A Saint.

Today I confessed all the sins of my life. What confusion to behold that I'm such a sinner. I almost

240

believed that I was going to die of pain. When I prepared myself I didn't know what was happening: I saw in my poor soul mortal sins so great that I was horrified. I recite three Hail Marys to my Mother every day of my life so She'll preserve me from such a disgrace; I'd prefer to die before doing so. I offered up the sacrifice of not asking the priest if I had committed mortal sins, and imagine my joy when I heard the priest tell me: "By God's grace, you have never had the misfortune of ever committing any mortal sin. You've been exposed to sin and God, with love, preserved you from sin. Give Him the thanks of your heart. And because you have not lost your baptismal innocence, the vow by which you should consecrate yourself to God is not chastity, but virginity. Offer Him, then, your virginity."

I remained silent. How can I express what happened in my soul? In that instant I felt love, and that love was pure, virginal. Oh, how great is the mercy of my Jesus for His miserable spouse! How can I fully thank my Mother!

August 14, I feel sadness and abasement. I'm trying to repress it. On the other hand, I'm happy since they told me to take charge of a recreation class of little girls. I'm happy, since it's a proof of confidence on the part of Reverend Mother. I felt a little vanity, but I rejected it and spoke to Jesus, asking Him how I should act so as not to take enjoyment in it. Then He told me that He was giving me His grace so I'd be good, and not appear evil, as in reality I am. Today I had more fervor and above all, great love. When I approached to go to Communion, I began to cry. Oh, how good is my Jesus! I love Him. I feel that it's so difficult to fulfill my promises, but Jesus gave me encouragement, placing before me a view of His despised, humiliated face. I asked Him to give me strength.

241

From today on I desire to be always the least in all things, to occupy the last place, to serve others, to sacrifice myself always in all things and to unite myself more to the One who, being God, became a servant because He loved us.

I'll never excuse myself, even when unjustly treated. I'll do everything as well as possible so I can please not creatures but God. I'll love creatures because of God, in God and for God. I'll live constantly in that spirit of faith. I'll not pass up any occasion to humiliate myself and to mortify myself. At every moment I'll fulfill God's will. I believe that in love there is sanctity. I want to be a saint. Then I'll hand myself over to love, since that purifies, serves to expiate. He who loves doesn't have any other will but that of the Beloved; then I desire to do Jesus' Will. He who loves is sacrificed. I want to sacrifice myself entirely. I don't want to gratify myself in any way. I want to immolate myself constantly to become like the One who suffered for me and loves me. Love obeys without answering back. Love is faithful. Love doesn't vacillate. Love is the bond of union between two souls. For love, I will fuse myself with Jesus.

I've written nothing about my dealings with Carmel. Chela Montes went to Los Andes and showed them her books where I had written something. Then they asked her quite a bit about me, and Teresita, her sister, said that she had held me in her arms when I was a baby. Mother Angelica sent me a scapular and asked her to tell me I should write to them. So, I'm going to write to her.

August 15. Today, feast of the Assumption, I asked my Mother to give me her heart. With this treasure I'll have everything, given that in it is Jesus and all virtues. I found another way to mortify myself before going to sleep: putting my weight on the tips of my toes, causes additional pain. And also by not omitting any little act for Jesus.

242

## 31. I Wish To Be Poor. Tomorrow I Will be More Faithful. I Like The Carmelites.

Tuesday 16. My Jesus, pardon me. I'm so proud that I don't know how to accept with humility the slightest humiliation. Dear Jesus, teach me humility and send me humiliations, even though I'm unworthy of them. Dear Jesus, I want to be poor, humble, obedient, pure, as was my Mother and like You, Jesus. Make your little house a palace, a heaven. I long to live adoring You as the angels do. I feel my nothingness in Your presence. I'm so imperfect. I want to be poor as You were and, since I can't be this, I ask not to love riches in any way.

Monday 20. My God, why have you abandoned me? My Jesus, perhaps I've been ungrateful with You. I feel insensitive, cold as marble, powerless either to meditate or even to go to Communion with devotion. My Jesus, I offer you myself for my sins and for sinners and for the Holy Father and priests. I unite myself to your abandonment on Calvary.

Tuesday 21. I've been more united with my Jesus. I love Him. This morning He touched my heart and roused me from my lethargy. Oh, I love Him! He asked me to do three things: 1) keep silence; 2) live with a spirit of faith; 3) give thanks for Communion in the morning, and at night prepare myself for the next day.

I fulfilled the first one. Forgive me, Jesus, tomorrow I'll be more faithful.

Wednesday 22. If Jesus doesn't help me in my resolutions, I'll throw them all into an abyss so as not to remember them. But I place my trust in the One who comforts me. Let's see if tomorrow I'll be better than today, for when I go out I become distracted; I don't recollect myself as much.

I received a letter from Father Colom. He spoke of the elections at the Monastery. What should I do? Truly, I don't know what to do. On the other hand, they tell me that I shouldn't think about it since there's still time. But only one year still remains. I then desire to enter religious life when I'm 18 years old.

Thursday 23. Jesus told me I should obey my confessor. That I should place myself into His divine hands, and that I shouldn't be disturbed about anything, since He told me where I'll be. I examined what was bringing me to Carmel and the principal reason is that there I'll live already as in Heaven, since I'll never be separated from God for even a moment. I'll praise Him and will constantly sing His mercies, without mixing myself with anything in the world. Also, the rigors of penance attract me, since I feel a longing to be a martyr in my body, despising it with scourges, not giving into it in anything that pleases it, and making reparation for the time that I gave it pleasure and denied it to my soul.

I love the Carmelites because they are so simple, so joyful and Jesus must be that way. But I see also that the life of a Carmelite consists in suffering, in loving and praying. When the consolations of prayer are denied me, what will happen to me? I tremble. But Jesus said to me: "Do you believe I'll abandon you?"

Friday 24. I want to leave in writing an event that happened. Even though it's small it served to humiliate me. We were in class when a bee or another larger insect came near me. Without knowing how, in one leap I got out of the room; afterward, I was so ashamed of not having known how to conquer myself. But I finally offered the humiliation to God and came back into the room. Mother Izquierdo then looked at me with such a fixed and profound stare that I wished the ground would swallow me up as I was remembering the little control I have over my inclinations. Oh, I see myself so little and so miserable. I was alone. Jesus left me and I, without Jesus, what am I but misery? Afterward I went to ask Mother Izquierdo's pardon. I confess that it cost me; but I directed myself to my Mother Mary and she, as always, helped me. Mother Izquierdo immediately said it was all right. I think I'd have preferred to have her scold me. Then I recalled Jesus and His Mercy, when He looked at Peter and made his heart tender through His gaze. I thanked God for this event, since I didn't offend Him, but it served to humiliate me.

I went to confession on Friday. The priest told me I shouldn't be upset because of distractions, since they serve to humiliate me. He told me that when I had a doubt about anything, I should maintain a balanced frame of mind.

Saturday 25. How I love my Mother! How she loves me! Today is the feast of her Immaculate Heart. How tenderly they spoke of her during the sermon. I began to weep afterward. I love her so.

I'm sad. I don't know what's happening to me. How much it costs me to get used to considering myself always as the last. Jesus told me that He was always in the last place.

## 32. Exhausted. Sick. Fatigue Never Leaves Me.
### When I go to Communion I feel Courage.
### I Need Jesus.

Monday 27. I don't know what's happening to me, since I continually feel exhausted. Today at different times I've had to use all my strength of will not to permit myself to be overcome by sadness. Yesterday I made this resolution in my meditation: to be cheerful all day long. And I carried out this resolution. At times I've shown myself to be cheerful all day long. There were times I was almost unable to break out of this exhaustion of soul in which I found myself. I believe that it's the weakness I find in myself: a constant headache. And add to this the pain in my back. I don't know how I feel; but I'm happy, since I'm suffering. And I suffer with Jesus to console Him and make reparation for my sins and those of humankind. There is a moral sadness; but with the Psalmist I will say: "I'm surrounded by my enemies, but I place my trust in the Lord who will confound them."

August 28. Each day I feel worse. I have no courage for anything; but in the last analysis, finally, it's God's will. May this be done as He desires. My Mother, I place everything in your hands. Why have you abandoned me? Help me to know my lessons and do my compositions very well. My Mother, may I do "very well" in my compositions. Show that you are my Mother and give me everything, but above all humility. Jesus dear, give me sufferings. Suffering is no bother because in this way You love me.

Tomorrow I can't go to Communion. Obedience demands this of me. My Jesus, what can I do without You? Without Jesus, what will become of this miserable creature? Fortunately I have Him in my soul. There my Jesus dwells and I'll not let Him escape.

Today, August 30, I didn't receive Communion. I was unable to unite myself with God. And all this because of this body of clay. When will death be over and done with so I can live in God? My Jesus, You're my Life. Without You I'll die; without You I languish.

Today I feel badly. Fatigue will not leave me. What can I do since it's God's will? Today without Communion

I have been agitated. Silence, body; I only desire that the soul speak with God, so you be silent toward creatures.

The gaze from my crucifix sustains me. I see everything obscurely. My prayer is finished. They've forbidden me to make it during the night. They've denied me Communion; but I succeed because Jesus is everything and He's within my soul. What do all things matter? I only seek to consider the present, that is to say, to gaze at Jesus now. He enlightens me. The future nevertheless presents itself to me as darkness.

When I go to Communion I feel strong. Jesus gives me life, not only of soul but also of body. They take it away; they deprive me of Heaven. Dear Jesus, may Your will and not mine be done. Tomorrow I'll go to Communion. I have obtained permission. Oh, what happiness: tomorrow I'll have Heaven in my heart! Oh, I love You, Jesus, I adore You! I thank You and my Mother for this favor. I'm all Yours. You alone...no other creature!

September 1. I'm always sick. The future looks so bleak that I don't want to look at it. Today they told me they were going to take me out of school and, since H. V. *(Herminia Valdés Ossa, Juanita's second cousin)* was giving a dance, I'll be coming out next year. This frightens me. And, on the other hand, to think that because of my health I can't become a Carmelite. All this makes me exclaim: My Jesus, if it be possible, let this chalice pass from me; but not my will but Thine be done! And to think that I can't make prayer. But when I'm with Jesus, I don't know how to talk about my pains. Instead, I should console Him because He's suffering much more. So I remain silent. And my poor heart goes on sighing. Jesus looks at me with contentment. He tells me His....

I'm dying, I feel like I'm dying. My Jesus, I give myself to You. I offer You my life for my sins and for sinners. My Mother, offer me as a victim. Truly, yesterday I couldn't stand the pain in my chest. I was choking. I couldn't breathe and the pain left me exhausted. I am offering all this to Jesus for my sins and for sinners.

I'm at home. They made me come home because I couldn't go on. How painful it was to say goodbye to the girls and the nuns and my little ones. I love them so... but may God's will be done.

I didn't go to Communion. Last night I happened to dream that I was hungering for Jesus; but afterward, all day I was in a state of tepidity. I didn't make prayer or make a spiritual Communion. Oh, how bad I am. But today thanks be to God, I made up for it and made a spiritual Communion. I went to meditate. Then I fell asleep. Now I'm going to see if I can meditate. Tomorrow I'll go to Communion. How I long for this, my Jesus. I'm so bad. I need You to be good. Come, Love, come quickly and I'll give You my heart, my soul and all that I possess. My Mother, prepare my heart to receive my Jesus.


## 33. Mary Is My Mother And My All. Vocation To Be A Carmelite. Two Letters From Carmel.

September 7. Today is First Friday. Because it was raining this morning I was unable to go to Communion and they left me in bed. *(She was sick at home, not at boarding school).* How much pain I suffered. Nevertheless, I spoke with my Jesus. I hope I can go to Communion tomorrow, the feast of the Nativity of my Mother. Because I've been unable to offer many acts to my dear Mary, I'll begin a novena; but I don't know how to do it since, as I'm sick, I take pleasure in food and in almost everything; but from tomorrow on, I'll begin to celebrate my dear little Mary, because after Jesus she's my Mother and my all. Furthermore, I'll renew my vow till the 8th of December.

September 11. Since it was the anniversary of my First Communion I went to Communion. What an idea! For 7 years my soul has been united with Jesus. What an effusion there was in that first encounter! Jesus spoke to my soul for the first time. How sweet it was for me to hear that melody for the first time.

Today I went to Confession. I spoke with the priest for a long time about my vocation. He told me that as far as he could see, for now, I have a true vocation to be a Carmelite. Jesus might give me a vocation that is permanent, that is to say, forever, and I could enter Carmel. Or, He might give me a transitory or momentary vocation to free me from all evil in body or soul. Also, I must be true to my vocation, follow it if God gives the necessary qualities. Also, I can be a Carmelite spiritually, that is to say, follow the Carmelite way of life in my own home by getting up at a certain time, making an hour of meditation and then going to Mass, taking Communion and returning home and starting to work. I'd be in the presence of God all day long, and at night I could make another hour of meditation. Then I'd go to bed at a fixed time and visit as little as possible. After reflecting on it, he said, I should answer him, if that was agreeable to me. He then said that I should always look in the mirror of my soul; and when I was unable to meditate, I should conjugate the verb love, in the following way:

I, do I love God or do I love vanities?

You, soul, do you love yourself inordinately?

He (Jesus) loves me with an eternal love.

We love ourselves in God.

You love yourselves inordinately;

They love their passions and don't love Christ crucified.

I loved Jesus since my youth, etc.;

I'll love Jesus, and Him crucified, with the mercy of God, until death.

He told me that when I was very disconsolate and devoid of courage, I should first seek comfort in God and, if He doesn't grant it to me, I should seek a little from a person worthy of confidence who would take me to God. I should live like the crucified One, since Jesus would like me to be His Cyrenian. Jesus gave me a splinter of His cross; I should receive it with pleasure, and try not to allow it to dishearten me. More than ever I must live in God's presence. I should unite myself to Him. I'm to make a half-hour of meditation and, if I'm with people, take a book and read and meditate at the same time. I should be very careful. He forbade me all mortification. When I feel tired, I shouldn't force myself to meditate. I should concentrate on making ejaculatory prayers and acts of love.

September 13. Yesterday I went to see Rebecca, and Mother Izquierdo obtained for me the permission that they granted. I was happy although previously I had been anxious about coming to school. Later I was greatly amused when I had to change my dress and everything. I don't know what happened to me. There was such great interior sadness that I felt as though I was isolated from the whole world. Everything annoyed me and everything tired me. Finally, thank God, yesterday I was able to meditate and felt devotion and love, which our Lord hadn't granted me for a long time, even in Communion. In the end, those 2 months of suffering were 2 months of heaven, since even though I didn't unite myself very much to my Jesus because of my tepidity, still I offered everything to Him and asked Him to give me His cross.

My Jesus, as well as my Mother greatly besought me that I imitate them in the effacement of my person, that is to say, that I live very hiddenly and only for Him, that I should not manifest my feelings to anyone but to my confessor. So, I'll do this with God's help. Yesterday I made the resolution to live this day very happily exteriorly.

14. I carried out my resolution of yesterday. I went to see Mother Izquierdo. She recommended that I do everything for the love of God, that I seek not the consolations of God, but the God of consolations and that I live just for the day.

Yesterday two Carmelite nuns *(the other Carmelite Prioress was undoubtedly from the Carmen Alto Monastery)* answered me with beautiful letters. The nun from Los Andes sent me a photograph of the Virgin with a prayer, and a little medal of Our Lady of Carmel and the prophet Elias.

## 34. I Belong To Jesus.

### I abandon Myself To Whatever He Desires.

October 2. It's been a long time since I wrote. The vacation of September 18th ended and I returned to school. How happy I feel to be back in school again, without having given my heart to anyone. All for Jesus.

I want all my actions, desires, and thoughts, to bear this signet: "I belong to Jesus."

What delight I feel in again living in the house of Jesus. I have Him so very near to me. At each moment my spirit flies to the foot of the tabernacle. Nevertheless, it's been a long time since I've known what fervor is. I hear the voice of my Jesus, but don't see Him. I don't feel His love. I'm cold, insensible; but this helps me to see my nothingness and my misery. Thus it is that, when I'm with Jesus, I don't speak to Him, because my imagination flies to other things. But when I return to myself I cry when I see how ungrateful I am with my dear Jesus, since He comes to dwell in my soul which is so filled with misery and I scarcely speak with Him. In the end, I offer myself entirely to Jesus. I want to lose my nothingness in the abyss of His infinite love and power.

October 3. I don't know what to do with regard to mortifications, since the priest told me I shouldn't do any, but I've such an unusual craving to eat caramels. Today I had such hunger that I ate all those I could and the ones that tasted best. It pains me to see that this is the way I am. Truly I don't know what to do. I'll consult with Mother Izquierdo about this. Today I was very dissipated. What should I do with such misery? My Jesus, my Mother, have pity on me. Deliver me from my tepidity. I'm sick in my soul. I don't know what is happening to me.

October 4. Tomorrow is First Friday. I'll make a retreat, insofar as I can. And I'll explore the causes of my tepidity. I went to Confession. I'm going to be better. This week I'll mortify myself more.

October 5. Today I had more fervor. I believe my lack of devotion comes from the fact that I'm very attached to all that is earthly, to vanities. I want to renounce everything that is earthly. I want to live on the cross. There one finds abandonment, solitude.

October 7. Jesus demands that I become a saint, that I perform my obligations with perfection. My obligation - He told me - is the cross. And my Jesus is on the cross. I want to be crucified. He told me that I will save souls for Him. I promised Him this. I will also console Him; He Himself feels abandoned. He took me to His Heart and made me feel those... I feel He has taken possession of my being. I love Him.

October 9. I've been very united to Our Lord. Still, I don't feel fervor. I've been very strange. I had a strong desire to behave badly, to become angry, finally, to the point of crying. I believe all that comes from the way I feel physically. This morning I almost didn't make a meditation. And my thanksgiving after Communion was less than fervent, because I was exhausted. But Jesus told me that I shouldn't be upset, that I'm not culpable for this.

October 10. Today I wasn't good; I was presumptuous. Lord, I prostrated myself at Your feet for the thought of the pleasure I took in my facial appearance. And also for being dissipated. I don't know what I'm going to do with so much misery.

October 17. Today I had devotion. I was able to converse with Jesus in Communion. Also, today I went out. I preserved the presence of God 11 times, a thing that never happens. I'm indifferent to feeling or not feeling fervor. I surrender myself to what Jesus wants. I've offered myself to Him as a victim. I want to be crucified. Today Jesus told me that He suffered and that because He loved me He wanted me to suffer. I should forget myself and fulfill my duties. Thanks to those

253

counsels and to His grace, I've been better. My Jesus, I love You. I'm totally Yours. I give myself completely to Your divine will. Jesus, give me the cross, but give me the strength to carry it. It matters not whether You give me the abandonment of Calvary or the joys of Nazareth. I only want to see You contented. It doesn't bother me to be unable to feel, to be insensible as a rock, because I know, my sweet Jesus, that You know I love You. Give me the cross. I want to suffer for You; but teach me to suffer by loving, with joy and with humility.

Lord, if it please You that the darkness of my soul become deeper, that I not see You, it will not bother me because I want to fulfill Your will. I want to spend my life in suffering to make reparation for my sins, those of sinners and so that priests will be sanctified. I don't want to be happy, but I want You to be happy. I want to be like a soldier so that at every moment you can dispose of my will and preferences. I want to be courageous, strong and generous in serving You, Lord. You are the Spouse of my soul.

## 35. Rages And Doubts. I Need Jesus.
### The Goal Of The Carmelite. The Office of Martha.

Thursday, October 18. Today I had to do a great deal to conquer myself. I was very angry, and sorry that I disobeyed and did my own will. I was weary and thought that I didn't have a vocation, that it was an illusion, just an idea I would afterward despair of; finally, so many things. But I prayed devoutly to the Most Holy Virgin and in the depths of my soul I heard the voice of my Jesus: "Learn of Me because I am meek and humble of heart." And in this way my anger came to an end. Today one of the Sisters gave out a box of candy and, since she gave me a small piece, it made me furious and I threw it away; and then I wouldn't accept the other piece she gave me. Dear Jesus, what do You say about this soldier who is so cowardly and so imperfect? Forgive me. The next time I'll be better. I'll throw myself into that immense ocean of the love of Your Heart, to lose myself in It like a drop of water in the ocean and to abase my littleness in the greatness of Your mercy. I notice that I'm more proud, but, thanks be to God who has illumined me with His grace, from today forward I want to be humble. I want to forget myself entirely.

October 23. I couldn't go to Communion this morning because I was sick. Oh, how I hunger for Jesus. I love Him but don't feel the sweetness of His love. I don't see Him. It doesn't matter. I offer myself to Jesus for my sins, for those of sinners and for the sanctification of priests. I am much more recollected. What desires I have to go about entirely recollected, with my eyes lowered and remaining within my soul with Jesus. I love Him. Without Him I do not live. I die.

October 24. I showed Mother Izquierdo my little book and in it she noticed the goal I had in mind: to offer my deeds "for the sanctification of priests." She was not aware that the goal of the Carmelite is to pray for priests, because a Carmelite nun is also a priest. Being always at the foot of the cross, the Carmelite nun receives the blood of Jesus and pours it out through her prayers on the whole world.

October 25. I don't know what to do to get the priest to allow me to mortify myself. I have so many desires to fast, to wear hair shirts, since I see it is necessary for me to mortify not only my will but also my body. My Jesus, give me permission to do penance. My Mother, inspire the priest to grant me permission. Tomorrow is Friday. I must humiliate myself. I'll mortify myself by keeping silence, and by maintaining a posture that is uncomfortable. Today I did just this in French class.

October 29. Tomorrow is a recreation day for the lay Sisters, so the Children of Mary will take their places performing the office of Martha. How happy is the soul who lives by faith! Tomorrow I'm going to serve, to be a slave, a servant. That's fitting for me. But I'll be serving God and my Jesus in the person of my neighbor. Today I was unable to go to Communion because yesterday I marched in the procession of the Child Jesus for little Ignacio. God didn't perform a miracle, but something better happened. My father marched in the procession, which gave me great pleasure. Oh, how I asked my Jesus that He would heal my father. He was much sicker than little Ignacio. *(Juanita's godmother and aunt had been favored with a celebrated cure attributed to the Infant Jesus of Prague. Juanita and her relatives, hoping that the Divine Infant would miraculously cure the injured leg of little Ignacio, joined a procession that till this day the Carmelite Fathers of Santiago organize each year. Juanita hoped that her father would become better, as she loved him with great devotion. She uses excessively black ink here and on other occasions when she is worried about his moral situation. Those who lived close to him say "He was a very good person," and "I do not believe there was any bad conduct nor did he ever give any scandal." The truth is that Don Miguel Fernández, because of his meager education and lack of talent, did not know how to administer his goods skillfully. His family paid the consequences for this. Because of his helplessness, the family patrimony was decreasing. Possibly this was complicated by his wife's punctilious and demanding character. To avoid friction and his problems, Don Miguel spent long periods of time away from his family on his own lands or on the ones he rented and was cultivating. Living in the country, undoubtedly he grew a little careless in the practice of his religion, even letting a year pass without fulfilling his obligations in the church. But his life was never intemperate. He changed a great deal after Juanita's death, living more piously during his last years, when he went to Communion almost every day and, of course, recited his rosary. He died on August 21, 1923. Juanita on numerous occasions recalled her father's disinterested life of sacrifice, his good sentiments and his attitude as a believer, and showed that she was proud of him and thanked God for having given her a father who was so Christian).*

I don't know how many times I offered up my life. Last night I went to bed very late and this morning I awoke at 7. Thus I couldn't go to Communion. Still, perhaps if I'd been more prompt in getting up I might have succeeded. How sorry I feel. I didn't experience the presence of Jesus, but I did spend today united with Him.

October 30. I served as a Sister all day. I enjoyed it, because I imagined I was serving Jesus. Today I spoke quite a bit with Jesus. He made me see the necessity that a Carmelite nun has to always live at the foot of the cross and there learn to love and to suffer. To suffer in three ways: (1) A Carmelite must mortify her flesh following the example of the suffering Jesus. (2) She must mortify her will by denying herself all pleasures and by submitting her will to God and to her neighbor. (3) By suffering in her spirit the abandonment of our Jesus in her prayer, in her struggles of her soul, etc. As Jesus exclaimed on the cross: "My God, why have you abandoned me?"

The life of the Carmelite is reduced to this: to live to attain the most perfect union with God, and to totally immolate and sacrifice herself in all things, since sacrifice is the oblation of love.

## 36. When Will I Be A Carmelite? All With Mary.

October 31. I'm suffering, because every time I ask my father for money he tells me that he doesn't have any. *(This statement and "perhaps we will not go to spend the summer" in the following chapter confirm that economically her father was not doing well).* What am I going to do when I ask him to give me a dowry to become a Carmelite nun? Oh, my dear Jesus! I believe he's not going to want to let me go. I see so much hostility against the Carmelite nuns. My Jesus, I trust in You. You are all-powerful. Come steal me away and do it quickly, very quickly and forever. Tomorrow is the feast of Heaven *(the feast of All Saints).* My soul's a heaven, because Jesus is present in it. Because tomorrow is my feastday I'll sing all day long. I'll be the praise of glory for my God.

November 1. I spent the whole day with an atrocious pain in my stomach. Finally, may the will of God be done. I don't know how I made my meditation and thanksgiving, since I was so exhausted I had to go to bed. God will dispense me. Today we recited the Office of the Dead. It is so beautiful. What I understand enchants me. When will I be a Carmelite to sing the praises of the Lord every day?

November 2. I went to Confession. How God communicates peace to me through this sacrament! Now I feel the courage to suffer for my Jesus. I told the priest that if he wished I would change my particular examination of conscience. He told me that I should make it about my devotion to the Virgin. During the first week I should meditate on the greatness of Mary; during the second, on the goodness of her heart; during the third week, on the maternal love of her heart; during the fourth week, on how I must honor, love and place all my confidence in her. He told me that everything should be given to Mary so she can present it to Jesus. He told me I must do everything possible to live without consolations and satisfactions in prayer. I should do all in the same way, even when I don't find consolation; I must resign myself to live in this way. He gave me permission to use a knotted cord.

I'm sick. I can't eat anything. I fast. I'm happy. How good is my Jesus who gives me His cross. I'm happy. Thus I'll show Him my love. Furthermore, my shoes hurt me. I don't want to complain about this, so I offer it to the Virgin. I'm alone. I don't go to Communion, but I'm on the cross and on it my little Jesus is present. I live, then, in permanent communion. Jesus, I thank You for the cross. Make my cross heavier, but give me strength and love. Jesus I know that I'm unworthy to suffer with You. Pardon my lack of gratitude. Have pity on sinners. Sanctify priests.

## 37. Conquering Souls With Jesus.

November 16. Last night I spent one hour with Jesus. We were speaking intimately. He reproached me because in my pains and doubts I didn't have recourse to His Heart as I used to. He desires that I be a virgin, without being touched by any creatures, because I must belong entirely to Him. I rested myself on His Heart. Then He spoke to me about poverty. I came away from Him without a thing. Everything belongs to Him. Everything passes away and is vanity. Afterward He spoke to me about humility of thought, action and empty knowledge. Finally, He opened His Heart to me and showed me that because of my prayers He had written the name of my father there. He told me I should resign myself to not seeing the fruit of my prayers, but that I would obtain everything. Afterward He manifested His love to me, but in such a way that I began to cry. He showed me His greatness and my nothingness, and told me He had chosen me as a victim. I must climb Calvary with Him. Together we should undertake the conquest of souls: He the Captain, and I the soldier. Our motto, the cross. Our cry love. He told me that I should suffer with joy and with love, and every day I should remove a thorn from His Heart. He told me that I should love Him and that I will become a Carmelite; that I should not be discouraged; that I should not talk about this, since they'll try to dissuade me from my vocation. And finally, that I should belong to Him alone: a virgin, intact and pure.

November 21. I'm very afflicted. I went out and was given the news that perhaps we will not go to spend the summer. I asked the Virgin that my father go to Confession, that peace return to the family. Each day I feel worse. I always feel exhausted. Now my back hurts as well as my chest; but in the end, may God's will be done. Little Ignacio also needs to go. Luís is very weak. My little Mother.... Oh, what I would give to work and let them go! My Mother, tell Jesus what I need. And beseech Him intensely for this favor. My Mother, to your maternal heart I entrust all my troubles.

I can't do any more. Unless Jesus sustains me, I don't know what I'll do, because I'll be spending the whole day lying down and doing nothing. I live in a state of confusion. I have a constant headache that makes me see everything in different colors. My God, Thy Will not mine be done. I offer You my sufferings for my sins, for sinners and for the sanctification of priests.

Death, what is more desirable? To die and to live in God for an eternity and have fruition in God, can there be any greater happiness? My dear Jesus, every time I feel bad, I feel homesick for You and for that Heaven where I'll nevermore offend You; where I'll be inebriated with Your love, Jesus, where I'll be one with You, since I must have my being and movement in You.

November 23. Today I exercised my apostolate. A little girl whom they had severely upbraided and threatened to take away her sash was so filled with despair that she was going to persuade Mother Izquierdo to take her sash away from her. I prayed a *Memorare* to the most Holy Virgin, and I told the little girl all that Mary inspired me to say in order to encourage and console her. I spoke to her of the Virgin, that she should tell Mary all her troubles and ask her protection; that if she suffered with patience, she would have a great reward in heaven.

November 25. Today I contemplated Mater Admirabilis *(Mother Most Admirable, a Marian devotion traditional in Sacred Heart schools. A curious fact: at this school the students used to call Juanita "Mater Admirabilis" because of her exceptional goodness and conduct).* in the temple, in that majestic silence whereby she united her whole being to God. In this way she went about adoring Him and recognizing her nothingness before God. I tried to keep recollected and remained as long as I could with my eyes lowered and in the presence of Jesus.

## 38. Not To Have My Own Will. Availability.

November 26. I felt so bad today that I thought I was going to have to go to bed, since I was unable to stand on my feet. But Jesus sustained me and I only had to ask permission to go out to take a little air in the garden, and thus I felt better very quickly, even though I had pains in my chest and was unable to breathe. May God's will be done.

November 29. Mother du Bose follows me everywhere I go. I feel my blood boiling with anger. I did not look at the creature but I consider that it's God who put into her head the idea to follow me around. May God's will be done, and in this way I became peaceful.

November 30. I went to see Mother Izquierdo. She spoke to me about my vocation and repeated one more time that I had neither a vocation nor the health to become a Carmelite. We spoke for quite a while. I came away distressed. She's the only one who doesn't think I have a vocation to be a Carmelite. I finally put everything into the hands of my Jesus. It's so easy to abandon oneself entirely to Jesus.

December 3. Yesterday we went out for the day. I see the love that I still have for vanities in dressing myself, in making a good appearance; but fortunately or by the grace of God, I didn't give consent, but rejected all these thoughts. In spite of that, I caught sight of myself in the mirror and looked at myself.

December. I went to confession. The priest gave me permission to renew my vow till Easter. *(A vow of chastity that she renewed periodically from December 8, 1915, when she made it for the first time).* I told the priest what Mother Izquierdo had said, that she didn't believe I had a vocation to become a Carmelite. Then he said that God did not choose a religious to manifest His

262

will, that He gave light to the confessor. He said I shouldn't pay attention to her and I shouldn't put confidence in her. He spoke of what I should strive to do- given the fact that Jesus desires that I be a victim-if I am to put my ego to death.

Consequently, so as not to have my own will, I shouldn't speak of myself either favorably or unfavorably, but as of a being who didn't exist; as about a nothingness, since that is what I am, and not only a nothingness but a criminal nothingness. He said I should annihilate myself in the presence of God; that I should recognize His greatness and at the same time my nothingness and my baseness.

Afterward he asked me if I was disposed to suffer desolations, doubts, aridity, etc., in Carmel. Yes, I answered. Even now I'm asking Our Lord for them. Finally, he asked me if I would like to suffer humiliations in my exams and prizes. And I answered, no. But he told me that if it would be for the good of my soul, I should desire it. Thus for that reason I do desire it if it will be the better thing.

December 8. I renewed my vow. Jesus asked me for total union with Himself, without any mixture of creatures or anything of the earth. I walked in the procession, I wanted...

December 10. Today, thanks be to God, I didn't excuse myself when reprimanded. Jesus helped me. I felt myself to be so wicked. I was very exhausted and a terrible pain began in my shoulder. My back hurt me as well as my head. Oh, Jesus, when will I be able to live in You! May Your Will be accomplished and not mine!

December 14. I'm leaving school. I'm so distressed I'm almost unable to cry. Only Jesus knows what I'm suffering. I will forever be leaving this place where I've spent so many happy hours. Here one lives as if in Nazareth, given that one lives with Him, without any danger to our innocence and where we are taught virtues. All this I'm going to leave to enter the world, full of snares. I'm afraid that vanities will enslave me. Lord, I only ask that You grant me suffering. It will bring me to You.

My Mother, I know you are my Mother. Remember that I gave myself to you. In your Immaculate Heart, keep me pure, a virgin. May your Heart be my refuge, my hope, my consolation, my solitude. I place myself in your maternal arms so you may put me in the arms of Jesus. I abandon myself to Him. May His holy Will be done.

## YEAR 1918

### 39. Pain. Dryness. Abandonment. Darkness.

March 12. Thank you, my Mother, for having freed me from all dangers and for having made me spend my vacation very well. Thank you, my Mother. I would like, my Mother, to tell you many things. But oh, my language is so poor that it trembles in just telling you that I love you. My Mother, I'd love to sing your praises at your virginal feet, but my voice is so weak that I can only formulate a prayer. I have pain because, despite having asked and at the same time having mortified myself, I have not obtained my request that my father, Miguel and Luís make a retreat. But may God's will be done.

Holy Wednesday. Abandonment, dryness, agony. I'm at the point where I can do no more. My chest and my shoulder pain me greatly. Everything looks so bad, because I won't become a Carmelite if my health is so frail.

April. I'm suffering abandonment, but in a horrible way. Jesus has abandoned me because I'm unfaithful. And He doesn't hear my prayers and He leaves me to conquer myself without His grace, so that I'm without hope. My Jesus, have pity on me. You know that I love You. My Mother, help me in this darkness. *(During these months Juanita was maturing by means of the spiritual purification the mystics call "the dark night").* Nothingness. Jesus is not in my soul. The Virgin doesn't answer me. Jesus, have pity on your unfaithful spouse. Yes, I love You. Do not abandon me. Oh, thank you! With Your word, Jesus, You can completely dispel the storm.

April 10. I'm in a terrible state.... Angry. With desires to be mischievous. Mad at the nuns. Without taste for prayer, because I encounter dryness in it. I feel despondent. At each moment I'm failing in my duties. And Jesus told me today that it was because I was attached to creatures. I want to be loved by them. I cry because I don't know what is happening to me and I have no one to counsel me or help me. Mother Izquierdo was angry and that is tormenting me.

April 13. Mother Ríos was sick. May God's will be done. I'm going to try to be very good so that she may feel better, if it be the will of God.

April 16. Jesus told me that I should always carry out His will with joy, even though my spirits are low. That I may remain in peace, I shouldn't look at the future. I want to keep this maxim before me. Today I am beginning the work of my....

## 40. How Can I Not Be Mad For Jesus? Jesus Is The Only One Capable Of Enamoring Me.

May 25. I went to confession to Father López. I enjoyed a peace that I hadn't found in 3 months. He told me that I should ask Our Lord to give me the strength to be good; He will grant it to me. If I'm in that state now, it's because Jesus relied on me to immolate myself even more. I should renew my resolution every hour and offer myself entirely to God, without determining anything regarding my vocation. I should live in a spirit of faith. I should often repeat the ejaculatory prayer: Jesus meek and humble of heart, etc.

Feast of Mother Barat. I'm very grateful because she granted me a great favor. They preached on the marvels of education, which consists of God taking possession of our faculties. Prudence is the science of the saints and of the wise. Prudence and modesty are the picture frame in which the other virtues attain their proper order. The education of the woman is more important than that of the man, since she will form him.

May 28. I have an admirer. Because she has a high regard for me, I'm troubled because this is going to make me lose all I have gained regarding humility. My God, I ask You that I be forgotten, unappreciated. My Jesus, I don't desire the love of creatures.

June 7. Feast of the Sacred Heart. It was a year ago today that I received the Child of Mary medal. Oh, what graces my Mother has granted me! I promised Our Lord that I would completely renounce my will, always do what is displeasing to self. I ask myself why will I not become mad with love for Jesus who is worthy of all my veneration, love and watchfulness. How little do I love Him in comparison with how much He loves me. Why do I not become mad for Him?

June 8. I'm suffering so much. Mother Izquierdo is angry with me. I don't know what I've done. She's not the same mother toward me that she used to be. I continue to have the same affection and trust toward her. This frightens my soul. Why, my Jesus, are You placing this coldness around my poor heart? Ah, it is because You love me. You want to encircle me only with your love so I will not be attached to any creature. This helps me see that love doesn't exist on earth, but in God alone; because, if favored, chosen and holy souls forget or are indifferent, what will other people be like? You, Jesus, are the only One capable of inspiring me to fall in love.

I'm contented, happy and very thankful to Our Lord and to the Virgin, because all have gone to Communion this year. My Jesus, be the Jesus of Bethany for me.

## 41. Fiat. Suffering Without Tears.
### My Leaving School Has Been Determined.

July 11. *Fiat voluntas tua*, this is my prayer. I don't ask for any other things. This morning Jesus asked me not to cry because of my departure from school, since that is His will. And I told Him that then the nuns would think I was unappreciative; but He made me see how attached I was to what creatures said. I'll show my appreciation by praying for them. I'm going to offer up the sacrifice for my father and brothers.

July 15. My Mother, prostrate at your feet, I promise you to fulfill the rule perfectly so that he be converted. My Mother, I offer you the sacrifice of not shedding a tear when leaving school. You know that I love you. Likewise Rebecca... My Mother, I offer up all for him. I'll even begin by taking no candies until I leave.

July 17. Yesterday I said to Jesus that if it was true that He was speaking to me that He should make Mother Izquierdo ask me this question: "Do you love Our Lord?" How I was moved today when I heard Mother say to me: "Do you love Christ?" I blushed with emotion and became silent. She said to me: "And are you not answering with all your soul?" I replied: it would be monstrous if I did not love Him. Oh, how good Jesus is with this vile slave! Oh, Jesus, Your love annihilates me and confounds me!

July 19. Our Lord asks me to mortify myself in all things. Not only by not gratifying my taste, but even in eating; that I eat a little of everything. During the day I feel weakness, but I offer it to Jesus. One priest told me that I should not deprive myself of food; another priest gave me permission to fast once a week. I don't know what to do. I believe the best thing is to consult Jesus about it.

July 20. I've suffered as never before in my life. I'm happy. It's been heavenly for me. They were going to pull out one of my teeth, but it split and they were unable to extract it. The pain was so great that I nearly went out of my mind. I felt confused that I had cried, but was unable to do better. I offered all this to Our Lord for them. I suffered all day long and pretended not to be in pain. Oh, Jesus, I want to suffer everything for my own sins and for them!

July 21. My tooth hurts a great deal, but I'm saying nothing. I want to suffer in silence for them.

Reverend Mother: There are only 15 days left before I leave school and even though I'm sad, I want to fulfill God's will with joy. Pray a great deal for me; I'll begin to struggle with the world and I think that during the vacation I'll ask permission to go to the Carmelites. I see

268

that it's God's will, since many difficulties that previously seemed insurmountable have been taken care of. In my home, I think I'm living a life of prayer: I get up at 5:30 and meditate from 6 to 7. At 11:30 I make my examination of conscience. At midday I do my spiritual reading and, in the evening, one hour of prayer.

July 28. I have great pain because there's only one week before I leave, but I want to make the sacrifice heroically, without shedding any tears. What is increasing my pain is Mother Izquierdo's indifference towards me. After having loved her as I loved her, and having let her read my soul, here is what I receive. This is teaching me that not even the holiest creatures know how to love. Farewell to all human affection. In Jesus alone do I encounter constant love, love without limit, love that is infinite.

July 29. My departure from school is settled. I'm sorrowful because I'm going to leave this school where I live with Our Lord, isolated from all the dangers of the world.

July 30. I went to Mother Vicar. She gave me very good and very wise advice. She told me that I should be resigned to my departure, since that is God's will. I should be a guardian angel for the family. Every day I should get up for Mass and make my meditation. I should remember that I'm a Child of Mary. I should imitate her, be humble, put up with humiliations. I shouldn't allow myself to be carried away by impressions, but always preserve a serene countenance, despite contradictions and sorrows.

I should be very affectionate with my mother, and now the time has come to thank her not only with words but with deeds for all she has done for me. I'm going to spare her pain, console and help her in every way. I must be very affectionate with my father, be an angel and offer counsel to my brothers and sisters, and be so virtuous and mortified as to make virtue attractive to all. I should study, because today more than ever a woman must be informed. Finally, she told me that I will always retain the affection of the Sisters and that I can count on their prayers and sacrifices. I should look on the Most Sacred Heart as my own home. When I need counsel, I should go and seek it in the Sacred Heart of Jesus.

July 31. They extracted my tooth, but thanks be to God, only after I was given chloroform. It's impossible to describe how that tooth made me suffer. I spent two nights without any sleep and yesterday I cried from the pain; but during the night I resolved not to cry but to offer it to God. I bore the pain all night without complaining. I love that tooth because it made me suffer.

August 2. Today is First Friday. I didn't go to Communion because I was unable to get up. I have a lot of pain, but in my heart I'm with Him. Yesterday I spoke quite a while with Herminita, asking her to become more pious. I'm going to propose that she change herself completely. May Jesus be our union, and our friendship be a continuous act of praise of glory.

## 42. Speak, Lord! (Retreat of 1918).

August 7 *(Juanita wrote July 7)*. I went on retreat: "Speak, Lord, for your servant is listening" *(1 Samuel 3: 9-1)*. With the most Holy Virgin I want to say: "Be it done unto me according to Your Word" *(Luke 1:38)*. My little house is closed to all the world and open only to heaven. Like Magdalene, I'm going to listen to Our Lord who is "the one thing necessary" *([Luke 10:42)*. I want to keep silence and mortify my sight.

**OUR GOAL.** To love and serve God and thus attain Heaven. What greater goal: to know God, God who is infinite in perfections, God who is eternal, immutable, all-powerful, merciful and good. That's the God who is my goal. Who are You, my God, and who am I? I'm a creature formed by Your hands, a creature taken from nothingness, formed from clay, but with a soul that's like unto God, a soul that's intelligent and free, destined to give You the glory of the visible world. My God, we're so miserable that we rebel against You, our Creator. Pardon me! For instead of loving You, we offend You. There's only one commandment You have imposed on us and we don't fulfill that one. What does it profit us to gain the whole world if we lose our soul? What do riches, honors, glory, human affections matter, for they pass away and end? How do they compare with my soul, which is immortal and has been made worthy by the Blood of Jesus Christ, my God? How precious must a soul be since the devil will be watching out to destroy it. Either I'm going to save my soul or I'm going to condemn it forever. That's why I'm resolved to save it.

**RESOLUTIONS.** My goal is to love and serve God. For if I love God, I'll fulfill His divine will. What is His Will? That I follow Him and be perfect. How can I most easily attain perfection? By means of the evangelical counsels: obedience, chastity and poverty. I must follow Jesus Christ wherever He calls me, since that is my salvation.

**GOD.** God who is holy. One sin was enough to make the angels fall instantly into hell. Original sin was the event that brought death into the world and, finally, it crucified Our Lord on Calvary. Oh, what horror, my God! I'd rather die a thousand times than offend You even slightly, since You are my Father, my Friend, my adored Spouse. You frequently punished Sarah, Moses, David,

271

etc. for one venial sin; and yet, You are not punishing me for having offended You thousands of times. Grant me pardon!

**DEATH.** We must all die. All things pass away and we ourselves, too. Every day we draw closer to that eternity. Why do we attach ourselves to things that perish? Honors are unlike virtue, and miserable are the creatures who bestow such honors. Riches are easily lost. They're worth nothing and give no happiness. Applause and affection die out and are extinguished by the slightest misunderstanding. Only God can satisfy us. He is truth and unchanging good. He is eternal love. Oh, my Jesus and my Mother, may I belong to Him forever. May nothing on earth claim my attention but the tabernacle. Preserve me pure for Yourself so that when I die I can say: how happy I am now that at last I can now lose myself in the infinite Ocean of the Heart of Jesus, my adored Spouse.

**JUDGMENT.** There are three things we will be judged on: Your blessings to us, our sins and our deeds, according to what our intention was. Oh, my God, I'm not a saint even though You have filled me with blessings! Pardon me so I may be a saint from now on. My Mother, make me become a saint!

I went to Confession. I'm very much consoled. I told the priest everything. He left me completely satisfied. He wants me to get 7 hours of sleep. He gave me permission to wear the hairshirt three times a week, for one hour. He told me that I should make prayer for three-quarters of an hour in the morning and for one-quarter in the evening. I may renew my vow until the 8th of September.

**HELL.** Hell doesn't frighten me so much. But Saint Teresa's thought does: "The condemned are unable to love God."

**THE PRODIGAL SON.** My Jesus, there's something here that moved me so much: Your love Oh, Jesus, for so ungrateful a creature. I prostrate myself at your feet and then, filled with confusion, I beg pardon. Yes, my Jesus. From now on I want to live always by Your side. Oh, Love, consume this miserable creature!

**THE LAST SUPPER.** When they speak of the Eucharist I feel something so strange in myself that I'm unable to think or do anything. It's as though I'm paralyzed and I believe that if in that instant there came to me impulses of love I'd be unable to resist them. My Jesus, I annihilate myself before Your love! You, God of heaven and earth, of the seas, of the mountains, of the star studded firmament; You, Lord,who are adored by the angels in an ecstasy of love; You, Jesus in your humanity; You, the living bread! Oh, to be annihilated, all this would be so little! If they had left a relic of You it would be a token of love worthy of our veneration; but You Yourself remain, knowing that You would be the object of profanations, sacrileges, ungratefulness, abandonment. Lord, are You mad with love? You are not just in one place on earth for us but in all the tabernacles throughout the world. Oh, Lord, how good You are, how great is Your love that You make it appear to be nothing. What is more, You disappear by letting them see a creature, a criminal nothingness.

**THE PASSION.** He suffered from the time He was born, because He saw what He was going to suffer. He desired to suffer and scolded the scandalized Saint Peter, when Peter said He would not die. He suffered because He wanted to and because He is an infinite God who suffers for the sins of one of His vile and miserable creatures. He suffers injuries in His spirit as well as in His body.

**OBEDIENCE.** To obey with a spirit of faith, seeing God in superiors; to obey as Our Lord in Nazareth obeyed.

**HEAVEN.** To possess God. To see Him face to face, to love Him for an eternity. To understand all His mysteries and to know Him. What felicity!

## 43. I'm Leaving School. Resolutions.

I have spent heavenly days. *(She refers to the retreat days that allowed her to spend more time in prayer).* On each walk I went to talk with Him in the little chapel, united to Him. We used to speak for such a long time.... I was experiencing many doubts about my vocation. I had doubts whether I would become a Carmelite, but Jesus told me that it was His will.

I'm leaving school. It's impossible to describe what I'm suffering. Oh, my God, how everything passes away and comes to an end! How much we attach ourselves to what's transitory. I haven't cried, but my heart is torn to pieces. I was present for the opening of the semester and, seeing that I would have no responsibility, I felt that my heart was being destroyed. Farewell, Sisters, who have taught me the way of virtue, who have shown me the road to the most complete happiness here on earth and the way to heaven. Farewell, dwelling place of the Heart of Jesus, where for 3 years I've lived with You. Farewell, my dear companions. Farewell. Your affection will always remain in my memory. Farewell, farewell to everyone. I'm going with Him. I'm going to follow Him and I'll be happy. I won't cry. With generosity I want to make my sacrifice to God. All for You, Jesus, until death.

Resolutions for my entire life:

1. I'll never miss my meditation, my Communion and Mass.

2. I'll make my particular examination of conscience and recite my morning and evening prayers on my knees.

3. I'll make my spiritual reading and preserve recollection in my soul, for it'll keep me united with Jesus and completely separated from the world.

4. I'll maintain a good character. I'll never allow myself to be governed by feelings or by my heart, but by reason and by conscience.

5. I'll joyfully fulfill the will of God in sadness and in joy, without ever betraying on my face what's going on in my heart. I'll never cry, ever keeping in mind the words of Saint Teresa: It's imperative to have the heart of a man and not that of a woman.

6. I'll never allow myself to be carried away by human respect, whether in my manner of conducting myself or in my words.

### 44. "My Leaving School"

Glory to God alone!

How many different impressions I'm experiencing! Sadness because I'm leaving my beloved school as well as the Sisters and my companions, to whom I am so grateful. How good they are to me, what affection they show me, although I was so unworthy of that! I carried out my sacrifice without crying. Truly, I felt a strength in myself that was superior to my own; it was Jesus who made me so strong in that instant. I felt my heart was being destroyed when I said farewell to my life as a student, but I didn't cry because I had promised our Lord to prepare myself for the great sacrifice I must accomplish in a few months. On the other hand, I feel the attractiveness of home life, of life with my family

275

that I had abandoned when I was so young; of returning to a life of intimacy with my own in order to do good and to sacrifice myself for each one of them at every moment. But I also had to leave Rebecca. That was the first time we were separated. It was a prelude to our separation here on earth; but in it I see the affectionate hand of my good Jesus, who in this way is preparing our hearts to make the sacrifice.

My heart is also seized with fear. An unknown path is opening before my eyes, and the unknown always produces distrust. On top of that, I'm going to enter the world, that world so perverse. I'm going to be submerged in a cold atmosphere, glacial in its social indifference. Will I succumb to it? God alone knows what I've suffered! Over and above that, the Sisters at school believed I was leaving because I wanted to. How far I am from doing my own will. Circumstances forced me to leave my dear little school, that refuge of peace, innocence and joy. It was, above everything, God's will that was urgently calling me. Today, I now find myself in the world and see what my life is, I find that life in God can be continued even more than in the school. How many sacrifices that are unknown to all! Besides, my life is more prayerful. I spend a lot of time alone in my room with God alone. Study used to take up my thoughts much more. Now I must think only of Him.

## 45. A Friend Who Is An Angel. At The Theater.

August 25. I left school 14 days ago and thank God my life, which seemed to be a mystery when I was in school, is now unfolding very peacefully. Every day I go to Communion and make my prayer for three quarters of an hour. I'm trying to live continually in the presence of God.

How good Our Lord is! How can I not help but love Him? The very day I went out into the world He gave me a friend who is an angel. *(Elisita Valdés Ossa, second cousin of Juanita. Elisita had the same vocational problems. For some time she even had a place reserved at the Monastery of Los Andes, but she did not enter. She did great things in social and charitable work. Conscious of the importance of the teaching of religion, in 1936 she founded the Juanita Ossa Valdés Catechetical Home, which she headed and for which she worked tirelessly until her death (7/22/1973). Juanita said in a letter, "l had hardly left school when Our Lord gave me a true friend, whose name I will not reveal so as not to compromise her. We have the same ideals, the same feelings and tastes and even the same character. With us all is one. We share our most intimate thoughts. Each day we encourage and strengthen each other to belong more and more to God").*

We think the same way in everything and have souls that are alike, even though she's a little saint and I'm a miserable person. We have lived through similar circumstances and we must dissimulate them very well, so much so that we pretend we're not friends, but we go out together and then we take advantage of this situation by conversing with one another.

Today in meditation Our Lord made me see His great love: how He humbled Himself and reduced Himself to the point of seeming to be crazy, a sinner, a blasphemer, impure, a thief. He told me that in striving to unite myself to Him entirely it was necessary to die to myself and to love Him more than myself.

He taught me how I must die: 1. By seeking humiliations and not seeking honors and fame, etc.; 2. When thoughts of pride come to me, to humiliate myself before Our Lord, comparing His infinite intelligence with my puny understanding, and say disparaging things about myself so as to be humiliated like Christ who was considered to be a fool; 3. To mortify my will by not taking pleasure in anything and by loving humiliations; 4. By living united to Him in my soul and there loving Him. Oh, I love Him! No one is like to Him! He is eternal, while creatures die. He is immutable, while creatures change. He is all-powerful, while creatures are impotent. He is wise. He knows the past, the present, and the future, and we creatures know scarcely anything. Our Lord is freeing me from all social outings. The only exception was the time I had to go to the theater. What an impression it produced in me that first time. What great indecency! How sorry I felt to see those women so lacking in shame. How God was offended there. My soul remained united to Him. The Virgin protected me in an extraordinary way. I didn't remember to bring my little rosary to recite and I was upset by this. When I went out to the lobby, Luís told me that he found a little rosary. He showed it to me and, without thinking, I kept it and afterward I was able to recite it. How many thanks my soul directed toward that Mother who is jealous of the purity I entrusted to her. At other times they played very beautiful pieces of music. I didn't know how to thank my Jesus. How many temptations I had to conquer not to enter a courtship. I can't deny it. It was delightful for me to court as a diversion. Nevertheless, I can see I can't do this, because it would be a lack of gratitude for my Jesus.

## 46. Counsels of Father Joseph. Pains Of Soul.

September. Father Joseph *(Father José Blanch, C.M.F.)* came to visit us. I went to Confession to him.

He told me he believed I should go to Carmel in another year. When I become a Carmelite, he advised me, I shouldn't perform extraordinary penances outside the Rule, and I should be very prudent. Even if the novices tell me I should ask permission to mortify myself more, I shouldn't do this, because it's more important to fulfill the Rule perfectly than to mortify myself more than is required, and become ill and thus forced to ask for a dispensation. Even when I'm allowed to perform such mortifications because of necessity, I must always protest to the Superior that I'd prefer to follow the Rule. He also told me that I should never give an account of the state of my soul to the Mistress of novices and Superior, nor of the special inspirations given by Our Lord, because afterward I would remain uneasy.

When asking for the permission, he told me that if my father didn't give it to me, I should tell him that God was able to snatch me away forever by sending me sickness and death. I should speak about everything with the Monastery so that, once the permission was given, I should not have to wait. When I have temptations or scruples, I should always manifest them to my confessor or another priest, because God gives them light, and not to a lay person. I should be very faithful to Our Lord, rejecting all thoughts that are not about love for Our Lord, nor should I go courting or even desire this, because these are temptations against virginity. I should never raise my eyes to a young man and, if I had to converse with him, I should look at him with indifference and modesty. I'm to make a particular examination of conscience at noon and in the evening.

October 14. To suffer! That word is the cry of my heart. But now I'm suffering like never before. These are pains of the soul. It's necessary to die to myself and to live hidden in Christ. I have no consolation either in prayer or in Communion and, still, I feel in my soul foolish desires to unite myself to Him. I don't hear His voice. Nothingness. Darknesses. I'm unable to meditate or do anything. Our Lord asked me to offer myself as a victim for the abandonment and ingratitude He suffers in the tabernacle. He told me He would make me suffer by being despised, experiencing ingratitude, humiliations and drynesses. Finally, He wants me to suffer. That's my only desire: to want to suffer, and even when I do suffer, I desire to suffer more in order to unite myself with our Lord.

October 15. Feastday of my Holy Mother, Saint Teresa of Avila. I wrote to Carmel. I asked Saint Teresa to allow me to celebrate her feastday in Carmel next year. Yesterday I spoke with Him; and He told me that three things are needed to come to complete union within myself: 1. I should never speak about myself, or give my opinion unless they seek it; 2. I should prefer all others to myself, and consider myself as the least one and as the servant of all; 3. I should consider the little I am worth and humiliate myself interiorly, seeing how miserable I am; 4. I shouldn't take pleasure in anything but give thanks to Him when any sacrifice is asked of me. With my neighbor: 1. In all my dealings with people I should always maintain a spirit of faith, seeing God in my neighbor; 2. Whenever I converse with any young man I have Him present and see His beauty. With God: 1. Humble, annihilated before Him. 2. Loving and seeking charity.

# Year 1919

## 47. To Be A Religious Of The Sacred Heart
## Or Become A Carmelite?

January 1, 1919. I suffered great pain when I see seeing the forgetfulness in which people live with respect to God. They live in unbridled pleasure; they offend Him, without thinking that each year they are closer to death.

I have a lot of doubts regarding my vocation. I wonder whether I should be a Religious of the Society of the Sacred Heart or a Carmelite. I spoke with Mother Vicar. She gave me an intimate understanding of the life of a Sacred Heart Sister. It can be summed up this way: it is a mixed life of prayer and action; they must live a very deep interior life, since they must keep God within themselves, and yet give Him to souls. They must always remain with Him.

They have five hours of prayer every day, counting the examinations and the Office. Their life is a continual prayer. That their work may be fruitful for souls, they must recur to God and do so at every moment. Their principal aim is to glorify the Most Sacred Heart, and to attain this goal they must save many souls. They save souls by continual abnegation. From morning to night they sacrifice themselves for souls. They are dedicated to educating rich and poor girls. They have chapters of the Children of Mary and of teachers in training. They must deal with the world but must show themselves to Him as religious, as those crucified for Him. They live by seeing comforts but without possessing them. They have no convent that is their own. Their homeland is the whole world. They can be sent to other countries without knowing the language or knowing anyone.

I'm very attracted to this life of immolation; but Carmel presents itself with all the attractions needed to fill my soul. Besides, Our Lord has manifested to me so many times that I am to become a Carmelite. When I'm in prayer Our Lord tells me that He has chosen me for that life which is so perfect and so filled with union with Himself because He loves me greatly among those chosen by his Divine Heart. To Magdalene He said "You have chosen the better part," although Martha served Him with love. The Most Holy Virgin, my Mother, was a perfect Carmelite. She always lived contemplating her Jesus, suffering and loving Him. Our Lord lived 30 years of His life in silence and in prayer, dedicating only the last 3 years to evangelizing. The life of the Carmelite consists in loving, contemplating and suffering. She lives only with her God. There are no creatures between her and Him, there is no world, there isn't anything, therefore her soul attains the fullness of love, becomes one with His Divinity and attains perfection through contemplation and suffering. She only contemplates God and, like the angels in Heaven, sings the praises of the Being par excellence. Solitude, detachment from everything on earth, the poverty in which she lives, are powerful elements that favor the contemplation of God who is Love. Finally, suffering intensely purifies her. The Carmelite silently suffers the trials of the spirit, which perhaps may be more horrible than those of the body. Jesus Christ in His Passion didn't complain even once; but when His soul suffered the weight of the Passion, He was unable to say less than: "My soul is sorrowful unto death. My Father, if it be possible, let this chalice pass from Me; but not My will but Thine be done" *(Mt 26:38-39)*. What will be the sorrow experienced when the spirit has its own suffering that the Man of Sorrows said was enough to make Him die!

Another time, Jesus exclaimed from the cross: "My Father, why have you abandoned me?" *(Mt 27:46)*. The Carmelite often sees herself surrounded by darkness that hides her Beloved. She sees herself rejected and unprotected. Is it possible that there is any greater suffering for a soul who has abandoned all to follow the God she loves than to see herself alone without Him? The Carmelite has no distractions that can take her away from her pain. She lives for Him and no one can make her forget her pain for an instant. She remains in solitude.

She suffers in her will: she strives to despoil herself of self to become like God. She must only love because never again will she do what pleases her. Because of Him she's left the ones she loved the most. And never again will she be able to caress her loved ones because the grilles keep her separated. She suffers in her body from the austerities to which she is subjected. She suffers hunger and cold. And many times she offers herself to God as a victim for souls, and God accepts this offering by making her suffer horrible sicknesses that no one can cure. But what joy is expressed on her face, what peace shines through her deeds! It is because she remains submerged in a divine atmosphere. Even when she feels unable to perform penances, when she encounters discouragement in that life so full of sacrifices and solitude, she follows her Rule with cheerfulness. She knew this before entering the cloister and, knowledge notwithstanding, she preferred the cross.

The Carmelite is poor. She possesses nothing. She must work to live. Her bed is a straw mattress. Her tunic is coarse. She doesn't even have a chair on which to sit. Her food is rough and scarce. *(In painting the life of the Carmelite nuns she darkens the colors, above all by exaggerating certain austerities, with the mind set of one who lives outside the cloister. When she is actually living that life, in her letters she presents the life much more attractively: as an anticipation of heaven).*

But she loves, and love enriches her; she gives it to her God. But why is that attraction for suffering born in the depths of my soul? It is because I love. My soul desires the cross because Jesus is on it.

## 48. The Trip To The Carmelite Monastery Of Los Andes.

January 11, 1919. I have no words to express my gratitude to my Jesus. He's too good. I annihilate myself before His favors. I abandon myself into His arms. I allow myself to be guided because I am blind and he is my Light. I am a soldier who follows my Captain. Where He is, there His soldier is. I am nothingness. He is everything. Oh, how the soul who places her trust in Him has no reason to fear, because all obstacles and difficulties are overcome by Him! The trip to Los Andes that seemed to be impossible for me, I entrusted to Our Lord. If He wanted it, good; and if not, that is also good. Every day my doubts increased more. I was in a state of such great distress that I didn't know what was happening to me. Lo and behold, all at once all the little children went off to the farm with my father, making it possible for us to go with my mother, who was so good as to take me.

We took the morning express train and had to transfer to another train; but that one was delayed, and we had to wait one full hour and were unable to return on the afternoon train, but instead had to take the one at night. God allowed that so I could spend more time in my little Convent. When we arrived at Los Andes I found a house, poor and old, that was going to be my Convent. Its poverty spoke to my heart. I felt myself attracted to it. Afterward a young girl came out to open the door and told us Mother Angelica was expecting us after lunch. At 11:30 we returned. I entered the speak room and Teresita Montes *(the sister of Juanita's friend Graciela Montes)* came to the turn. We spoke with her. I didn't know what was happening. She went to call Mother Angelica. For the first time I heard her voice. I felt happy. I remained alone with her. We began to talk about the Carmelite life. She explained it all to me. She spoke of the Divine Office: how the religious replace the angels by singing the praises of God. Afterward the bell rang for Vespers and she told me we could go to the church. It was dark there. In the back there was a grate and one could hear the sisters reciting the Office with such great devotion that truly one believed oneself to be in heaven. I was not praying. I was annihilating myself before my God. My soul was weeping with gratitude. I felt happy and satisfied. I saw Our Lord with His smiling face and it seemed that He said He was happy there, listening to the praises of His brides. I was thinking that I would one day unite myself to that choir; I, so sinful, so miserable, would unite myself to those angels. I was crying because I didn't know what was happening to me. After that they recited the Litany and I had the happiness then of uniting myself with them. It was my first prayer to my most holy Mother in union with the Sisters.

After that I went to the speak room. It's impossible to express the great peace and happiness that I was feeling. I clearly saw that God wanted me there and I felt I have the strength to overcome all obstacles so as to be able to become a Carmelite and enclose myself there forever. We spoke of the love of God. Mother Angelica did it with an eloquence that seemed to come from the intimate depths of her soul. She made me see God's great goodness in calling me and how all that I had came from God. Afterward she spoke to me of humility: how this virtue was so necessary; that I should always consider myself to be the least; that I should humble myself as much as possible; that when I am scolded I should say interiorly: "I deserve that and much more." She spoke to me of my dear Sisters, of how good they are. I spoke with her alone until 4:30. Then she asked my mother to take a little tea. Teresita Montes came to ask if I would like to make the "visit of visits" *(The presentation of the aspirant to the community so the religious could get to know her, was called "the visit of visits).* Mother Angelica gave her permission and then Teresita went to call all the Sisters.

In the meanwhile the curtain was drawn back from the grilles and each Sister began to enter and approach the grille. I was kneeling. I considered myself unworthy to be on my feet in the presence of so many saints. All the Sisters with their veils raised came to greet me with such affection that I was embarrassed. At first my emotion was so great I could scarcely speak, but then afterward we spoke with the greatest confidence. They showed a joy and at times a familiarity among themselves that enchanted me. They asked me when I was coming. I told them in May. Then one went to look at the calendar to see whether the feast of Saint Joseph or the Holy Spirit came first.

It turned out the seventh was the Feast of Saint Joseph, and they commended me to him. *(Until the*

*institution of the feast of Saint Joseph the Worker, there
was a great celebration in Carmel on the feast of the
Patronage of Saint Joseph on Wednesday of the second
week of Easter, which in 1919 was on May 7).*

After a while all the Sisters left, saying goodbye, and
I remained with Mother Angelica, who asked me to have
some tea. I obeyed even though I didn't want to, since I
felt full. After half an hour I returned; but then my
mother spoke with her and I went to prayer.

Afterward she called me to give me some books and
other things that I had asked for. With sadness I said
goodbye, and yet at the same time my soul was full of joy.
How God had turned the storm into fair weather;
disturbance, into a holy peace!

On the way home we prayed to God that we wouldn't
meet anyone we knew, and so it happened. Blessed and
praised be my God! We arrived home at 11:30 P.M. Only
Rebecca was waiting up for us. No one else had
suspected. How God in His goodness takes care of me in
all things without my doing anything.

### 49. Prayer That I Had.

January 15, 1919. I'm at the farm. *(From January
14 till March 7 they were at the ranch of San Pablo (near
Saint Javier de Loncomilla) that her father had rented).*
What pain I have, since I cannot make prayer, because I
can't even be alone. Yet I'll be united to my Jesus. I
offer everything to Him, since this is His will.

The prayer that I had. During the nights I had a
great deal of fervor and Our Lord made me understand
His grandeur and at the proper time my own
nothingness. From then on I longed to die, to be reduced
to nothing so as not to offend Our Lord, nor go on being

unfaithful. At times I desire to suffer the pains of hell so I can love Him and in some way repay Him for His graces.

January 27. This morning I read The Spiritual Summa of Saint John of the Cross *(This book, edited in Burgos in 1904, concerned John's precautions and sayings)*. I have so much love because God is not separated from my thoughts. Such is the intensity of love I'm experiencing that I feel I have no strength and am dead. Almost as though I were in another place, not in myself.

I felt a strong impulse to go to prayer. I began with my spiritual Communion but in making my thanksgiving my soul was dominated by love. One by one the perfections of God were presented to me: His goodness, His wisdom, His immensity, His mercy, His holiness and justice. There was a moment when I didn't know anything. I felt that I was in God. When I contemplated the justice of God, I began to be fearful. I would have wanted to flee or hand myself over to His justice. I saw hell, whose fire was enkindled by the anger of God, and annihilating myself I begged for mercy and felt that I was filled with it. I saw how horrible a thing sin is. I want to die before committing it. I promised to see God in His creatures and to live in great recollection. He told me to strive to be very perfect and, in a practical way, He explained to me each one of His perfections. I should do all my actions with perfection so that between Him and me there would be union, since I would not have it if I did something imperfect. Afterward I remained as though not knowing what was going on in my head, and I was afraid to present myself before the others, because I believed I still had something that would make me conspicuous. I believe that more than an hour went by.

288

In the evening I didn't have much fervor, but I was recollected.

January 28. I made my prayer. I felt love and union with God, but I had very little recollection. For a long time I kept on without thinking of anything. I just remained there passively receiving the rays of the Divine Sun. Our Lord asked that I should obey through faith. He told me that He desired of me the greatest purity possible. I should live without worrying about things of the body, as though the body didn't exist. I should look for no comfort. I should live only by seeing God and my soul in all things. I should not touch others unless necessary, not even my own mother. Afterward I felt the pain of separation and even fear of such an austere life that I'm going to live. But then I grew calm by putting my confidence in God.

## 50. Counsels Of Father Cea. Pact With Him.

February 10. How good my God is! We made the Mission. The Most Holy Sacrament was exposed, we received Communion and had two Masses each day. I spent time kneeling at His feet. Many times I felt I was swooning with love. I annihilated myself in His presence in seeing myself so miserable despite being filled with graces. I do everything for His love. I live continuously in Gods presence. The priests who came are very holy. One, Father Cea *(Father Julián Cea, C.M.F., with whom Juanita kept up a correspondence)*, seems to fathom souls. I went to confession to him and told him I desired to be a Carmelite. He thanked God for that, since he considers them to be saints. I consulted him about my prayer and he told me I should pay no attention to interior locutions, but to the effects they were having on my soul, that I should tell my confessor everything that Our Lord was telling me.

He told me that the first thing needed to attain union with God is to be detached from creatures; 2. To despise oneself; 3. The continual presence of God. He told me that I should do all for God and for His love, having this goal alone. He told me I should often reflect on the goodness of God, on His grandeur and my nothingness; on the number of souls that are being lost, and on how the Blood of Our Lord is being lost. I should console Him and make reparation for so many sins. On Saturdays I should think of the virtues of the Virgin and every day I should seek something new so I will not grow tired: Fridays, on the Passion, etc.

I should acquire humility by humiliating myself, considering myself a sinner and the least of all. When I see a defect in other persons, I should think of their good qualities and that those defects may be permitted by God to humiliate the person who has them, and in exchange may be interiorly very pleasing to God, while I have worse and still more defects than she has. I should see the little I'm worth in the sight of God and serve everyone as though I were a slave, since that is what I am through sin.

After that I made a general confession to humiliate myself and to know how evil I am, and also the favors God has worked in me. He told me that we should make a pact: he would pray very much for me and I should do the same for him. He gave me a picture of Saint Teresa with a verse on the reverse side and a picture of another saint with the ideal of the Carmelite and a prayer of Father Claret to the Virgin. He left a book with me called, "A Treatise on Religious Perfection" by Neeremberg. How good, Lord, You are with this criminal nothingness. How is it that You are the One who takes such interest in bringing me to Yourself? I don't know how to repay You.

## 51. In Perpetual Communion With Jesus.

February 21. I finally started to bring my diary up to date.

I'm just finishing my meditation. First of all, I read in a book the priest gave me about the excellent values of the vocation. Before that I made a spiritual Communion and Our Lord told me He wanted me to live with Him in perpetual communion because He loved me greatly. I told Him that if He so desired, I will be able to do it because He is all-powerful. After that He told me that the Most Blessed Trinity was in my soul, that I should adore it. At once I remained very recollected, I contemplated the Trinity and it seemed that I was filled with light. My soul was annihilated. I saw His infinite Greatness and how He abased Himself to unite Himself to me, a miserable nothingness; He, Immensity, with littleness; Wisdom, with ignorance; the Eternal, with a limited creature; but above all, Beauty, with ugliness; and Holiness, with sin. Then in the intimate depths of my soul, very quickly He made me understand the love that made Him go out of Himself to seek me; but, that happened without words and by an enkindling in me of God's love. Afterward I meditated on how God called me by preferring me to so many other beings who never would have offended Him and would have corresponded to His love by being saints, while I fail to correspond to His favors. Then I asked Him why He was calling me. He told me that He had made my soul and determined all that I should do and how I should do it; that He saw how I would correspond ungratefully and, despite that, He loved me and wanted to unite Himself to me. I saw how He didn't even unite Himself with the angels and yet, He wants to unite Himself with so miserable a creature. He wants to identify her with His own being

291

by removing her miseries. He wants to divinize her in such a way so that she might possess His infinite perfections.

All this makes me almost go out of myself, and when I open my eyes it seems I've come from another world. I asked Him what He wanted from me? How should I correspond to His love? He told me I can do this by avoiding all sin and by obeying His inspirations. I offered myself to console Him. I said to myself: how can I serve and console God, I who am nothingness? But He told me that He loved me, that He was concerned about me and my desires were pleasing to Him. Then I united my desires for reparation to the desires of Our Lord, to those of the Virgin and to the angels and saints.

**IN THE EVENING.** I meditated on the Prayer in the Garden. Our Lord drew me close to Himself. I saw His dying face. I felt He was cold. He prayed for me to His Father so that at least I wouldn't abandon Him and that I would remain faithful. I felt fervor but pain for having offended Him.

February 22. I'm in meditation. Our Lord told me I should meditate on the purity of the Virgin. She, without saying anything to me, began to speak. I didn't recognize her voice and asked if it was Jesus. She answered me that Our Lord was within my soul, but that she was speaking to me. She told me I should write down what she was telling me about purity. 1. To be pure in thought: that is to say, I should reject any thought that's not from God so I'd constantly be living in His presence. For this I must strive to have affection for no creature. 2. To be pure in my desires, in such a way that I desire only to belong to God more each day; to desire His glory and to be a saint and perform all my deeds with perfection. To this end, never to desire either honor or praise, but to be despised and undergo humiliations, since in this way I am pleasing to God. To desire no comforts or anything that flatters my senses. To desire neither to eat nor sleep but only to serve God better. 3. To be pure in my deeds. To abstain from all that can defile me and from all that is not permitted by God who seeks my sanctification. To do all things for God as best I can, not because creatures are looking at me. To avoid every word that's not spoken for God and for His glory. In my conversations, always bring in something about God. I'm to look at nothing without necessity, but contemplate God in His works. To imagine that God is always looking at me. In my tastes to abstain from what is pleasing to self. If I eat anything I should take no delight in it, and I should offer it to God, because for me it is necessary to serve Him better. I should mortify my sense of touch by not touching myself without necessity, or any other person. In a word, my whole spirit should be immersed in God in such a way that I forget my body completely. Mary lived this way since she was born; but it was much easier for her since she was always full of grace. I should do all on my part to imitate her, since by so doing God will unite Himself intimately to me. I should pray to obtain this grace. In this way I'll reflect God who is in my soul.

Night of the very same day. Thanks be to God! I was continually thinking about God.

## 52. Without Recollection Or Fervor. My Diary.

24. I was unable to recollect myself, but our Lord, from the intimate depths of my soul, told me that I should adore Him and I remained very recollected. In the evening I went out to consecrate homes to the Sacred Heart. With what love and pleasure I do this. But what

pain it gives me that my Jesus cannot take up His dwelling in all homes *(She succeeded in having 30 houses consecrated to the Sacred Heart).*

25. When I was making my prayer I was interrupted. But Our Lord permitted me to remain united with Himself.

February 26. I made my prayer. I had no recollection, that is to say, no internal recollection or fervor. Neither did I feel love, nor hear Our Lord's Voice. Still, I felt consoled in being with God. At the end of my prayer, I desired to die so I would not go on offending God and I felt I'd like to pour out my blood when I see my ingratitude and God's goodness and mercy. Finally, God enabled me to understand His infinite love. In the evening I was very recollected, adoring Him with great love. I feel sad I'm unable to be in Carmel to live always adoring Him. My meditation was, because Our Lord told me this, about the Three Divine Persons; how the Father, by knowing Himself, engendered the Word and, by loving Himself, the Holy Spirit, and the operations that each Person exercises in souls. But I was not in that kind of prayer the whole time, since afterward I meditated on the words of the Lord: "Watch and pray so you do not fall into temptations" *(Mark 14:38).* I made a resolution to be very recollected.

February 27. I had no fervor in prayer. Great aridity. But God manifested Himself to me, without speaking to me very interiorly. I meditated on the vow of poverty which consists in possessing nothing, not even our own will or judgment, and having no desire for anything. No comfort. To reject every thought of ambition. To desire to be treated as a poor slave. To be poor in a way that we may appear such before all. Let's never complain about a thing. To give thanks to God when we lack anything. God made me understand that I was attached to sensible consolations and tastes for divine union. I suffer when I see that Our Lord, to attract me, gives me consolation. What a miserable person He must find me to be! And I also suffer in seeing that I do nothing for my God. I'd like to be a martyr in my body to demonstrate my love to God. He also made me understand that divine union does not consist in sensible recollection, but in the perfection of my soul in imitating Him and suffering with Him. Not in locutions, since I shouldn't pay attention to them, but pay attention to truly being holy and having His perfections.

I've lived in recollection. My resolution was to renounce every comfort, my tastes and even my own will, knowing that I'm a poor slave who possesses nothing, but that God gives me everything. I kept my resolution.

April 3. It's been some time since I wrote in my diary, whose pages I will very quickly consign to the fire. When I enclose myself in Carmel it's necessary that all those memories of exile die so I may live only a life that is hidden in Christ. My mother and Rebecca have asked me for it, but there are such intimate things in my soul that no one, no creature is permitted to penetrate them. Only Jesus can read it. His divine Hand has the sufficient delicacy to touch me without wounding me. Moreover there are enclosed in these pages so many miseries, such infidelities and all the love of that Divine Heart toward this unfaithful soul, that for that reason alone I'd be pleased if they'd read it. But there are favors that God grants to chosen souls that must not to become known; and only the soul is to keep them in remembrance.

Today my little niece was born. I've been awaiting her birth with indescribable anxiety and fear. How great is the power God made manifest in the work of human generation! What wisdom fills the heart and understanding when it contemplates this!

### 53. Will My Father Give His Permission?

(April 3]). I wrote to my father requesting his permission, but have received no reply. What my soul is suffering is indescribable. He is going to come home and I must go to welcome him, without knowing what kind of a welcome he will give me. Will I have to endure his looks full of sadness and the bitter reproach with which he will look at me? Or maybe he'll adopt an attitude of indifference. Oh my Jesus, what a cruel martyrdom! But all for love of You. If it weren't for You, I'd never have had sufficient strength to give him this pain. But since it is You, everything disappears.

My brothers are worried because I don't like to go out, and they'd like me to go out. They even reproached me for not going out. The same day I sent the letter, everyone was against me; but even though I'm suffering that and much more, can it compare to the great good I'll enjoy? Jesus, I'm happy because I am suffering. I desire to suffer more, but I don't ask You for any other thing than that Your divine will be accomplished in me.

Today I felt annihilated, but I held my crucifix tightly and I only told Him: "I love You." That was enough to revive me.

Our Lord is too good. In the evening my father wrote to my mother and was filled with tenderness for me, saying that he believes he's obligated to give me his consent; but that he'll think about it. Could I find words for my Jesus? No. He reads what my soul is experiencing in the presence of the exquisiteness of His

296

love. I remain indifferent to His Divine Will. For me it's the same whether he (my father) gives permission for me to go in May or doesn't give his consent. It's the same whether he does or does not allow me to become be a Carmelite. It's true that I'll suffer. But as I seek Him alone and to keep Him contented, what does the rest matter to me? If He permits it, I submit to His good pleasure, since I have done what He commanded me.

April 4. My father still hasn't arrived. He's coming tonight. I believe that tomorrow, Saturday, the Most Holy Virgin will want to be the bearer of God's will. I notice that my soul is almost asleep. I sometimes experience fervor in prayer, at other times I don't, yet I'm anxious to make prayer. During these days I don't have any fervor, but when I do want to meditate I can't do so discursively. It seems like a dense cloud is hiding my Beloved from my heart, and my soul would like to submerge itself in contemplation of the perfections of that adorable Being, but I'm unable to do so. I'm suffering greatly. I love Him. I feel that love, but don't find any consolation. It seems that my soul desires to be suspended above the earth, and while it feels so attracted to God, it can't elevate itself; it's unable to contemplate Him.

I assisted at the Holy Hour. Father Falgueras spoke of the means to unite oneself to God, to conform human thought with the divine, to appreciate what God appreciates, to despise what Christ despised, to desire sufferings and humiliations and to despise honors, riches, vanities. Do I despise them as I should? No. I like to be praised more than despised. And neither do I like to appear poor. I nevertheless did ask my mother not to worry about my dress and thus He has heard me, because they didn't buy me clothes, since it's not worthwhile if I'm going to go to the Convent. I also asked for humiliations, all that His Divine will wants to send me.

He also said how necessary it is to unite our will to the will of God by being faithful to His inspirations, by denying Him nothing. It's certain that at times I don't respond to His call, but I almost always do. I begged His pardon for my sins. I felt myself to be so sinful that I threw myself at His feet and asked Him to cure my wounds.

He also spoke of how necessary it is to live constantly contemplating God, above all Jesus Christ, since the Humanity is the gate through which one must pass to enter into the Divinity. In prayer we should penetrate into the sentiments and affections of that divine Heart to imitate Him and be transformed by them. I promised Him to live only for Him, not to omit my prayer without a serious motive or impediment, and to live according to my schedule, since I find I'm wasting time.

## 54. I'm In Carmel 8 Days.

May 14, 1919. I'm now in Carmel 8 days. Eight days of heaven. I feel divine love in such a way that there are moments when I believe I'm unable to endure it. I want to be a pure host and continually sacrifice myself for priests and sinners. I made my sacrifice without tears. What strength God gave me in those moments. How I felt my heart torn to pieces on hearing the sighs of my mother and brothers. But I held on to God and He alone was enough.

Our Lord reproaches me for my minor imperfections and asks the smallest sacrifices, but it's inconceivable how much they cost me. He asked me to live in continual recollection and to look at no one. And I'm to do everything out of love. I should obey at the slightest indication and have a great spirit of faith.

May 17, 1919. I am greatly aware of divine love. In prayer I felt that the Sacred Heart was united to mine. And His love was so great that I felt my whole body embraced in that love and yet with no experience of my own body. All this touched me so that I had to sit down and a sensation so disagreeable was produced in me that I began to quiver. The love of God was manifested to me in such a way that I was unaware of what was happening. I spent almost an hour and three-quarters in this way. Our Lord told me that I should abandon myself totally to Him and that I would attract many souls to abandon themselves completely. I offered myself as a victim so that He would manifest His infinite love to souls. He told me that I should do all this by uniting myself to Him.

May 20. I went to Confession to Father Avertano. *(Father Avertano of the Most Blessed Sacrament, the only Carmelite spiritual director Sister Teresa had. He was born in Bilbao in 1877 and died in Santiago on July 9, 1953, after 44 years of fruitfully exercising his apostolate in Chile.)* I gave thanks to God for having given me a director so learned and holy. He told me I should be prudent about the locutions that I experience interiorly. I should never ask anything from Our Lord, not even ask Him for a cross, because He'll grant sufferings that will be equal to the pains of the condemned. I feel happy to be able to suffer something for God. I should pay no attention to any voice I hear speaking to me interiorly if it commands me to do something extraordinary, unless it does so for the fourth time, and then I should consult him.

When I feel disturbed or when it commands me to do something contrary to my state in life, I should pay no attention to it, the priest said. Only if Our Lord teaches me to practice the virtues or corrects my faults, only in that case should I listen and pay attention to it. My intention must be to please God alone. I should make my particular examine about this point. I should work in such a way as to be independent of creatures, and I should believe myself to be the only one in the Convent. I shouldn't seek to draw to myself the sympathies and affection of creatures; on the contrary, I should seek only to be despised and exteriorly I should not be singular in anything. In trying to purify my intention, I should run through an account of conscience *(a kind of rosary with beads to count one's acts of virtue or one's faults)* and, when I try to please creatures, I should make an account of my defects.

I should be equally amiable with all my Sisters. And I shouldn't be more attentive with the one who esteems me more or who speaks with me more. I should not seek to be despised, but always keep myself indifferent. The same regarding the cross. Regarding obedience, I should not oblige myself to what is prejudicial to my health. Regarding mortifications, never try to kill the body, but to inconvenience it. In prayer I shouldn't seek to form any image, but the pure concept of God; because if I was imagining Him, I'd be making Him less than He is.

## 55. The Pain Of Separation. Human Ingratitude.
### Submerged In Our Lord's Agony.

[May 20]. At night I felt an immense pain of separation. I was imagining Rebecca alone in our room and crying. I ardently desired to hug and embrace each of the ones I left for Jesus. I didn't know the pain I was going through and whether I should tell this to our dear Mother Superior, since it seemed to me that I was seeking consolation from creatures. But I told Our Lord that if she comes in to leave us in the novitiate, I'll tell her; otherwise, I'll be silent. But Our Lord, as usual, spoiled me and, contrary to our custom, permitted her to come. *(Mother Angelica, being at the same time Prioress and Mistress of Novices, did not ordinarily accompany them when they retired to the novitiate. She appointed a substitute to be with the novices while she herself stayed with the community).* I told her my sorrow and she took me to the choir where I began to tremble because of the violence of the pain. Thanks to the prayers of our dear Mother I remained more in peace and was able to sleep afterward.

May 22. In prayer Our Lord showed me how He was ground and converted into a host for us. He told me that to be a host it's necessary to die to self. A host-a Carmelite-must crucify her thoughts by rejecting all that's not of God. She must have her thoughts always fixed on God, her desires directed to the glory of God and to the sanctification of her soul. A host doesn't have a will of her own as to where she is to be taken. A host doesn't see or hear, doesn't communicate exteriorly, but only interiorly.

Then He showed me how, despite His agony on the altar, creatures did not love Him or make reparation to Him. That made me sad all day long. It's a kind of martyrdom, since I feel myself to be without any strength to love Him as I should, very, very miserable and incapable of offering Him any consolation. Furthermore, I see the ungratefulness of men and women. This produces an indescribable bitterness in me. To add to my torment, a letter arrived from my mother telling me to pray that Our Lord take Miguel *(Juanita's older brother. Undoubtedly he was very sick and his mother asked the Lord to take him after he had repented but before he became shamefully lost. Miguel was very gifted; he was a poet but lived a bohemian style of life and often drank excessively. His mother used to reprimand him bitterly. Juanita was more understanding and dealt with him with delicacy and sweetness. In addition, she used to ask her mother to correct him with more kindliness. Referring to Juanita, Miguel used to say, "There was one who was a true saint." It's worth reading what he wrote to her on the day she entered Carmel)* to Himself because he is very sick. That caused me to be beside myself, because it was my own blood that was offending God. I'm absolutely helpless. Such is the love I'm experiencing and the bitterness for sins I'm feeling. After Communion, Our Lord told me I should console Him. He is present to me at every moment just as He was when He was dying. It's dreadful! He told me I should caress Him, kiss Him, because that served to console Him.

May 26, 1919. For 3 days I've been taken into Our Lord's agony. He is represented to me at each instant as dying, with His face on the ground. His hair is red with blood. His eyes are livid. Without a countenance. He is pallid and emaciated. His tunic covers only half of His body. His back is covered with a multitude of lance wounds, which I understand are sins. In His shoulder blades He has two wounds that allow us to see his white bones, and nailed to the holes of these wounds are lances that penetrate into His bones. In His spine He has lances that hurt Him horribly. On both sides the blood flows down in torrents, inundating the ground. The Most Holy Virgin was standing at His side, weeping and asking the Father for mercy. I see this image with such vividness that it produces in me a kind of agony. I can't cry, but perspiration pours over me and my hands grow cold and my heart pains me so that I feel shortness of breath.

With this vision, everything becomes bitter to me and I find pleasure in nothing else than staying united with Our Lord. But I find it's more perfect to do everything without exteriorly displaying anything of my pain. I talked with my Mother Superior, since I feel it's necessary that souls not as miserable as mine should console Him. Our Lord told me that our dear Mother and Sisters as well as I have greatly consoled Him. I don't know how to thank our Lord who is making me a participant in His sufferings and who finds consolation in me, a miserable sinner. The only thing He asks is that I not speak of myself, that I live only for God and to console Him, that I suffer in silence. But as there are times when I can do no more, I unburden myself with my Mother. How long will I seek creatures? I desire not to die until the end of the world so as to always live at the foot of the tabernacle, comforting the Lord in His agony.

## 56. Retreat Of The Holy Spirit.

Yesterday I went on retreat. Our Lord told me I should go to His Father through Him. The one thing I should strive for in this retreat is to hide and submerge myself in the Divinity in order to know God better and to love Him, and to know myself better and to abhor myself. He desires me to allow myself to be guided entirely by the Holy Spirit. My life should be a continuous praise of love. I should lose myself in God and always contemplate Him without ever losing sight of Him. For this reason, I should live in silence and forgetfulness of all created things, since God by His nature always lives alone. In Him, all is silence, harmony, unity. And to live in Him it's necessary to become simple, to have no other thoughts or activity: to praise.

God is communicating Himself to my soul in so ineffable a way during these days in the Cenacle. The love I feel is not sensible, but much more interior. In prayer there are things happening that never happened before: I remain completely steeped in God. I can't make reflective prayer. It's as though I'm sleeping in God. In this way I experience His greatness and so great is the joy I'm experiencing in my soul, as something coming from God. It seems to me that I find I'm completely immersed by the divinity.

Three or four days ago while I was in prayer, I felt God was abasing Himself to me, but with such a great impetus of love that I believe that if it had lasted just a little more I'd have been unable to endure it, because in that moment my soul was about to leave the body. My heart was beating with such violence that it was awful. I felt that my whole being was as though suspended and that it was united with God. They rang the bell and I didn't hear it. I saw the other novices leave and tried to follow them but was unable to move. It was as though I were nailed to the ground. Almost on the point of tears I begged Our Lord to allow me to leave since all were going to notice this. Then I was able to get up, but my soul was as if in another place.

Not everything has been enjoyment. The cross has been very heavy. First I had to accompany Our Lord in His agony. Then horrible doubts against faith came to me so I was tempted not to go to Communion and afterward, when I had the Sacred Form on my tongue, I wanted to spit it up, because I thought that Our Lord was not there nor had He ever existed there. I didn't know what was happening to me and I asked our Mother Superior about this. She assured me that I hadn't given consent. With that I remained more at peace and she told me that I should pay no attention to that thought. Thus the temptation disappeared. But our Mother Superior told me that I shouldn't abase myself excessively, that I should be more of a woman. Our Lord reproached me for discharging my cross onto our Mother Superior, and He asked me to suffer without saying anything. My third trial was most horrible. I felt the whole weight of my sins, as well as God's numerous favors and love. I still didn't know what was happening in seeing that I didn't correspond to Our Lord. My pain increased more in the refectory when I heard what the primitive monks did. I began to cry in my cell, being prostrate, with my head on the ground. That's the way I was when Our Mother came looking for me to go into the garden and she kept me conversing all during the recreation period. I was unable to do more; but I didn't tell her, nor did I give her reason to suspect. Quite the contrary. That night she asked me if I was peaceful and I told her yes, since I was so united with God's will, and I was overwhelmed with God's graces. She told me to go to bed, and that was worse, since I saw that Our Lord didn't even want me to praise Him. Afterward I remained with such pain that it was horrible. On the following day, Our Lord presented Himself to me when He was not in His agony, but with His face so sad. I asked Him what was wrong, but He didn't answer me, making me understand that He was angry with me. But afterward, as I persisted in asking Him, He told me that He didn't want to speak with me, and that I was a sinner. He told me all the sins of my life in a moment and He continued to be very sad. I remained with great pain and confused because of my sins. But I was unable to believe He was that angry, since He had told me that He had pardoned me. And furthermore, He's all goodness and mercy.

The fourth trial was terrifying. It took place after prayer, when I saw myself inflamed and transported in God, without being able to move. The thought came to me that all this was the deceit of the devil, and the proof was that I had not obeyed the bell. The darknesses were most horrible, since I believed that I was without God's protection. Furthermore, I felt the greatest pain in seeing that all were noticing something strange in me. This filled me with pain, since I desire to remain unnoticed.

Today, the day before the feast of Pentecost, I felt my whole being carried off in God with great violence, without being able to conceal it. Three times I returned to myself and was then again transported. I suffer greatly, since I don't know if these are illusions, and I don't have anyone to consult about this matter. Finally, I surrender myself to God's will. He's my Father, my Spouse, my Sanctifier. He loves me and desires my well-being.

To come to live in God, with God and for God, which is the ideal of a Carmelite and of Teresa of Jesus, and to be a host, I understand that four things are necessary: 1. Silence, both interior as well as exterior. Silence in all my being. Avoiding every useless word. 2. to never speak of myself. And if it's necessary to do so to entertain others, to do it in the third person. Never speak of my family. 3. Absolute denial of the flesh. Never seek pleasure in any way or to seek my own inclinations, so I can deal with God with more ease. 4. To see God in all creatures, since everything is found in His immensity. I'll read these resolutions every day and I'll examine myself on these points.

## 57. Retreat of 1919. September.

I belong to God since He created me. I must live only for God and in God. In bringing me to the cloister, God drew me into this life in Himself, since the cloister is the antechamber of heaven and in it God alone exists for the soul. A soul that doesn't live in God in the cloister profanes it. The cloister is totally pervaded by God. It's His dwelling place. Religious souls are the angels who constantly adore Him. A religious must keep her vows, given that her sanctity is based on them. The vow of obedience encircles the other two and is the one that makes her a religious. It's the greatest offering that one can make to God, since by it we renounce our own desires, and to fulfill this vow with perfection we must attend to the least details of the *Rule, Constitutions and Ceremonial Book.* When obeying we must see only the authority of God and prescind from creatures. Even though the creature allows herself to be dominated by passion and orders things that seem unjust, we must obey, seeing in it only the will of God who wants to make us perfect and draw us closer to Himself. A Carmelite must always live in God by faith, hope and charity. The life of faith consists in only appreciating and judging things and creatures according to the judgment God has of them. For example, with a spirit of faith a humiliation is received with joy, since by it the soul is made more like Jesus who was humiliated. Hope consists in complete distrust of ourselves, by having confidence in the grace of Jesus and forgetting our sins when the enemy takes advantage of them to make us distrust the mercy of God who is Love. Charity consists in appreciating God and preferring Him to all things and creatures.

From the spirit of faith and charity is derived the spirit of sacrifice which consists in a continual renunciation of creatures, things, and of our own concupiscence. A soul that is sacrificed from morning to night will conquer herself and wage war against her passions. Union with God or holiness consists in living in a spirit of faith and charity. Faith must be my guide to go to God. I must detach myself from all the consolations and pleasures I find in prayer. I must try to forget the favors God grants me, fixing my attention on the love that He shows me on the cross and in the tabernacle.

(Prayer). You who created me, save me. Since I'm unworthy to pronounce Your most sweet name because it would bring me consolation, I dare, being annihilated, to implore Your infinite mercy. Yes; I'm ungrateful. I acknowledge this. I'm a rebellious bit of dust. I'm a criminal nothingness. But are You not the Good Shepherd? Are You not the One who came in search of the Samaritan woman to give her eternal life? Aren't You the One who defended the adulterous woman and the One who wiped away the tears of Mary the sinner? It's true that they knew how to respond to your tender looks. They recognized Your words of life. And I-how many times have I not been transported by Your love, how many times have I not felt Your Heart beating within my own by listening to Your melodious accents-yet still I don't love You. But pardon me. Remember that I'm a criminal nothingness, that I'm only capable of sin. Oh, my adored Jesus, by Your divine Heart, forget my ungratefulness and take me to Yourself completely. Free me from all that's going on around me. May I live by always contemplating You. May I live submerged in Your love, so that it will consume my miserable being and transform me into You.

## 58. The Life Of A Carmelite. Resolutions.

Perfection of life consists in drawing close to God. Heaven is the possession of God. In heaven God is contemplated, adored, loved. But to attain heaven it's necessary to be detached from what is earthly. What is the life of a Carmelite if not one of contemplating, adoring and loving God incessantly? And she, by being desirous for that heaven, distances herself from the world and tries to detach herself as much as possible from everything earthly.

The house of Bethany was the delight of Jesus when He was on earth; it was His favorite dwelling. There He was intimately known by Lazarus, served by Martha and madly loved by Mary. The Carmelite being close to Jesus reproduces that intimate life now. She learns to love Him and serve Him according to His will. She is His refuge in the midst of the world, she with His chosen ones is His favorite dwelling place.

The Carmelite must ascend the Tabor of Carmel and be clothed with the garments of penance that will make her more like Jesus. And, as He, she wants to be transformed, to be transfigured in order to be converted into God.

The Carmelite must ascend Calvary. There she will immolate herself for souls. Love crucifies her; she dies to herself and to the world. She is buried, and her tomb is the Heart of Jesus; and from there she rises, is reborn to a new life and spiritually lives united to the whole world.

Feast of the Presentation of the Virgin
*(November 21).*

1. To live only for God, that is to say, with my thoughts fixed in Him, rejecting everything useless. To live completely hidden from creatures, not speaking

anything of self, never giving my opinion on anything unless asked; not calling attention to myself in any way, neither in my manner of speaking or laughing, nor in my expressions, nor even to speak about myself in order to humiliate myself, in a word, that the criminal nothingness may disappear.

2. To be faithful to all that Jesus is asking of me. To be faithful in the least detail. To be faithful in practicing what I'm advised to do, and to do things with perfection.

3. To keep the silence rigorously during the day and not to speak even with our Mother Superior, unless she first speaks to me.

4. To live in the present moment with faith.

5. Never to laugh or make signs to my dear sisters during the day.

6. During recreations to have great dominion over myself so as to be always cheerful, but without transgressing the limits of religious modesty.

7. To consider our Mother Superior like a tabernacle where Jesus is exposed, and my little Sisters as hosts where Jesus dwells in a hidden way. I'll love our Reverend Mother because for me she represents God's authority and His Divine Will. I'll love my little Sisters because they are images of God and because Jesus gave me a precept to do so.

8. Not to speak of spiritual things and to act as though I don't understand or grasp anything.

9. Never show that I'm suffering, unless Mother Superior asks me.

10. Never seek consolation in anyone, not even in Jesus, but ask Him to grant me strength to suffer more.

11. To always consider myself despicable, as much by creatures as by God, and to cheerfully accept

humiliations, forgetfulness by creatures and by Jesus, without becoming discouraged.

Finally, I'll always strive to do what I believe is most perfect.

# BIOGRAPHICAL GUIDE

### 1900

July 13: Juanita was born at 1352 Rosas Street in Santiago, Chile, at her maternal grandparents' house. She is the daughter of Miguel Fernández Jaraquemada and Lucía Solar Armstrong.

July 15: Baptized in the parish of Saint Anne by Father Baldomero Grossi and given the name Juana Enriqueta Josephina of the Sacred Hearts. Her godparents were Salvador Ruíz-Tagle and Rose Fernández de Ruíz-Tagle (sister of Don Miguel).

Her brothers and sisters were Lucía (born in 1894), Miguel (1895), Luís (1898), Juana, who died a few hours after birth (1899), Rebecca (1902), and Ignacio (1910). They live in Santiago but spend summers at the maternal grandfather's hacienda at Chacabuco.

### 1906

From her childhood she enjoyed hearing people speak of God. Attends afternoon classes for one month at the Teresianist Sisters' school onSaint Dominic Street, where she learns to read.

August 16: an earthquake destroyed Valparaíso and Viña del Mar.

Begins to attend daily Mass and begs to go to Communion, but her mother refuses her because she is too young.

**1907**

Becomes a day student at the school of the Religious of the Sacred Heart on the Alameda. The spiritual director is Father Artemio Colom, S.J.

May 13: Her maternal grandfather, Eulogio Solar Quiroga, dies. The hacienda at Chacabuco is auctioned off; Juanita's mother receives part of the property called Los Baños. The Fernández Solar family moves to 1652 Saint Dominic Street.

Juanita makes her first Confession and promises to recite the rosary every day.

**1909**

October 22: Receives the Sacrament of Confirmation.

**1910**

September 11: She receives her First Holy Communion from Monsignor Angel Jara in the chapel of her school. It was "a day without clouds" that marks her definitively.

From that time on she went to Communion every day and spoke with Jesus for long periods of time, but her special devotion was the Virgin: "From her I received everything."

**1911**

December 8: Because of different illnesses she was at death's door on the feast of the Immaculate Conception every year from 1911 to 1914

**1914**

Reads St. Thérèse of the Child Jesus' *Story of a Soul*. The family moves to 475 Ejercito Street.

December 30: Operated on for appendicitis at the Saint Vincent Clinic in Santiago. Experiences her first call to Carmel.

**1915**

July 13: Writes in her Diary: "Lead me by the way of the cross." At mid-term in July she begins attending the boarding school of the Religious of the Sacred Heart on Maestranza Street, which today is called Portugal Street. September 10: Has a decisive interview with Mother Julia Ríos concerning her vocation. Juanita assures her that she has been reading the life of Sister Thérése of the Child Jesus for some time.

December 8: Made her vow of chastity and will renew it periodically. Promises "not to admit any other spouse but Jesus Christ."

**1916**

April 15: Confides to her sister Rebecca the secret of her vocation: "I'm going to be a Carmelite nun. On the 8th of December I espoused myself."

**1917**

January 3: Offers her life to save her brother Luís from his religious doubts. Reads the *Autobiography* of Saint Teresa of Avila. Her new spiritual director is Father José Blanch, a Claretian. Again offers her life for the conversion of special people.

July 15: Receives the Child of Mary Medal (the highest distinction granted by her school).

Begins to read Elizabeth of the Trinity. Writes: "She enchants me and I feel close to her" because Elizabeth also dreams of living with Jesus in the intimate depths of her being and living her whole life as a praise of God's glory.

The family moves to 92 Vergara Street.

August: Goes on retreat. Makes a general confession and is assured by the priest that she never committed a mortal sin in her life.

September: Writes to the Prioress of the Los Andes Carmel, expressing her ardent desire to become a Carmelite. She is aware that the vocation of a Carmelite is "to suffer and to pray." Asks God for strength to overcome obstacles to enter Carmel: delicate health, incomprehension on the part of her family and economic problems regarding her dowry.

December: awarded many prizes at school.

**1918**

Continues her correspondence with the Prioress of Los Andes.

Spends her summer at Algarrobo; forms a parish choir and teaches catechism classes.

March 12: Returns to the Sacred Heart School on Maestranza Street.

July 15: Her sister Lucía marries.

Receives first prize in the Sacred Heart schools of that area for her composition "Destroyers and Creators."

August 12: Leaves school forever. Takes Lucía's place helping her mother at home.

September 7: Writes to the Prioress of Los Andes, asking to be admitted to the Monastery. Receives an affirmative answer by return mail. Reads *The Way of Perfection* by Saint Teresa of Jesus. Visits her first cousins Elisa and Herminia Valdés Ossa at Cunaco. Writes her family the now-famous letter on "her propensity to laughter." Helps at the parish Mission. Is troubled for several weeks by doubts: Should I become a Carmelite or a Religious of the Sacred Heart?

**1919**

January 7: Travels to Los Andes with her mother to be interviewed for entrance into Carmel. Impressed by the simplicity and joy of the Sisters. Captivated by the poverty of the Monastery.

January 9 to March 7: Spends time with her family at the San Pablo estate near San Javier de Loncomilla; consecrates homes to the Sacred Heart; goes for a little rest to her relatives at San Enrique in Bucalemu.

March 25: Writes a tender letter to her father, begging his permission to enter Carmel.

April 3: Birth of Lucía's daughter Lucecita, her first niece.

April 6: Her father gives his permission. Juanita sends him a moving letter expressing her thanks. That night she writes Mother Angelica at the Los Andes Carmel to say she has her father's permission and will be ready to enter on May 7.

April 7-15: Returns to Cunaco. Juanita prepares to enter Carmel; suffers greatly because of the impending separation from her family.

May 7: Enters the Carmelite Monastery of the Holy Spirit at Los Andes. Changes her name to Teresa of Jesus. Her letters radiate happiness; she brings many friends to the religious life.

October 14: Receives the Discalced Carmelite habit and begins her Novitiate.

**1920**

First days of March: Assures Father Avertano, O.C.D., her confessor, that she will die within a month.

April 1: Holy Thursday. Spends almost the whole day in choir until 1:00 of the following day.

April 2: Good Friday. At dawn she returns to the choir. Recites the Way of the Cross at noon and participates in the Three Hours devotion. The Novice

Mistress is surprised Sister Teresa's cheeks are so red, and discovers she has a high fever.

April 3: Suffers terribly.

April 5: Asks to go to Confession and receive Communion.

April 6: Goes to Communion again. Her mother arrives. She receives Extreme Unction.

April 7: At 12:30 A.M. makes her religious profession because she is in danger of death. Her condition is diagnosed as advanced typhus. Receives Communion for the last time.

April 12: Dies at 7:15 P.M. Her life lasted only 19 years, 9 months; 11 of these months were spent in Carmel.

April 14: Funeral followed by burial in the Monastery cemetery.

November 23: Rebecca enters the Los Andes Monastery.

**1940**

August 15: The Community moves to a new Monastery on Sarmiento Street.

October 17: The remains of Sister Teresa transferred to a new tomb in the Monastery Choir on Sarmiento Street.

**1942**

December 31: Rebecca dies.

**1947**

March 16: Her brother Miguel dies.

March 20: Diocesan Process for her beatification begins; closes on March 4, 1971.

**1955**

April 12: Her sister Lucía dies (on the same day Sister Teresa died.)

**1976**

November 2: Her brother Ignacio dies.

**1978**

March 18: Closing of the Informative Process; results sent to Rome.

**1984**

April 7: Luís Fernández Solar, her brother, dies.

**1985**

December 3: A favorable and unanimous decision is reached on the heroic virtues of Sister Teresa.

December 4: During a fire in Santiago, a young volunteer fire fighter of the Sixth Company of Firemen, Hector Uribe Carrasco, falls from a high roof and received electrical charges. Doctors declared him "clinically dead." His mother and her friends recommended him to Sister Teresa of the Andes, and within a few minutes vital signs began to reappear. An account of these events was sent to Rome and the miracle was approved on February 25, 1987. This was the official miracle approved for the beatification of Sister Teresa.

**1986**

March 18: The Congregation of Cardinals and Bishops recognizes that Teresa of the Andes practiced the evangelical virtues to an heroic degree.

March 22: Pope John Paul II signs decree recognizing and approving the heroicity of her virtues. From that moment, Teresa of the Andes was officially declared "Venerable."

**1987**

March 16: Pope John Paul II signs decree for her solemn Beatification.

April 3: The same Pope beatifies Sister Teresa of the Andes at 5:30 P.M. during an outdoor ceremony at O'Higgins Park in Santiago, Chile. She is now known as Blessed Teresa of Jesus, though she is more popularly and affectionately called Blessed Teresita of the Andes.

**1987**

October 18: The Discalced Carmelite Nuns move to their new Monastery.

**1988**

December 11: Cardinal John Francis Fresno, Archbishop of Santiago, assisted by Cardinal Enrique Silva, Bishop Francis de Borgja Valenzuela Ríos of Valparaíso and Bishop Manuel Camilo Vial of San Felipe, presides at an elaborate ceremony during which the remains of Blessed Teresa were brought to their definitive resting place at Chacabuco on land donated by Luís Alberto Fernández. On her tomb are inscribed the words Pope John Paul II used in his Beatification homily, "Love is stronger than all things."

December 12: The following day, the feast of Our Lady of Guadalupe, Patroness of Latin America, the National Shrine in honor of Our Lady of Mount Carmel where the remains of Saint Teresa of Los Andes are preserved was solemnly consecrated by Cardinal Fresno, Archbishop of Santiago. Apostolic Nuncio Giulio Eunaudi and 29 bishops were present.

**1989**

July 13 has been assigned officially by the Holy See as her liturgical feastday. Thus she will forever be a part of the Novena in preparation for the feast on July 16 of

Our Lady of Mount Carmel, the patronal feast of her Order and the titular feast of her country.

**1992**

July 11, Pope John Paul II signed decree which approved the miracle granted to Marcella Antúnez through the intercession of Teresa of the Andes. This miracle was presented for the canonization.

**1993**

March 21, Teresa of Jesus of the Andes canonized by John Paul II in Saint Peter's Basilica.

April 18, Archbishop Carlos Oviedo of Santiago declares Teresa the patron of children, especially the homeless or those in minor prisons.

# PAPAL HOMILY AT THE BEATIFICATION OF SISTER TERESA OF LOS ANDES

Blessed Teresa Gives Us a Message of Reconciliation:

1. There are three things that last: faith, hope, and love; and the greatest of these is love" (1 Cor 12:13). These words of St. Paul, the culmination of his hymn to charity, resound with new tones in this eucharistic celebration. Yes, "the greatest of these is love."Such are the words brought to life by Sister Teresa of Los Andes, whom today I have the grace and joy to proclaim

Blessed. Today, my dear brothers and sisters of Santiago and of all Chile, is a great day in the life of your church and nation.

A most beloved daughter of the Chilean church, Sister Teresa is raised to the glory of the altar in the country that gave her birth. In her, God's pilgrim people find a guide in their journey toward the heavenly Jerusalem.

I wish to extend my cordial greetings to my brother Bishops present here, particularly to His Eminence, the Cardinal Archbishop of this dear Archdiocese. I wish also to greet the civil authorities, the Superior General of the Discalced Carmelites, the men and women religious, the beloved faithful of this pilgrim church in Chile who today rejoice over a young girl, a Carmelite religious, a model of virtue.

Moved by faith, hope and love, we walk as pilgrims toward God who is Love, and our souls are filled with joy as we discover that this spiritual pilgrimage has its crown in glory, to which Christ Our Lord wants to lead all of us.

At the beginning of the ceremony we read a brief biographical profile of Sister Teresa of Los Andes, a young Chilean girl, symbol of the faith and goodness of this people, a Discalced Carmelite, captivated by the heavenly Kingdom in the springtime of her life; the first fruits of the holiness of the Teresian Carmelites in Latin America.

In her brief autobiographical writings, she has left us the witness of a simple and attainable holiness, centered on the core of the Gospel: to love, to suffer, to pray and to serve.

The secret of her life completely directed toward holiness is summarized in familiarity with Christ as a

Friend who is constantly present, and with the Virgin Mary, a close and loving Mother.

Ever since she was a child, Teresa of Los Andes experienced the grace of communion with Christ, which developed within her with the charm of her youth. She was full of vitality and cheerfulness, never lacking a sense of healthy amusement, play, and contact with nature, just as a true daughter of her time. She was a happy and dynamic young girl, open to God. And God made Christian love blossom in her, an open love profoundly sensitive to the problems of her country and the aspirations of the Church.

The secret of her perfection could be none other than love; a great love for Christ, who fascinates her and moves her to consecrate herself to Him forever and to participate in the mystery of His Passion and Resurrection. At the same time she feels a filial love for the Virgin Mary, who draws her to imitate her virtues.

For her, God is infinite joy. This is the new hymn of Christian love that rises spontaneously from the soul of this young Chilean girl, in whose glorified face we can sense the grace of her transformation in Christ. She possessed an understanding, serving, humble and patient love, a love which does not destroy human values, but rather elevates and transfigures them.

Yes, as Teresa of Los Andes says: "Jesus is our infinite happiness." That is why this new Blessed is a model of Gospel life for the young people of Chile. Teresa, who heroically practiced the Christian virtues, spent the years of her adolescence and youth in the normal environment of a young girl of her time: in her daily life she showed her piety in collaborating with the Church as a catechist, at school, with her friends, in works of mercy and in times of rest and recreation. Her exemplary life evidenced a Christian humanism with the unmistakable seal of a lively intelligence, a delicate sensitivity, and the creative capacity typical of the Chilean people. In her we see an expression of the soul and character of your country as well as the perennial youth of Christ's Gospel that enthused and attracted Sister Teresa of Los Andes.

Today the Church proclaims Sister Teresa of Los Andes Blessed, and from this day on, venerates and invokes her with this title.

Blessed, joyful, happy is the person who has made the evangelical beatitudes the center of her life and has lived them with heroic intensity. In this way our new Blessed, having put the beatitudes into practice, incarnated in her life the most perfect example of holiness, Christ Himself.

In effect, Teresa of Los Andes irradiates the joy of those who are poor in spirit, meek and humble of heart, of those who suffer in silence, for this is how God purifies and sanctifies his chosen ones. She hungers and thirsts for justice, she loves God intensely and wants Him to be loved and known by all. In her complete immolation, God made her have compassion for priests and for the conversion of sinners. Peaceful and reconciling, she shows understanding and dialogues with all around her. Her life above all reflects the beatitude of purity of heart. In effect, she surrenders her life totally to Christ and Jesus opened her eyes to the contemplation of his mysteries.

What is more, God allowed her here on earth to experience the joy and happiness of union with God in the service of her neighbor.

This is her message: only in God can one find happiness; God alone is infinite joy. Young women of Chile, girls of Latin America, discover in Sister Teresa the joy of living the Christian faith to its ultimate consequences! Take her as your model!

In our Mass today in which we are elevating one of the beloved daughters of Chile to the honors of the altar, we pray especially for reconciliation. In the responsorial psalm we invoked God with these words: "Show us, Lord, your mercy, and grant us your salvation. Mercy and fidelity meet, justice and peace shall kiss" (Ps 84:8-11).

The action of reconciliation, which in the Holy Mass is expressed in the initial penitential rite as well as in the sign of peace, continues like a cry of all individuals and peoples to the God of the covenant, to this very God who has reconciled all humankind to himself in Christ, His only Son, who died on the cross. This same God has handed over the ministry of reconciliation to the apostles and to the Church (cf 2 Cor 5:18 ff).

As I mentioned in my apostolic exhortation *Reconciliatio et Paenitentia:* "The message of reconciliation has also been entrusted to the whole community of believers, to the whole fabric of the church, that is, the task of doing everything possible to witness to reconciliation and to bring it about in the world. In intimate connection with Christ's mission one can therefore sum up the Church's mission, rich and complete as it is, as being her central task of reconciling people with God, with themselves, with their neighbor, with the whole of creation" (n. 8). Yet we must not forget that reconciliation is a gift from God and fruit of the grace "of Christ the Redeemer, Reconciler, and Liberator of people from sin in all its forms" (ibid., 7).

The Church on her part lives most intensely and expressively in the eucharistic celebration her condition of being a reconciled community and sacrament of our communion with God and with all humankind (cf. *Lumen Gentium 1)*. In effect, the celebration of the Eucharist requires the firm resolve of reconciliation and forgiveness. That is why in our prayers we ask the heavenly Father to forgive our offenses, and we show the sincerity of our petition by forgiving those who have offended us (cf. Mt 6:12).

The new spirit of the Kingdom of God that Jesus reveals to us is also expressed in His exhortation which the Christian community will always view in an eucharistic context: "If, then, you are bringing your offering to the altar and there remember that your brother has something against you, leave your offering there before the altar, go and be reconciled with your brother first, and then come back and present your offering" (Mt 5:23-24).

We can therefore see, dear brothers and sisters, how demanding the Lord's call to eternal reconciliation is. In a humanity afflicted by so many divisions that have their ultimate cause in sin, reconciliation is not only a necessity, but also a condition for survival: if peace and harmony do not exist among individuals and nations, then conflict may take on truly tragic proportions.

In this ceremony of the Beatification of Sister Teresa of Los Andes, I wish to give thanks to the Lord with all my soul, because through a spirit of dialogue and reconciliation, peace between two sister nations, Chile and Argentina, was preserved with the solution of the dispute over the southern area. Let us thank the merciful God for having sustained the strength of the Successor of Peter and his collaborators during the mediation. Let us thank the God of history for having inspired sentiments of peace and understanding among the rulers and peoples of these neighboring countries, thereby avoiding so much suffering and unforeseeable consequences for the entire American continent.

Permit me to speak now, as I did in my meeting with the Chilean Episcopate, about internal reconciliation, that is to say, reconciliation within your country.

Certainly, all are convinced of the need for an atmosphere of dialogue and agreement, which is not alien to the well-known democratic tradition of the noble Chilean people. In agreement with the path your country has followed is the conviction, deeply rooted in the Chilean conscience, that this reconciliation is expressed in the convergence of wills toward obtaining the common good, toward that high goal which confers a proper meaning and reason for being upon the function of the political community. As the Second Vatican Council teaches us: "The common good embraces the sum of those conditions of social life by which individuals, families, and groups can achieve their own fulfillment in a relatively thorough and ready way" *(Gaudium et Spes, 74).*

We must admit that active participation in public life in order to promote the common good and foster all that will assure proper conditions of justice, peace and reconciliation corresponds to the social and community dimension, as the very same Council indicates: "It is in full accord with human nature that juridical-political structures should, with ever better success and without any discrimination, afford all their citizens the chance to participate freely and actively in establishing the constitutional bases of a political community, governing the state, determining the scope and purpose of various institutions, and choosing leaders" *(ibid, 75).*

The Church, in conformity with her inalienable mission, has been and will continue to be "a sign and safeguard of the transcendence of the human person" *(ibid., 76),* the image of God. As the same pastoral constitution *Gaudium et Spes* points out: "The Church founded on the Redeemer's love contributes to the wider application of justice and charity within and between nations. By preaching the truth of the Gospel and

325

shedding light on all areas of human activity through the teaching and the example of the faithful, she shows respect for the political freedom and responsibility of citizens and fosters these values" *(ibid.)*.

With this same evangelical freedom and with my heart set upon the good of this beloved nation, I pray to the Lord that He graciously grant you this reconciliation, which entails greater awareness of human dignity for everyone.

The search for the common good also demands the rejection of all forms of violence and terrorism, whatever their origins may be, which thrust people headlong into chaos. Reconciliation, as the Church proposes it, is the authentic path of Christian liberation, without recourse to hatred, class struggle, retaliation, or an inhuman dialectic that does not look upon others as brothers and sisters, children of a common Father, but rather as enemies to be combatted. We will never tire of repeating everywhere that violence is neither Christian nor evangelical, nor does it lead to the solution of the real problems of individuals or nations.

In this Park, *(O'Higgins Park)* which bears the name of one of the most illustrious fathers of this country, I wish to manifest my encouragement and support for the efforts made toward peace by the Chilean Episcopate, particularly by the pastor of this Archdiocese in his pressing calls for peace and understanding and his energetic condemnation of violence and terrorism.

Working for reconciliation supposes a universal, patient and generous love, firm in the proclamation of the truth and unbending in resisting all forms of violence.

It has as its foundation the very mission of the Church, which proclaims the communion of the children of God in a single family, respect for one's neighbor, especially for the most needy, and working for the common good.

In this perspective the Church in Chile cannot renounce the task of convincing and uniting all Chileans in a joint pledge of solidarity and participation to attain the good of the nation.

As your bishops have proclaimed: "Chile has a vocation to understanding and not to confrontation." There can be no progress by deepening the divisions; it is the hour of pardon and reconciliation. St. Paul exhorts us: "Let yourselves be reconciled with God" (2 Cor 5:20). This search for peace with God, on which the apostle insists, is a task that does not allow rest; it is a program of life that must take ever deeper root in the consciences of all persons until the end of time

To reach this goal, our path is illuminated by the lifestyle of the beatitudes. There is agreement in truth when we fearlessly confess that the Kingdom of God belongs to the poor in spirit, when the sorrowing are comforted, the peacemakers rule the destiny of the world, and compassion and mercy are practiced.

There is true reconciliation among the sons and daughters of a single nation when, with their contributions toward an open and sincere dialogue, prejudices and envies disappear, when the pure of heart try to feel, talk, and act as builders of peace; then God will call them his sons and daughters and bless them with happiness.

There is union of minds and wills when, out of love for justice and truth, the dignity of each person is respected and the wisdom of the cross is learned, experiencing the cost and profound meaning of love and forgiveness in communion with Christ.

Suffering for the sake of love, truth and justice is the sign of fidelity to the God of life and of hope. It is the blessedness of those who suffer for Christ, who fall to the ground like grains of wheat and are promised life and resurrection.

This is how the future is built, through a patient and understanding love that always believes and hopes, because it entrusts itself to God who holds the reins of history in his hands.

Dear brothers and sisters of the Chilean nation! Together with all of you today, I address my prayer to the Lord, asking for the inestimable good of reconciliation, for the gift of peace and justice for your society. "The fruit of justice is peace" (Is 32:17).

The Gospel of the beatitudes is the magna carta of the kingdom of God. The words of Jesus ring out like an invitation and a challenge, to choose the Gospel way of peace, which is the fruit of justice, against every temptation to violence, with the patience and effectiveness of one who knows how to build peace by creating the necessary conditions to renew hearts and reform unjust structures. This is the style and talent of the disciples of the Master of Peace and Love. "Blessed are they, for they shall be called children of God" (Mt 5:9).

In this Eucharist we have asked the Lord for his light and grace, so we may perpetually build peace based on justice, love, and freedom. Peace is a gift of God, which the Pope implores with all of you through the intercession of Teresa of Los Andes from Him who is Lord of all, the God of life, the Prince of Peace.

"He is our peace" (Eph. 2:14). In Christ, God the Father has reconciled the whole of humanity to himself, all the sons and daughters of the first Adam. "God so loved the world that he gave his only Son, so that all who believe in him may not perish, but have life everlasting" (Jn. 3:16). The saints and the chosen souls are exceptional witnesses of this love of the Father. Blessed Teresa of Los Andes is one of these witnesses!

Today, as we give thanks to the Lord for inspiring the desire for peace and reconciliation among individuals and social groups, let us ardently ask for the mature fruit of this reconciliation for your nation. Let us never forget that Christ has reconciled us with God in the perspective of eternal life! Let us never forget it!

This is a joyous day for the Chilean nation, for Sister Teresa of Los Andes has been raised to the honors of the altar. It seems as if she is giving us a message of life, the words she learned from her father and teacher, St. John of the Cross: "Where there is no love, put love, and you will find love."

Here on earth there are three things that last - faith, hope and love. They lead us toward eternity, to eternal salvation in God the Father, Son and Holy Spirit, to union with God who is love. That is why the greatest of these is love.

# HOMILY OF POPE JOHN PAUL II FOR THE CANONIZATION OF ST. TERESA OF JESUS OF THE ANDES

His Holiness Pope John Paul II
March 21, 1993
St Peter's Basilica, The Vatican

**I am the light of the world. (Jn 8:12)**

Today, the fourth Sunday of Lent, could well be called *the day of light.* In fact, during the first centuries of Christianity, in the process of preparing catechumens for Baptism, today's liturgy, permeated with many references to the biblical theme of light, gave them a foretaste of the moment in which through baptismal cleansing, the eyes of their souls would be opened to the light of faith. Thus they would join the community of the Church.

The sacrament of Baptism makes the passage from death to life through participation in the mystery of the crucified and risen Christ. Christ is the life; *and the life "is the light of the world.* The Word which came into the world, the Son who is consubstantial with the Father, is himself the "Light from Light." Those who welcome him welcome the light. They open their eyes; they open the inner vision of their soul to see "the wonderful works of God" *(magnalia Dei)* (Acts2:11).

In the account of the cure of the blind man, the Gospel of the fourth Sunday of Lent shows the none too easy way which *leads to the discovery of this light.* In how many diferent ways the event narrated by the evangelist John is renewed in the life of human beings of every era!

There are different ways, but the result is always the same: the light shines in the inner and outer darkness. The person sees. Even more: the person becomes a witness to the truth which comes from God.

*I am the light of the world. Whoever follows me will...have the light of life" (Jn 8:12). "You are the light in the Lord. Live as children of light" (Eph 5:18).*

## St Marie gave example of heroic forgiveness

Today the Church wants to speak the words of St Paul with particular reference to two of her daughters who, have become "light in the Lord": Marie of St Ignatius (Claudine Thévenet) and Teresa "de Los Andes" (Juanita Fernández Solar). These children "of light" distinguished themselves as Christ's witnesses: in the "old" world of Europe, Thévenet, and in the "new world" Fernández Solar. As we are still celebrating the 500th anniversary of the evangelization of the great American continent, we pick a beautiful blossom which the Good News and the grace of Baptism raised among the populations of the "new land."

They both received this Baptism in the Church which gave them birth into the life of God. By her Christian childhood Claudine Thévenet was prepared *to meet the great trial of her adolescence,* the execution of her two brothers under the guillotine. Crossing through the "valley of darkness" (Ps 22:4), she relied entirely on God. Her vocation has its origin in this wound. One aspect of *her heroic forgiveness,* inspired by her own brothers, was that it impelled her to turn in faith and love toward those around her whom she saw wounded by life. In the face of the hardship born of the upheavals and wars of

331

her era, she wanted to give only *love's response*. In those troubled times, who needed to be accompanied and supported if not those who in their frailness were at risk of being deprived of everything-the poor and abandoned children, exposed to exploitation of every type?

We have heard the words addressed to the prophet Samuel: "Man sees the appearances, but the Lord looks into the heart" (I Sm 16:7). In the frailty of a child Claudine Thévenet discerned the power of God, the Creator; in the child's poverty the glory of the Almighty who does not cease calling and who calls us to share the fullness of life which He possesses; in the child's abandonment, Christ crucified and risen who is ever *present in His brothers and sisters, the least of people*. That is why the saint of Lyon wanted to devote her life to restore children and young people to the life of society in sound and dignified conditions. Giving a Christian upbringing to girls of all conditions was her mission; that is her message.

Her concept of education combines a sense of human realities with a sense of the divine. Were not the homes which she founded for the poorest girls called *"Providences"*? Indeed it was necessary to teach the young girls to manage a good household doing the smallest chores with as much care and love as the greatest. *A burning charity* places her at the service of the young with respect and affection in order to permit each one to give the best of herself. Thus she reveals one of the secrets of her activity. "The best director", she writes, "is not the one who inflicts the most punishment, but the one who has the talent of helping to avoid faults". She ceaselessly invoked *God's goodness*.

In order to accomplish her mission, Claudine Thévenet inspired a group of young girls who, filled with zeal like hers, drew their energy from *the fountain of the Heart of Christ and of His Mother.* With a strong link of unity between constant attention to God, love of Jesus and Mary as well as faithful obedience to the Church, Mother Marie of Saint Ignatius founded the religious of Jesus and Mary which allowed her work to spread. Through the generous activity of her companions "the works of God" were made visible (Jn 9:3), as the Lord Himself desired in healing the man born blind. Claudine's holiness would bear fruit in the life of her sisters and the missionary dynamism of the Congregation. Our joy is great at having been able to beatify one of them last evening, Blessed Dina Bélanger.

**St. Teresa teaches us, God alone suffices.**

But in each person there is, or could be, a blind person cured of his affliction and called to receive the Savior's light. They need guides, medicine, educators who can help the young people throughout the world to receive this light.

Sister Teresa "de los Andes," Teresa of Jesus, is the light of Christ for the whole Chilean Church. This Discalced Carmelite, the first fruits of holiness of the Teresian Carmel of Latin America, today is enrolled among the Saints of the universal Church.

As in the first reading which we heard from the Book of Samuel, Teresa does not stand out because of her "appearance or...lofty stature." "Not as man sees, because man sees the appearance but the Lord looks into the heart" (1Sam 16:7). Therefore, in her short life of little more than 19 years, in her 11 months as a Carmelite, God made shine forth in her in an admirable way the light of his Son Jesus Christ, so that she could be a beacon and guide to a world which seems to be blind to the splendor of the divine. In a secularized society which turns its back on God, this Chilean Carmelite whom to my great joy I present as a model of the perennial youth of the Gospel, gives the shining witness of a life which proclaims to the men and women of our day that it is in loving, adoring and serving God that the human person finds greatness and joy, freedom and fulfillment. The life of Blessed Teresa cries out continually from within her cloister "God alone suffices."

She shouts it out particularly to the young people who hunger for the truth and seek a light which will give direction to their lives. To young people who are being allured by the continuous messages and stimuli of an erotic culture, a society which mistakes the hedonistic exploitation of another for genuine love, which is self-giving, this young virgin of the Andes today proclaims the beauty and happiness that comes from a pure heart.

In her tender love for Christ Teresa finds the essence of the Christian message: to love, suffer, pray, and to serve. In the bosom of her family she learned to love God above all things. In feeling that she belonged to the Creator alone, her love of neighbor became more intense and definitive. She stated as much in one of her letters; "When I love, it is for always. A Carmelite never forgets. From her small cell she accompanies souls wherever they are in the world" (Letter of August 1919).

Her burning love led Teresa to desire to suffer with Jesus and as He did: "To suffer and love, like the Lamb of God who took upon himself the sins of the world," she tells us. She wants to be a spotless victim offered in continual, silent sacrifice for sinners. "We are corredeemers of the world," she says a little later, "and the redemption of souls is not obtained without the cross" (Letter of September 1919).

The young Chilean Saint was an eminently contemplative soul. For long periods of time before the tabernacle and the cross in her cell, she prays and adores, pleads and expiates for the redemption of the world, with the power of the Spirit animating the apostolate of missionaries and, in a special way, of priests. "A Carmelite, she tells us, "is a sister of the priest" (Letter of 1919).

However, being a contemplative like Mary of Bethany did not excuse her from serving as Martha did. In a world which relentlessly seeks to excel, possess and dominate, she teaches us that happiness is found in being the least and the servant of all, following the example of Jesus who came not to be served but to serve and to give his life in ransom of the many (Cf.Mk 10:45).

## We turn to Christ, the light of the world

Now in eternity, St. Teresa of Los Andes, continues to intercede as an advocate for an endless number of brothers and sisters. What she found in her heaven on earth as a spouse of Jesus, she now contemplates without veil or shadow, and from her immediate closeness, intercedes for those who seek the light of Christ.

*The Lord is my shepherd* (Ps 23 [22]:1).

Whole generations of disciples, faithful followers of Christ in the "old" and "new" worlds, from north and south, turn to Him who is the Good Shepherd, the shepherd of souls, to Him who redeemed us by the blood of His cross, to Him who is "the light of the world."

Behold, in the *name of all those generations these two saints speak to us today:* Marie of Saint Ignatius and Teresa of Los Andes.

They give thanks to the Father for all "goodness and righteousness and truth" (Eph 5:9).

Yes, they give thanks.

And, at the same time their voices overcome the darkness, ceaselessly invoking light. They proclaim to every persons threatened by the darkness: "Awake,...and arise from the dead, and Christ will give light" (Eph 5:14).

This is the Lenten message of today's canonization: *Christ is the light of the world!*

Whoever follows Him "will have the light of life."

# REFLECTIONS OF THE SUPERIOR GENERAL OF THE DISCALCED CARMELITES

Returning to Rome from the impressive beatification in Santiago, Chile, where he had represented his Order, Father Philip Sainz de Baranda, the Superior General of the Discalced Carmelite Order voiced his personal impressions in his official letters to the Discalced Carmelite Nuns throughout the world. In one of the letters he expressed his heartfelt gratitude to God for the beatification of Teresa of Los Andes as a significant and joyous event for the Teresian Carmel and also for the whole Church.

Putting this solemn matter into wider perspective, he emphasized these important points. First, he stated, it has been argued in the public press that because Sister Teresa of the Andes lived such a short life and such a deeply contemplative life while still in the world, it can be said that she was a saint when she came to Carmel and therefore she should be presented to the world primarily as one who sanctified herself in the world and thus has a message for the world, rather than the message of a saintly cloistered Carmelite. While admitting the truth of how she was sanctified while still in high school and living with her family, the Superior General of the Order stressed that this claim does not do full justice to several important aspects of her life and spiritual personality. That's why he wrote to the Carmelite Order:

*We should not forget or underestimate two facts that certainly prove to be decisive in her human and spiritual biography. The first is that it was precisely in Carmel where, after a long and hard search, she discovered her vocation. The realization of one's vocation is a definitive event in life, the thing that gives completeness and fruitfulness to one's life. At the same time one's vocation is one's Christian destiny and human project of life. Teresa of the Andes is the model of the person with a vocation, 'one who is called'.*

*The other point to be made is that it was in Carmel that the young woman, Juanita Fernández Solar, lived a new spiritual experience. The Monastery with its austerity and silence, the community with its good sense and joy, and above all, prayer and solitude, introduced her to an inundating spiritual experience, and carried her into an encounter with God of extreme radicality and theological vibrancy. It was in Carmel in the last year of her life where the definitive events of her human and spiritual life shaped her to be the person that she is for the Church today, so that she could offer her message to the world and to the religious life, and be an*

*example to young women in the world, as well as for
young women called to Carmel.*

## Looking to the Future

In another letter to the Carmelite nuns, written just before Christmas 1987, Father Sainz de Baranda made a very telling and practical consideration of the providential meaning and significance of any beatification. For a religious family, he said, a beatification is more than an honor, it is also a challenge to the Order. It looks to the past approvingly, yes, but it does more. It forces us to look at our lives today and is a shining light to aid us as we face the uncertainties of the future in this changing world. "A beatification is not simply a title to glory for a religious family or for a local Church," wrote the Superior General of Carmel. "If on the part of the Church it signifies approval, characterized as exemplary, of a vocation and a spirituality and a life, then in this case, particularly for the Sisters of the Blessed, the beatification must bear the force of a message that invites to renewal, to still greater fidelity and comprehension, to the assumption, with greater determination, of the demands of a vocation and life which they share with her."

## Balance in Her Vocation

This point needs to be emphasized because it shows that Juanita Fernández Solar possessed the psychological aptitude to profit from her vocation to Carmel. Father Sainz de Baranda emphasizes this important point with these words:

*We are able to know the vocation and spiritual road
that the Blessed walked in Carmel, thanks to as*

338

*many as 71 letters she wrote during her 11 months*
*as a Carmelite postulant and novice. Through these*
*it is easy to detect some personality traits: 1) the*
*perfect balance she maintained between her human*
*temperament and the spiritual demands of Carmel,*
*between her very open and sensitive psychology and*
*the evangelical radicalness of her vocation; 2) a*
*strong sense of vocation (the theme of vocation*
*constantly appears as evidence of her desire to*
*understand more every day her particular vocation*
*as a Discalced Carmelite and to live it to the fullest);*
*3) the joy and happiness she lived at every moment*
*and in everything, including suffering and*
*renunciation.*

## An Ode to the Joy of the Carmelite Vocation

The joy that is associated with Teresa of the Andes is
not a sign of a sentimental or superficial person. Quite
the contrary. Father General discerns her personality
accurately when he writes of her love for and
appreciation of the depths of the contemplative vocation
God gave her. He writes:

*The letters of Blessed Teresa of the Andes are an ode*
*to the contemplative vocation of the Discalced*
*Carmelite Nuns and to the joy of being a Carmelite.*
*It is hard to find a letter in which she does not*
*express in one way or another the joy of her vocation,*
*happiness in the silence of her cell, happiness in*
*small things, in recreation with her sisters, in*
*prayer's solitary encounter with God, in the simple*
*life free of enslaving social and human pressures.*
*Can such happiness be written off to the initial*
*and untested enthusiasm of a postulant and novice,*
*to one still in the discovery and novelty of the first*

*experiences of Carmel? If anything appears clearly in her biography it is that she was never shallow or superficial, never subservient to passing emotionalism. She had a strong temperament, profound convictions, and vibrant spiritual depth.*

## Happiness in Her Vocation

It would not be possible to persevere in a vocation without joy and happiness. When there is spiritual joy and happiness, God is present, we are told; when joy and happiness are absent, any vocation is to be considered suspect. "Happiness in the life of anyone is the fruit of fidelity," writes the Superior of the Carmelite Order. He continues:

*Fidelity to something, fidelity to someone, with all the renunciation that such happiness imposes every day in certain moments and circumstances...this is also the law of happiness for the Discalced Carmelite Nuns: the happiness of a contemplative and Teresian vocation shouldered without the compromise that diminishes its radicality and without projects that evade the demands of fraternity, of prayer, abnegation, solitude.*

Uncovering the deepest roots of joy and happiness for her vocation, Father Sainz de Baranda concludes his words on Teresa of the Andes in this way: "Happiness, as joy, will always be the fruit of the Spirit (cf Gal 5:22). Vocational happiness grows day by day as love for one's vocation with all its demands increases. But joy has an intimate relation with that fraternity to which every consecrated soul is called, fraternity that is spiritual communion and open friendship with the whole community. Teresa of Los Andes experienced and lived the happiness of a community that was simple, fraternal, joyful, prayerful."

340

Proof of the divine joy Teresita found in her vocation, is the subject of the Superiors concluding words. "From Carmel, Teresa wrote on May 14, 1919: 'To live joyfully always. God is infinite joy.' And in the same month she wrote: 'When one loves, everything is joy. The cross does not weigh down. Martyrdom is not felt. One lives more in heaven than on earth. The life of Carmel is love. This is our vocation.'"

## Conclusion

In this book we have attempted to present the life and holiness of Saint Teresa of the Andes with clarity and simplicity. The book attempted to present her as a true contemplative of Carmel, one who, as she herself declared, was specially chosen, loved and favored by God. The title *God, the Joy of My Life*, draws attention to the fact that the divine joy that filled her life is a true seal of holiness, for the Bible again and again assures us that blessed are those who take their complete joy in the Lord unceasingly.

Devotion to God's servants is always important, but it is only true, genuine and authentic if it can stand the test of prayer that is inspired by the Holy Spirit and if it leads to prayer and intimacy with God. We are especially filled with joy in joining the faithful in their prayer to God in honor of the young and joyful Saint Teresa of the Andes, the special glory of Chile and the pride of all Latin America.

We are well aware that the last words have yet to be written about this beautiful spiritual jewel of the Carmel of Los Andes. But it is already evident that her charming and attractive example is leading many to experience love, joy and peace, the most special and precious fruits of the Holy Spirit. The desire that her spiritual mission in the world grow ever stronger, especially among the youth of our times, is expressed with especially touching grace and beauty in the official liturgical prayer of her feastday. This feast is annually celebrated in the liturgical calendar each year on July 13, during the novena in preparation for the feast of Our Lady of Mount Carmel to which she was so devoted and which is also the patronal feast of her native land, Chile. We will always joyfully beseech this young Chilean Carmelite to pray for us and with us as we say the prayer that the Church assigns to her feastday:

*Merciful God, joy of the saints, who inflamed the youthful heart of Saint Teresa with the fire of virginal love for Christ and His Church and who made her a joyful witness of charity even in the midst of suffering, grant us through her intercession that, inundated by the sweetness of her spirit, we may proclaim in the world, in word and deed, the gospel of love. We ask this through Our Lord Jesus Christ. Amen.*

Juanita's mother, Lucia
Solar Armstrong

Juanita's father, Miguel
Fernandez Jaraquemada

Juanita's grandfather with brother, Luis

Juanita at 18 months of age

Juanita on the day of her first communion

Juanita at Algarrobo with family and friends

Aunque por mí le suplico, yo me
acuerdo siempre de V Reverenda Madre
y de todas "mis hermanitas" las quiero
tanto, y aunque poco valen mis oraciones

Querido Papacito:

Antes de irnos al colegio hemos querido enviar
le muchos cariños, y de expresarle lo mucho
que hemos rezado por su pronta mejoría
todas las noches antes de dormirnos le
rezamos a la S. Virgen para que lo proteja
ya que está tan lejos de nosotros.
Cuanto deseamos Papacito, estar afuera
para poder acompañarlo en el campo
y cuidarlo y regalonearlo a nuestro gusto.
Adiós ya nos vamos a ir lo esperamos
el Jueves pues esperamos salir para
verlo. Lo abrazan y besan mil veces sus
hijas que mas lo quieren.
Juana y Rebeca

Lunes 3 de Mayo de 1918

Cell arranged as Sister Teresa's
was in the monastery

Juanita with her sister, Rebeca

Rebeca in the habit

The card in honor of Sister Teresa's beatification